THE CHURCH'S HOPE:
THE REFORMED DOCTRINE OF
THE END

DAVID J. ENGELSMA

THE CHURCH'S HOPE:
THE REFORMED DOCTRINE OF
THE END

the coming of Christ

REFORMED
FREE PUBLISHING
ASSOCIATION
Jenison, Michigan

© 2022 Reformed Free Publishing Association

All rights reserved

Printed in the United States of America

No part of this publication may be reproduced, stored in a retrieval system, or transmitted in any form or by any means—electronic, mechanical, photocopying, recording, or otherwise—without the prior written permission of the publisher. The only exception is brief quotations in printed reviews

Scripture cited is taken from the King James (Authorized) Version

Italics in Scripture quotations reflect the author's emphasis

Cover design by Erika Kiel
Interior design by Katherine Lloyd, the DESK

Reformed Free Publishing Association
1894 Georgetown Center Drive
Jenison, Michigan 49428
616-457-5970
mail@rfpa.org
www.rfpa.org

ISBN 978-1-7368154-2-7
Ebook ISBN 978-1-7368154-3-4
LCCN 2022937267

To Ruth—in this too, a help.

CONTENTS

INTRODUCTION 1

1 THE PRECURSORY SIGNS 3
    Introduction   3
    The Structure of Revelation   8
    The Identity of the Signs   11
    The Practical Purpose of the Signs   18

2 THE UNIMPORTANT DATE OF REVELATION 21
    Introduction   21
    The Contemporary Issue of the Date   22
    A Presupposed Conclusion   22
    Fundamentally Unimportant Date   30

3 THE SIGN OF THE PREACHING OF THE GOSPEL 35
    Introduction   35
    Preaching as the Sign   36
    How the Sign of Preaching Appears   40
    The Sign of the Gospel and Antichrist   41

4 APOSTASY 45
    Introduction   45
    The Nature of Apostasy   46
    Apostasy and Antichrist   54
    Apostasy and the Providence of God   57
    Apostasy and Faith   58

5 THE SIGN OF ANTICHRIST 63
    Introduction   63
    The Nature of Antichrist   64
    The Futurity of Antichrist   66
    Seeing the Sign   68

6 IDENTITY OF ANTICHRIST 71
    Introduction   71
    A Kingdom   72
    The False Church   77

	The Man	85
	The End of Antichrist	88
7	ANTICHRIST-RELATED EVENTS	93
	Introduction	93
	The Abomination of Desolation	94
	The Great Tribulation	97
	Battle of Armageddon	100
8	THE *PAROUSIA*	103
	Introduction	103
	What It Will Be	104
	Biblical Terminology	108
	Confessional Statements	110
	The Purpose and Nature of the Coming	112
	The Nearness of the Coming	114
9	THE RESURRECTION OF THE DEAD	121
	Introduction	121
	What It Is	122
	Features of the Resurrection	130
	Saving Implications of the Resurrection	131
10	THE FINAL JUDGMENT	137
	Introduction	137
	What This Judgment Is	138
	The Judge	146
	Standard, Basis, and Source	147
	Further Features of the Judgment	149
	The Purpose of the Judgment	152
	The Purpose of Proclaiming the Final Judgment	154
	Contemporary Controversy over the Final Judgment	157
	The Outcome of the Final Judgment	159
11	THE FINAL STATE	163
	Introduction	163
	The Eternal Destinies of Humans	164
	The Future of the Cosmos	172
EPILOGUE		177
INDEX		181

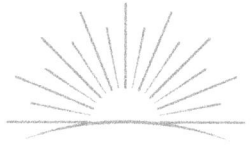

INTRODUCTION

Volume 1 of this two-volume treatment of the Reformed doctrine of the last things explains the biblical teaching of the intermediate state, sometimes called individual eschatology, and the biblical truth of the millennium, or the thousand years of Revelation 20. As explained in volume 1, any treatment of the biblical doctrine of the last things must reckon with the truth of the millennium at the very outset. This is not because of the overwhelming importance of the doctrine of the millennium in comparison with other aspects of the doctrine of the last things, but because of the decisive influence of a right understanding of the millennium upon all the rest of eschatology.

Volume 1 therefore treated the subject of the millennium at length and in depth, defending what is known as amillennialism and exposing the two main millennial errors—postmillennialism and dispensational premillennialism—as false doctrines concerning the end.

The eschatological field thus having been cleared, as it were, it is now possible to set forth, develop, and defend the leading truths of eschatology proper. The truth central to all this eschatology is the second coming of Jesus Christ itself, what the Greek of the New Testament promises as the *parousia*, literally the *presence* (of Jesus Christ). Since all the other aspects of the biblical doctrine of the coming of Jesus are subordinate to this coming, either as leading to it, accompanying it, or proceeding from it, the proper subtitle of this volume is *The Coming of Christ*.

But the title of this volume, as of volume 1, is *The Reformed Doctrine of the End*. The coming of Christ Jesus, with all that is related to it, will be the "end." Such is Jesus' own description of his coming in Matthew 24:14: "And then shall the end come." *End* in the Greek original is *telos*, which means *goal*. Matthew 24:14 might be paraphrased, "And then shall the goal be reached." The coming of Christ, with all that precedes and follows, is the goal of God, not only with the events of the last days but also of all history. All the events belonging strictly to the last things, all the history of the New Testament church, all the history of the world beginning with its creation, and all the doctrines of the Christian faith have the coming, or presence, of Jesus Christ as their goal.

This is the importance of the content of this volume.

This is why the outstanding promise of the gospel is that uttered by Jesus himself, "I come quickly" (Rev. 22:12).

This is why the fundamental prayer of the church is, in response, "Even so, come, Lord Jesus" (Rev. 22:20).

1

THE PRECURSORY SIGNS

INTRODUCTION

Leading up to and forecasting the coming of Christ are what Christian theology calls the "precursory signs." These are "all the events in the realm of nature, as well as in the history of the nations and in the church, which more or less clearly indicate that Jesus is coming and that the end of all things is near and approaches quickly."[1] More popularly, they are known as "signs of the end" or "signs of the times."

In determining the truth of the precursory signs, Reformed theology, in keeping with Christian theological thinking generally, reckons with the biblical passages that teach the *reality* of such signs. These passages invariably warn the disciples of Christ to observe these signs. All of Jesus' instruction in Matthew 24–25 about events leading up to his coming is his response to the disciples' question in chapter 24:3: "What shall be the sign of thy coming, and of the end of the world?" The word of Christ in verse 33 makes plain that the events described earlier in the chapter are indeed precursory signs of his coming, which the church is to observe so as to live in the expectation of that coming: "So likewise ye, when ye shall see all these things, know that it [the coming of Christ] is near, even at the doors."

The parallel passage in Luke 21, referring to events in nature, speaks of signs explicitly:

> 25. And there shall be signs in the sun, and in the moon, and in the stars; and upon the earth distress of nations, with perplexity; the sea and the waves roaring;

---

1 Herman Hoeksema, *Reformed Dogmatics* (Grand Rapids, MI: Reformed Free Publishing Association, 2005), 2:487.

26. men's hearts failing them for fear, and for looking after those things which are coming on the earth: for the powers of heaven shall be shaken.

That these happenings are precursory signs of the coming of Christ is put beyond question by the verse that immediately follows, verse 27: "And then shall they see the Son of man coming in a cloud with power and great glory." What the practical purpose of the signs is, verse 28 makes plain: "And when these things begin to come to pass, then look up, and lift up your heads; for your redemption draweth nigh."

Having established the reality of signs of the coming, Reformed theology then discovers from Scripture what these signs are and arranges them in their biblically determined order. This latter is important inasmuch as the signs are dependent upon each other, functioning to serve the coming of Christ in their proper order. For example, lawlessness and apostasy work together to bring about the appearance of antichrist, and according to 2 Thessalonians 2, antichrist must come on the scene before Christ returns.

Immediately, at the very beginning of the treatment of general eschatology, we are reminded of the truth that was set forth at large in the preceding volume, namely, that in the matter of the precursory signs Reformed eschatology differs radically from millennialism, that is, from both postmillennialism and dispensational premillennialism. Reformed theology holds that there *are* precursory signs that the church must observe. These events in nature, in the wicked world, and in the sphere of the nominal church signify to the people of God that Christ is coming and that his coming is near.

Millennialism, both pre- and post-, in contrast, denies precursory signs to the church. According to premillennialism, there are no signs for the church of the coming of Christ. Christ will come in the rapture at any moment, completely without warning. Such events as the antichrist and the great tribulation will follow the rapture of the church out of the world and its history. John F. Walvoord speaks for all dispensational premillennialists when he declares that the coming of Christ for the church in the rapture is imminent and that imminence means that there are no signs of this coming: "The return of Christ to take the saints to heaven is…an imminent hope. There is no teaching of any intervening event. The prospect of being taken to heaven at the coming of Christ is not qualified by description of any signs or prerequisite events."[2]

According to postmillennialism, all the signs of the end forecast by Scripture

---

2   John F. Walvoord, *The Rapture Question*, revised and enlarged edition (Grand Rapids, MI: Zondervan, 1979), 73.

have already occurred either in the destruction of Jerusalem in AD 70 or in the persecution of the church by the Roman Empire in AD 65–320. Therefore, just as in the teaching of premillennialism, there are no signs of the coming of Christ, except of course for the millennium, which some postmillennial theologians extend to such great length that it becomes impossible to determine the coming of Christ even from the millennium.

Gary DeMar expressed the postmillennial denial of any sign of the second coming of Christ: "Can Christians ever assert that Jesus' return is near? To ask it another way: Can we point to *any* signs that would indicate that Jesus' coming is imminent? The answer is no…There are no observable signs leading up to His bodily return!"[3]

Implied by the reality of the precursory signs, which include the preaching of the gospel among all nations and the appearing of antichrist and his world kingdom, are both that the coming of Christ was distant regarding the church in the apostolic age and that the church must expect these and other events to precede this coming.

Second Thessalonians 2 is conclusive for the truth of the precursory signs as taught by Reformed amillennialism. The subject is the coming (Greek: *parousia*) of Jesus and the church's being gathered to him at this coming (v. 1). Literally, the apostle beseeches the Thessalonians and the church down the ages *in the interest of* the coming. The coming of Jesus is the interest, or subject, of the teaching of the apostle in chapter 2. At once, the apostle warns that the church must not suppose that the day of Christ is "at hand" (v. 2). The warning of the apostle is that the church must not suppose that Christ could come at any moment, precisely the error made by premillennialism in disregard of this admonition of the apostle. To teach that Christ could come at any moment is deception (v. 3). This teaching has the effect that the church is "shaken in mind" and "troubled" (v. 2).

Before the coming of Jesus, two great events must occur in the history of both the church and the world. They are "a falling away [Greek: *apostasia*] first," that is, before the day of Christ, and the revelation of "that man of sin…the son of perdition," that is, the antichrist (v. 3).

The apostle's doctrine of precursory signs in 2 Thessalonians 2 is his own explanation of his teaching in 1 Thessalonians that the day of the Lord comes as a thief (5:2) and that the life of the believer in the time of the new covenant must be a waiting for Jesus (1:10). Whatever these passages mean, they do not mean that Christ can come at any moment or that there are no signs of his coming. No doubt, some in the church of Thessalonica misunderstood the apostle's

---

3 Gary DeMar, *Last Days Madness* (Atlanta, GA: American Vision, 1994), 150–51.

teaching of Jesus' coming as a thief. The apostle corrected this misunderstanding in the second epistle.

There are signs of the coming—enormous, highly visible, and unmistakable signs—and these signs are of such a nature as to demand the passing of many years before their realization. This indication of the passing of many years before Christ comes is in harmony with the implication of the outstanding sign in Jesus' instruction in Matthew 24: the gospel must be "preached in all the world for a witness unto all nations" before the end comes (v. 14). The gospel is not preached in all the world in a few years after the ascension.

Other passages also teach that the coming of Jesus is distant, in terms of time and history, from the disciples and church of the New Testament. Matthew 25:19, which is part of Jesus' eschatological discourse in chapters 24–25, has the lord of the parable coming back to conduct the reckoning with his servants "after a long time." Luke 19:11 prefaces the parable of the pounds with the statement that Jesus taught the parable "because they [his disciples] thought that the kingdom of God should immediately appear." The parable disabused the disciples of the mistaken notion that the appearance of the kingdom of God would, with the coming of Jesus, be immediate.

Second Peter 3 disarms the power of the eschatological scoffers who tempt the church by asking, "Where is the promise of his coming?" (v. 4). Implied by the mocking question is a seeming delay of the coming, the passing of many years. The response of the apostle to the scoffers is that the Lord is "longsuffering," not willing that any of us, his elect church, should perish, but that all of us should come to repentance (v. 9). Divine longsuffering demands the passing of many years between the ascension and coming of Christ, rather than the passing of only a few. Christ suffers *long*. Besides, the apostle reminds the church, and the scoffers, a thousand years with the Lord is "as one day" (v. 8). According to the reckoning of the Lord, which is the reckoning that counts with regard to his coming, not even two days have passed since Christ ascended into heaven.

These passages of Scripture are the refutation of a popular theory among theologians regarding the coming of Christ that calls itself "the delay of the *parousia*." This theory contends that the apostles, and even Jesus himself, supposed that his coming with its establishment of the kingdom of God in perfection, in all the world, was to occur at once in the days of the apostles or very soon thereafter. But their expectation was mistaken. They had no idea that the *parousia* was far distant.

This eschatological thinking about the end necessarily calls into question the inspiration of Scripture, which is guilty, according to these theologians, of the eschatological mistake of the delay of the *parousia*. It charges both Jesus and his apostles with this erroneous thinking and with teaching it—teaching it in the New Testament Scripture. It is unbelieving modernism.

In fact, apart from attributing major eschatological error to Jesus and the apostles, it is seriously in error to speak of a delay of the coming of Christ. If there is one truth about the coming that the church in all her warfare, struggles, and suffering in the world needs to hear and be assured of, it is that the Lord Christ does not delay his coming, his coming to her and for her. Christ does not delay. He comes quickly, as quickly as possible.

Where the theory of the delay of the *parousia* goes wrong, in its explanation of the end, is its understanding of the biblical teaching that the coming of Jesus is near and at the door and that Jesus comes quickly. The right understanding of these passages requires that the church and the believer understand the relation of the precursory signs and the coming of Jesus.

The idea of precursory signs in relation to the coming of Christ is not so much that the signs are events that occur in the stream of history that remind us of the end. They are not signposts along the way that alert us to, and assure us of, the fact that eventually we arrive at our destination. Rather, they are inner, constituent elements of history that are due to Christ's coming, that themselves serve this coming, and that indeed *are* this coming. They are not the final, bodily coming, but they are the coming in its preliminary, progressive, preparatory stages.

Rather than think of the signs as so many indicators along the highway that the city is increasingly close, one should think of them as harbingers of a terrific thunderstorm. There is the noticeable change of the atmosphere, the heat and humidity. There is the darkening of the sky off in the southwest. There are the faint flashes of lightning. There are the far-off rumblings of thunder. All of this is not so much occurrences that certify that a storm will happen as it is the thunderstorm itself on its way.

Jesus is coming throughout the age of the new covenant. He began coming as soon as he ascended into heaven. The precursory signs are significant aspects of his coming, as the heavy, black clouds far off in the distance are the coming of the storm, although the storm does not break upon the town for hours.

The reality of Jesus' coming throughout the present age is a reminder that there are distinct phases of his coming. He came in his incarnation, which was the culmination of his coming throughout the age of the Old Testament. This coming began with the mother promise of Genesis 3:15.

He came in the outpouring of his Spirit on Pentecost Sunday, as he promised in John 14:18: "I will not leave you comfortless: I will come to you." As verses 16 and 17 make plain, this coming is a coming by the gift of the "Comforter," the "Spirit of truth."

There is a coming of Jesus for the believer individually at the believer's death: "I will come again, and receive you unto myself; that where I am, there ye may be also" (John 14:3; see also 2 Cor. 5:1).

There is also his coming in history in the various events that lead up to and serve the bodily coming that is the end. Jesus' coming throughout the history of the present dispensation is the meaning of his assertion in Revelation 22:20: "Surely I come quickly." The verb is present tense, not future: I *come*, not I *will* come. Jesus is presently coming. He is on the way, as the thunderstorm, far off in the distance, is coming. And as he assures his church in Revelation 22:20, he is coming quickly, as quickly as is possible with a view especially to the perfect salvation of all the church.

That Jesus comes throughout the new dispensation especially in the preaching of the gospel is the meaning of his otherwise puzzling response to the high priest in Matthew 26:64: "Hereafter shall ye see the Son of man...coming in the clouds of heaven." There will be a future fulfillment of this prophecy, as Revelation 1:7 teaches: "Behold, he cometh with clouds; and every eye shall see him, and they also which pierced him: and all kindreds of the earth shall wail because of him. Even so, Amen." But that future fulfillment will be the full reality of the coming of Jesus throughout the history of the new dispensation, indeed throughout all of history. *Hereafter* in Matthew 26:64 translates a phrase that means "from now on." Inasmuch as the condemnation of Jesus by the Jewish council is an aspect of Jesus' coming at the very end as the exalted Messiah, the meaning of Matthew 26:64 is that Jesus comes, "from now on," in what Caiaphas and the other Jewish leaders were doing to him at that very moment.

Upon his resurrection and ascension into heaven, the exalted Jesus Christ executes the counsel of God, which counsel has him and his coming as its purpose and goal—its *end*. This is the message of Revelation 5. The "Lion of the tribe of Judah, the Root of David, hath prevailed to open the book" that was in the right hand of God (v. 5). All that follows in the book of Revelation is the largely figurative account of the unfolding of the history of the present age under the sovereign direction and control of the risen Jesus Christ. He looses the seven seals of the book of the counsel of God that determines the course of New Testament history, with regard particularly to the history of the church.

THE STRUCTURE OF REVELATION

Here, it is fitting to take note of the structure of the book of Revelation. This book, which in its entirety reveals the end, that is, the bodily coming of Jesus as the culmination of his constant coming throughout the present age, is structured by the opening of the seven seals of the book by the Lamb that had been slain (chapters 4–6).

Chapters 1–3 concerning the seven churches are significant introduction to this history of the opening of the seals in that they require that the subsequent history be understood as applicable to, and centering upon, the church. Therefore, the argument of dispensational premillennialism that all of Revelation after chapter 3 treats of the nation of Israel inasmuch as the church is not mentioned in these chapters is of no consequence. The first three chapters of the book set the stage for the entire book. The book of Revelation is about the church manifested by the seven churches of the first three chapters. The history of the book is church history from the all-important point of view of the warfare between the kingdom of Christ and the kingdom of antichrist.

This history unfolds by the Lamb's opening the seven seals of the book of the counsel of God (chapter 6). The seventh seal dissolves into seven trumpets (chapters 8, 9, 11). The seventh trumpet becomes seven vials (chapters 15, 16).

Comforting the church and magnifying Jesus Christ in the midst of all this account of the tribulation of the church, of judgments upon a wicked world, and of the raging of Satan are chapters that testify to the security of the church and to the majesty of the exalted Christ Jesus. These chapters may be regarded as interludes. Such, for example, is chapter 7, which testifies of the preservation of the saints, who have been "sealed" (v. 3), and of the victory and reward of those who have been martyred. Chapter 14, immediately following what might otherwise be a terrifying prophecy of the beast and his persecution of the church toward the end of history, reveals the Lamb standing calmly and triumphantly on mount Sion, about to rise for the destruction of the foe and the deliverance of his persecuted church.

In its symbolic prophecy of the history leading up to the end at the return of Jesus Christ, which return is the content of chapters 19–22, Revelation is neither strictly preterist (past) nor strictly futurist. Rather, it sets forth the history of the present age from the day of the ascension of Christ to his second coming. This presentation of the history is not chronological, as though the historical account proceeds steadily, chapter by chapter, from AD 33 to the year of Christ's appearing on the clouds. Rather, the book takes the believing reader from the day of the ascension of Christ to the very end, again and again. The opening of the seventh seal brings about the end as the final judgment: the great day of the wrath of the Lamb is come (6:16, 17).

But chapter 6 is not the final chapter of the book. Following chapter 6, Revelation goes over the same history from Christ's ascension to the world's last day yet again, only this time by the figure of the blowing of seven trumpets. Again, the seventh trumpet takes the reader to the very end. The sounding of the seventh trumpet means that "the kingdoms of this world are become the kingdoms of our Lord, and of his Christ; and he shall reign for ever and ever" (11:15).

But neither does this spell the end of the book of Revelation. Yet again the chapters that follow chapter 11 reexamine the history of the last days, this time looking more closely at the time immediately preceding the coming of Christ. The figure this time of the unfolding of history is the pouring out of the seven vials (15:7). When the seventh angel pours out his vial, "It is done" (16:17).

Although the book goes over the same history again and again, each time there is new and fuller revelation of the history. The recapitulation of the history is not mere repetition. The history of the outpouring of the seven vials emphasizes the judgments of God upon the kingdom of Satan. This presentation of history has history ending in the battle of Armageddon, about which battle the previous tours of the history have said nothing.[4]

A. A. Hoekema has aptly described this method of revealing the history of the last days as "progressive parallelism."[5] The importance of recognizing this structure of the book of Revelation is hardly less than doing justice to the symbolic nature of the book. Viewing the book as setting forth the history of the end chronologically, as is usually the case with ordinary histories, sets the expositor the foolish and hopeless task of identifying what period of history corresponds to the events in each section of the book and invariably of locating exactly where the present generation finds itself in a particular chapter of the book.

Even as the seven churches in the first three chapters set the stage for the entire book of Revelation, thus establishing that the book concerns the history of the church in the world in the last days, so also do the references to the church in the final chapters of the book confirm that all that precedes is church history, rather than the history of nation of Israel, as is the teaching of dispensational premillennialism. The ending of history, particularly the destruction of the kingdom of antichrist, announces the marriage of the Lamb and his bride, the church: "The marriage of the Lamb is come, and his wife hath made herself ready…Blessed are they which are called unto the marriage supper of the Lamb"(19:7, 9; cf. also 21:2, 9 and 22:17). The bride of Jesus Christ is the church, as Ephesians 5 teaches.

All the history of the new covenant in particular tends toward the *parousia*, the coming of Jesus Christ. The risen, living, reigning Jesus Christ bends history

---

4 For a more detailed account of the structure of Revelation, as well as a sound, solid commentary on the book, cf. Herman Hoeksema, *Behold, He Cometh! An Exposition of the Book of Revelation* (Grand Rapids, MI: Reformed Free Publishing Association, 2000).
5 A. A. Hoekema, *The Bible and the Future* (Grand Rapids, MI: Eerdmans, 1979), 223.

toward himself at his coming, but then as the husband of his beloved bride the church and the consummation of the marriage.

The precursory signs are certain remarkable evidences of this coming in nature, among the nations, and regarding the church. How these events not only announce the end and its nearness but also serve the coming, indeed are aspects of it, can be illustrated regarding certain of the most outstanding of them. The preaching of the gospel worldwide is such a sign in that Christ must come at the end as savior of all the elect church from all nations. Regarding antichrist, Christ must come as vindicator of the righteousness of God to a world that has filled the cup of iniquity. The great tribulation serves the coming of Christ in that Christ can come only when the members of his church have completed the full measure of his suffering (cf. Col. 1:24; see also Rev. 6:11).

Christ himself pointed out the intimate relation of the sign of catastrophes in creation to his coming in Matthew 24:7–8: "Famines, and pestilences, and earthquakes, in divers places…are the beginning of sorrows." *Sorrows* translates the Greek word meaning *birth pangs*. Such is the relation of the sign of the catastrophes in creation, or nature, that in these catastrophes and upheavals creation is convulsing to bring forth the day of Christ and the new world. They are a sign of Christ's coming as the woman's labor pains are a sign of the birth of her child. In his creation of the universe, God impregnated especially the earth with the child of the coming of Jesus Christ. By his providence, God now brings creation to the labor pains attendant upon the birth of this coming. As the child is huge—the goal of all the ways of God with creation, history, and salvation—so are the labor pains enormous.

The truth that creation and, by implication, history are in labor to bring forth the coming of Christ defines time itself. It is well known that science and philosophy cannot define time. The wise men of the human race simply do not know what time is. The reason for this ignorance concerning a fundamental element of human life is that essentially time is not physical but theological. Time is the progressive realization in all things (Greek: *ta panta*) of the coming of Jesus Christ.

Implied by the signs of the coming of Christ is a distinctive philosophy of history. All of history, but the history of the new dispensation in particular, is single track, Christocentric, and eschatological.

THE IDENTITY OF THE SIGNS

Having established the reality and nature of the precursory signs, we must now ask after their identity. Since the single most important passage in Scripture on the signs is Matthew 24–25, a brief analysis of the passage is necessary. At the end of his earthly ministry, Jesus taught the doctrine of the last things, or end. He did so in response to the question of the disciples concerning the sign of his coming and of the end of the world (24:3). Apart from anything else, the question of the disciples, which was not corrected or qualified by Jesus, makes certain that Matthew 24–25 is Jesus' doctrine of the end in the full sense of his second coming. He may have taught an event that typified his coming, as indeed he did, but he taught that event not as the reality of the end, but as type of the end. The subject of his eschatological doctrine in Matthew 24–25, the one main subject, was not the type—the destruction of Jerusalem in AD 70— but the reality: his coming in the body on the world's last day.

The end of the world, after which the disciples asked, was typified by the destruction of Jerusalem in AD 70 by the Roman legions. Unwittingly, the disciples related this historical event to the coming of the end in their question about the end of the world in chapter 24:3. To Jesus' prophecy that the huge and magnificent temple would be destroyed (v. 2), they responded, "When shall these things [of the razing of the Herodian temple] be?" adding, as closely related to the destruction of the temple, the question about the end of the world (v. 3).

In fact, the destruction of the temple, and the destruction of Jerusalem of which the destruction of the temple was part, were closely related to the end of the world, although not in the sense that the disciples imagined. The one was a God-ordained type of the other. Therefore, in his answer to the question of his disciples Jesus referred to the destruction of Jerusalem. This is especially the case in verses 15–20. With reference to the type of the end of the world, that is, the destruction of Jerusalem and its temple, Christ foretold that "this generation shall not pass, till all these things be fulfilled" (Matt. 24:34). Against the preterist, postmillennial appeal to verse 34 in support of its claim that all of Matthew 24 was fulfilled, finally, in the destruction of Jerusalem, Herman Bavinck responded:

> In verse 34…Jesus…does not say that his parousia will still occur within the time of the generation then living. What he says is that the signs and portents of it, as they would be visible in the destruction of Jerusalem and concomitant events, would begin to occur in the time of the generation then living.[6]

The fact is that the destruction of Jerusalem was not the coming of Christ and the end of the world in their reality, about which the disciples asked. If Jesus contented himself with speaking only of the destruction of Jerusalem in

---

6 Herman Bavinck, *Reformed Dogmatics*, ed. John Bolt, tr. John Vriend, vol. 4: *Holy Spirit, Church, and New Creation* (Grand Rapids, MI: Baker Academic, 2008), 687.

AD 70, he failed to answer the disciples' question. Still worse, he failed to give important instruction to the church in all ages concerning his second coming. And since all the instruction of the apostles in the rest of Scripture is based on Matthew 24–25, all the apparently eschatological doctrine in the New Testament is, in reality, merely an account of the destruction of Jerusalem in AD 70, which is useless to the church today. Worst of all, inasmuch as the apostolic doctrine prophesies the content of Matthew 24–25 as future for the church after AD 70, the apostolic teaching is mistaken in that what they prophesy as future has already taken place.[7] When Paul, for example, in 2 Thessalonians 2:3–10 foretells to the church of the New Testament throughout the present age the future coming of antichrist, on the basis of Matthew 24:24, he is mistaken. The antichrist has already appeared in connection with the destruction of Jerusalem in AD 70.

The truth is that whatever reference the "false Christs" in Matthew 24:24 may have to men at the time of the destruction of Jerusalem, the reality of antichrist is still in the future, in connection with the seduction of and assault upon the church. The full reality of antichrist and the full reality of the coming of Christ, of which antichrist will be a sign, are future to the church today, as they were future to the church of the apostolic age.

Matthew 24–25 makes plain beyond all question and all doubt that its subject is the reality of the coming of Christ, that is, his coming in the body to raise the dead and to personally conduct the final judgment. Thus, the passage makes plain that all reference to the destruction of Jerusalem views this destruction merely as a type. "The coming of the Son of man" will be "as the lightning cometh out of the east, and shineth even unto the west" (24:27). "Immediately" before the coming of Christ "shall the sun be darkened, and the moon shall not give her light, and the stars shall fall from heaven, and the powers of the heavens shall be shaken" (v. 29). Nothing of these events happened in AD 70.

The coming of Christ that Christ himself taught in Matthew 24–25 is a coming that all the tribes of the earth will see: "They shall see the Son of man coming in the clouds of heaven with power and great glory" (24:30). It is the coming heralded "with a great sound of a trumpet," which, according to 1 Corinthians 15, raises the dead and thus "gather[s] together his elect from the four

---

7 Prophesying as future an event that is already past is a mistake, if not a deception, known as *vaticinium ex eventu*, that is, prophecy after the event. If Matthew 24–25 merely refers to the destruction of Jerusalem, all the teaching of the New Testament that prophesies as future the coming of Christ and the events leading up to this coming is foolish, indeed deceptive, *vaticinium ex eventu*. It would be as though I were to propound as prophecy that the Allies would defeat the Axis powers in a world war.

winds, from one end of heaven to the other" (Matt. 24:31). This did not take place in AD 70.

The coming of Matthew 24–25 has Jesus coming "in his glory, and all the holy angels with him." He will "sit upon the throne of his glory" to judge all persons of "all nations" (25:31–32). Implied in the appearance of all nations before Christ the judge at this coming is the resurrection of the bodies of all members of all nations. The sheep are "on his right hand" and the goats are "on the left" in their resurrection bodies (v. 33). This takes place at the bodily coming of Jesus, not at the time of the destruction of Jerusalem. The outcome of the judgment of Matthew 24–25 is the eternal state of both the elect sheep and the reprobate goats: "These shall go away into everlasting punishment: but the righteous into life eternal" (25:46). Also this is a reality at the bodily, future coming of Jesus, not when Jerusalem was destroyed in AD 70. Matthew 24–25 is the Lord's prophecy of the end, that is, of his bodily coming. This is what the passage is *essentially*. The destruction of Jerusalem enters in merely as an event that in some respects typified the end.

On the basis of Matthew 24–25 as prophecy of the last days culminating in the coming of Jesus and in light of the apostles' elaboration of the teaching of Matthew 24–25, the church can specify the signs and determine the order of their occurrence. Determining the order of the signs does not suggest that the one ceases altogether at the appearance of the sign, or signs, following. For example, the worldwide preaching of the gospel continues all the while that there are wars and social turmoil among the nations, and even to some extent during the time of the sign of apostasy.

Neither does the order of the signs imply that there is no reality whatsoever of the signs until their fullest and clearest appearance in history. For example, although there will be the fullest and clearest realization of the sign of antichrist and his persecution of the church in the future, shortly before the coming of Christ, antichrist and the persecution of the church have been constants throughout the history of the new dispensation, indeed throughout all of history. First John 2:18 declares that already in the days of the apostle "are there many antichrists," while recognizing that there will be the one outstanding reality of antichrist in the future: "antichrist shall come." Likewise, although the "great tribulation, such as was not since the beginning of the world to this time," still awaits the church (Matt. 24:21), there has been persecution of the church throughout the history of the New Testament, including that persecution of the church by Rome, which was the type of the tribulation at the very end.

Nevertheless, not only does Scripture identify the signs, but it also indicates a certain order of their appearance. First and foremost is the worldwide preaching of the gospel, the sign that began to take place already in the age of the apostles. This sign controls all the others inasmuch as this sign carries out the main purpose of God with history, namely, the gathering of the church out of all nations to the glory of his grace (Matt. 24:14; Rev. 6:1–2).

Among the earliest of the signs, although they continue throughout New Testament history, are catastrophes in nature, including earthquakes, storms, famines, pestilence, and the like, those calamities that the Lord described as the beginning of sorrows (Matt. 24:6–8). These contribute to the next sign, which is wars and various kinds of social turmoil—economic, political, racial, sexual—in and among the nations (vv. 6–7; Dan. 7). As long as this kind of social, national, and international upheaval continues, "the end is not yet" (Matt. 24:6), for as Daniel 7 teaches, the purpose of all this turmoil is to produce the beast out of the sea of Revelation 13, that is, antichrist. But it is a sign, and the church must view it as such. To this sign belongs the disease of Covid-19 that distressed the entire world beginning in AD 2020.

The abounding of iniquity is a vivid, dramatic sign: "And because iniquity shall abound, the love of many shall wax cold" (Matt. 24:12). In order to grasp the nature of this sign, it is important to know that the Greek word translated *iniquity* in the text is literally *lawlessness* (Greek: *anomia*). Lawlessness is not merely a violation, or breaking, of the law. It is deliberate, gross trampling upon the law out of sheer contempt for the law as the law of God. Lawlessness is a despising of the law of God because the sinner has decided that his will is his only law. Lawlessness is calling evil good and subsequently practicing the evil, not because the evil is experienced as better for the human than the good that lawlessness rejects, but simply because the good is approved and required by God and because he condemns the evil. Lawlessness is contempt for the law of God, not only as the law is taught in the word of God, holy Scripture, but also as the law is found in nature (Rom. 1:18–32).

Lawlessness is such a violation of the seventh commandment as not only approves homosexual relations and then vigorously promotes sodomy, but also legitimizes homosexual relationships as "marriage," by august decree of the Supreme Court of the United States of America, and then solemnizes the "marital" union in the name of Jesus by some alleged church and some reputed minister of the gospel. Lawlessness is the murder of unborn, nearly born, and partially born infants for one's own convenience with the official sanction of the government, whose duty from God is to protect innocent human life, and then to boast about the murderous act as an act that is good for the mother—for the *mother*, when the essence of motherhood is the loving care of offspring. Lawlessness is the thinking that approval of abortion is right and good, whereas opposition to abortion is hateful and evil. So far does lawlessness go that lawless law justifies abortion, while damning condemnation of abortion.

The ultimate expression of lawlessness, implicit in all the lesser forms, is the denial by word and deed that God—the God of Scripture, the God whose eternal power and Godhead are clearly seen from creation—is God and the affirmation that man is god. In myriads of ways, this lawlessness rages to dethrone God, even as the ultimate source of this lawlessness, Satan, once raged to dethrone God in the precincts of heaven.

The church in the early twenty-first century must take heed especially closely to the sign of lawlessness. This sign must awaken the church to the nearness of the end if the church has become eschatologically drowsy. According to Matthew 24:12, there is an effect of lawlessness upon the nominal church and the nominal member of the church: "Because iniquity shall abound, the love of many shall wax cold." Lawlessness cools the pseudo-love of many professing Christians for Christ. It also cools the love of many true Christians in their generations, as the genuine Christians yield in one way or another to the lawlessness of the age. In addition, this lawlessness paves the way for the coming of antichrist. Second Thessalonians 2:8 calls the antichrist "that Wicked," where the Greek word translated *wicked* is literally *lawless* one (Greek: *anomos*). Antichrist will be the lawless one in that he will hold up the law of God to contempt, exalting his own will, especially in the matter of worship and in that he will cause the world to despise Jesus as the Christ, substituting himself as the savior and lord of mankind. Thus, he will be the embodiment of the essential lawlessness of the fallen human race: man is god, and the personal revelation of the god of humanity is the man of sin rather than the Man of holiness.

Iniquity with its cooling of the love of many contributes to the sign of apostasy. Paul makes this a sign of the end in 2 Thessalonians 2:2–3, where he teaches that the "day of Christ" will be preceded by "a falling away first." In the Greek original of the text *falling away* is apostasy (Greek: *apostasia*). This is a grievous sign in the sphere of churches. As the English translation of 2 Thessalonians 2:3 accurately indicates, it is the departure from the truth of Scripture and thus from Jesus Christ himself. Whereas once churches confessed that Jesus is the incarnate Son of God, they now are doubtful, indeed deny it, holding him to be merely a man—a very good man, but only a man. Whereas once it was believed and confessed that salvation is by the grace of God through faith only, apart from the will and works of the sinner, now this is denied. Rather, salvation is said to be in part—the *decisive* part—by the free will and good works of the sinner.

Whereas formerly the church and its members confessed that Scripture is the inspired word of God, now, under the influence of the church's seminary, the

Bible is acknowledged to be significantly the product of weak, erring humans. It is open to criticism, and the theologians gladly engage in the criticism. Genesis 1–11 concerning creation, the historicity of Adam and Eve, the fall of mankind, and the judgment of a worldwide flood, all is mythical. Much of Old Testament history is unreliable, the concoction of a redactor. The account in the New Testament of the virgin birth is a fable—a lovely fable, to be hypocritically celebrated at Christmas, but a fable for all that. The tomb in which Jesus, if he ever existed, was buried still contains his bones. The doctrine of the epistles is not authoritative for modern man; no modern, humanitarian human can believe predestination. The hope of the early church for a bodily return of Jesus to raise the dead and conduct a final judgment was a quaint, ancient, pre-scientific form of the real expectation of good in the future, namely, man himself making this world a better place.

Apostasy is not an abrupt, overnight happening in a church. Rather, it is a slow, gradual development. One generation at a synod approves the unbelieving doubt of the truth of the days of creation in Genesis 1; the next generation is open to the doubt of all of Genesis 1–11; a later generation questions the inspiration of Matthew 1 and 2 concerning the virgin birth of the seed of the woman of Genesis 3:15. The next generation believes nothing at all of the Christian faith, except (as they conceive the faith) that we all should love one another and get along. Some theologians in the early church taught salvation by both the grace of God and the free will of the sinner. The result, in time, was the Roman Catholic Church with its "gospel" of salvation by the merits of the sinner.

Even though, as a Dutch theologian charged in his lament over the apostasy of his own Reformed denomination, "the theologians led the way,"[8] the members of the congregations are by no means free of guilt in the matter of apostasy. For as God exclaimed about the apostasy of Jeremiah's day, "The prophets prophesy falsely…and my people love to have it so" (Jer. 5:31). Especially clear as 2 Thessalonians 2 is concerning the sign of apostasy, it is by no means the only passage in the New Testament that forewarns the church of this sign. Among other passages, also 1 Timothy 4:1–3, 2 Timothy 3, and 2 Timothy 4:3–4 predict a falling away from the faith in the last times. And all of these and similar passages are based upon Christ's own instruction about apostasy in Matthew 24:11 and 24, where the apostasy of the end is referred to as "false prophets." Such is the threat of this sign to the people of God that, in verse 24, the Lord warns that if it were possible apostasy "shall deceive the very elect."

---

8 A. M. Lindeboom, *De Theologen Gingen Voorop* [The Theologians Led the Way] (Kampen: J. H. Kok, 1987).

On the wings of lawlessness and apostasy will appear the sign of the antichrist (Matt. 24:23–26; 2 Thess. 2:3–12; 1 John 2:18; Rev. 11–13). I will have much more to say about this sign later. One prominent aspect of the sign of antichrist will be the battle of Armageddon (Rev. 16:12–16). This will be the breakup of the antichristian world kingdom in history in a world war of universal extent.

Immediately following the great tribulation under antichrist, to which the battle of Armageddon puts an end, and immediately preceding the sign of the Son of man, will be signs in the heavens that must terrify the minions of antichrist and that will gladden the hearts of the saints who remain on earth. "Immediately after the tribulation of those days shall the sun be darkened, and the moon shall not give her light, and the stars shall fall from heaven, and the powers of the heavens shall be shaken" (Matt. 24:29). Luke calls these wonders "signs" and adds, "the sea and the waves roaring" (Luke 21:25).

Creation and firmament will then be heaving in the final "sorrow," or birth pang, to bring forth the coming of Christ, for this sign in the earthly creation will be followed by the "sign of the Son of man in heaven" (Matt. 24:30). This sign is the one main, outstanding sign of the coming of Christ. Although the events that precede in Matthew 24 are, in fact, signs of the coming of Christ, Jesus calls none of them a sign. Only of his appearing does he speak of a sign. This will be *the* sign of his coming about which the disciples asked in verse 3: "What shall be the sign [singular] of thy coming, and of the end of the world?" This sign is the one, great sign of which all the other, preceding events are so many preliminary aspects. Or the preceding events are the gradually intensifying development of this one, outstanding sign.

About the identity of this sign of verse 30, "the sign of the Son of man," there have been almost as many speculations as there are expositors of Matthew 24. The guesses are fanciful. For example, one popular theory is that it will be a gigantic cross in the heavens. There is only one biblical identification of the sign, and this identification is in Christ's own prophecy of the sign: the sign is the "Son of man in heaven." It is what the latter part of verse 30 describes more fully: "They shall see [what is 'seen' is a sign] the Son of man coming in the clouds of heaven with power and great glory."[9] The sign will be the appearance in the heavens of Jesus himself as he is returning.

THE PRACTICAL PURPOSE OF THE SIGNS

The passage Matthew 24–25 itself emphasizes the practical purpose of Jesus with disclosing the signs to his disciples and therefore the practical purpose of the

---

9   The genitive, "*of* the Son of man," is what grammar calls the genitive of apposition.

believer's seeing the signs. Before Jesus mentions any sign, he admonishes the disciples, "Take heed that no man deceive you" (24:4). He repeats this warning in various ways several times (see vv. 5, 11, 23–24, 26). Closely related is the purpose that the believer be vigilant, always looking for the coming of Christ, indeed living in a way that is determined by the eager expectation of Christ at his coming. Christ's own application of his revelation of the signs is, "Watch therefore" (v. 42). The warning in all that follows in chapter 24 is that failing to watch for the coming of Christ is spiritually and eternally fatal (vv. 43–51). Likewise the parable of the wise and foolish virgins with which Matthew 25 opens admonishes the members of the church, "Watch therefore" (v. 13). The parable that follows, that of the talents, adds that this vigilance is not to be inaction, but rather a watching that is profitable for Christ and his kingdom (vv. 14–30). The account of the final judgment in which the second coming of Christ culminates (vv. 31–46) further describes the vigilance of the elect believers as taking form in the help of needy Christians: "the least of these my brethren" (v. 40).

The practical purpose of Jesus with his instruction concerning the signs is, first, that we observe the signs as they appear. This requires a spiritual attitude of looking for them and then recognizing them as signs of the coming when we see them. Christ warned that some do not see the signs, regardless of their plain appearance. The lord of the evil servant "shall come in a day when he looketh not for him, and in an hour that he is not aware of" (Matt. 24:50). The evil of the servant (a *servant*—a nominal member of the church) is that he has no living hope for the coming of Christ. He is an apostate in a false church. The spiritually living member of a true church observes the signs because he hopes for the coming of Christ.

Second, the truth and reality of the signs undergird the hope of the Christian. Hope is the certain, lively expectation that Christ is coming, and that his coming is near. By this hope the Christian is saved, especially in the face of all the disappointments, struggles, and sorrows of his life, not least of which are his own struggle against indwelling sin, the reproach and mockery of the ungodly, the difficulties of his way as a stranger and pilgrim on earth, and his as-yet-unfulfilled longing for being at home with his heavenly Father (Rom. 8:24).

Third, the signs must stimulate the believer to vigilance, spiritual sobriety, and faithful service of the Lord and of his fellow saints. Concerning these virtues, Matthew 24–25 gives sharp warning. Luke 19:13, a passage parallel to Matthew 25, describes the active life of the believer of waiting for the Lord as "occupy[ing]" until he comes. The verb translated as *occupy* literally has the meaning of "carrying on a business." The business is spiritual, kingdom business, but it is *business*: learning the word of God; marrying and raising a family in the Lord Jesus; worshiping God on the Lord's day with a true church; indeed, engaging in all the activities of normal human life, whether farming, scholarship, or homemaking, according to Scripture, in the power of the Spirit, and to the glory of God. One who sees the signs does not flee ordinary earthly life, but he "occupies." One who is blind to the signs is not merely lazy; he does the devil's business. In the words of Jesus in Matthew 24:49, he smites his fellow servants and eats and drinks with the drunken.

Fourth, it is an aspect of the purpose of the signs that as the church sees the signs fulfilling, she prays with increasing fervor for the coming that the signs signify. The signs are the visible word of Christ, "Surely I come quickly" (Rev. 22:20). Seeing these visible words, the church responds in prayer, "Even so, come, Lord Jesus" (v. 20). Nor may it be overlooked that just as the coming of Christ will be divine vengeance upon the wicked world and apostate church that persecute the church, the prayer of the church for the coming of Christ is also the petition for the Lord's just judgment upon the church's and his cruel enemies. The church triumphant in heaven prays for this vengeance (Rev. 6:9–11). The church on earth prays for the coming of Christ with regard to this vengeance (Luke 18:6–8). The expectation of God's just vengeance at the coming of Christ upon the ungodly who ridicule and persecute them now, apparently victoriously, strengthens the patience of the godly.

In that both postmillennialism and dispensational premillennialism rule out signs of the end and strive to put doctrinal blindfolds on the eyes of the people of God with regard to signs, both of these eschatological errors are grievous false doctrines *practically*. They weaken watchfulness. They render their adherents unprepared for the man of sin and the great tribulation. They subvert the Christian hope, *by which hope the church is saved*, the one by presenting it as the illusory rapture and the other by the equally illusory golden age of a carnal millennium and the earthly reign of the saints.

2

THE UNIMPORTANT DATE OF REVELATION

INTRODUCTION

Consideration of the structure of the last book of the Bible raises the question of the date of the book, that is, the date of its writing by the apostle John. John himself informs us that he saw the visions that comprise the book when he was "in the isle that is called Patmos" and that he was in this island "for the word of God, and for the testimony of Jesus Christ," that is, as the object of persecution (Rev. 1:9). The persecutor was the ungodly, antichristian Roman Empire.

The Christian tradition, which has been almost universally accepted until recently, is that the persecuting emperor responsible for John's banishment to the island of Patmos was Domitian. Domitian ruled Rome from AD 81 to 96. When he demanded to be worshiped as "Lord and God" in AD 87, he launched cruel persecution of Christians, who of course refused this worship. "Tradition declares that [the] one who was banished for his faith was the Apostle John, who then wrote the Apocalypse on the island of Patmos."[1] John wrote the book, therefore, about AD 95.

This tradition of the date of the writing of the book is based largely, although not exclusively, on the testimony of the early church father Irenaeus, who lived from AD 130 to 202. He was taught by Polycarp, who knew the apostle John himself. In a book written about AD 180, that is, within eighty-five or ninety years after the event, Irenaeus stated that the book of Revelation

---

1 Peter Toon, in *The New International Dictionary of the Christian Church*, general ed. J. D. Douglas (Grand Rapids, MI: Zondervan, 1974), 308.

was "seen, not a long time ago, but almost in our own generation, at the end of the reign of Domitian."[2]

THE CONTEMPORARY ISSUE OF THE DATE

Of late, a group of theologians committed to Christian Reconstruction postmillennialism, or postmillennial Christian Reconstructionism (the Christian reconstruction of the world being fundamental), have contended for an earlier date of the writing of Revelation. They insist on a date prior to AD 70. This is the date of Rome's defeat of the revolutionary nation of Israel in Palestine and of the destruction of the grand temple in Jerusalem. One of this group, Kenneth L. Gentry Jr., has written an entire book devoted to proving that John wrote the book of Revelation before AD 70: *Before Jerusalem Fell: Dating the Book of Revelation*.[3] This 350-page book takes issue with the Christian tradition concerning the date of the writing of Revelation. It contends that the seemingly clear statement of Irenaeus does not, in fact, mean what it seems to mean. It examines the internal evidence of Revelation in order to prove that the content itself of the book demands a date prior to AD 70. Then it corroborates its finding of the early date by an examination of the history of the Roman Empire.

Gentry's conclusion is that the Christian tradition has been mistaken. John wrote Revelation sometime before AD 70, probably in AD 65 or 66, not during the reign of Domitian, but in the reign of Emperor Nero.[4]

A PRESUPPOSED CONCLUSION

There are two things seriously wrong with Gentry's conclusion, indeed with the book as a whole. First, Gentry did his research and wrote the book in order to buttress and defend a doctrine to which he was committed from the outset. His research did not lead him to his conclusion, but his conclusion drove and determined his research. The doctrine that decided when Revelation was written is Gentry's eschatology. This doctrine of the last things is postmillennialism.

---

2 Quoted in *The International Standard Bible Encyclopaedia*, vol. 4 (Grand Rapids, MI: Eerdmans, 1960), 2584.
3 The subtitle is *An Exegetical and Historical Argument for a Pre-A.D. 70 Composition* (San Francisco—London—Bethesda: Christian Universities Press, 1997). Gentry is not the only one in this school of eschatological thinking to date Revelation prior to AD 70. See also Gary DeMar in *Last Days Madness: Obsession of the Modern Church* (Atlanta, GA: American Vision, 1994), 182–83, and David Chilton, *The Days of Vengeance: An Exposition of the Book of Revelation* (Ft. Worth, TX: Dominion Press, 1987), 4 and throughout the book. Gentry himself argues on behalf of the early date of Revelation in another book, *The Beast of Revelation* (Tyler, TX: Institute for Christian Economics, 1989), 81–188.
4 Gentry, *Before Jerusalem Fell*, 336.

It is Gentry's theology that the future—the *earthly* future—of the church is bright with the promise that the church will gradually come to exercise dominion over all nations. This development will consist of the conversion of at least the majority of humans in every nation. In an outburst of postmillennialism's vaunted optimism, one of Gentry's colleagues prophesies the conversion of every human then living.[5] Responding in part to my charge that the revolt of hordes of Satan's minions against the reign of the saints at the end of the "golden age" of the millennium, as prophesied by Revelation 20:7–10 and grudgingly acknowledged by many leading postmillennial theologians, represents a fatal blow to the postmillennial claim that their theology is the victory of the kingdom of Christ at the very end, Selbrede contends that the passage in Revelation 20 does not teach a final apostasy. Such a view, argues Selbrede, amounts to "pessimistic postmillennialism."[6] On the contrary, during the millennium, prior to the second coming of Christ, every human then living will be saved; and all will obey the law in all its particulars, meaning apparently that all will be perfectly sanctified. This will be the eschatological universalism that alone does justice to the carnal victory of which postmillennialism dreams and to postmillennialism's preterist exegesis of Matthew 24–25.[7]

Regardless of the present objection to this eschatological universalism by such postmillennial theologians as Gary North, Greg Bahnsen, and Ken Gentry,

---

5 Martin G. Selbrede, "Reconstructing Postmillennialism," *The Journal of Christian Reconstruction: Symposium on Eschatology*, no. 15 (Winter, 1998): 146–224.
6 Successfully resisting the perverse pleasure of witnessing postmillennialists turning on each other with their favorite demeaning of amillennialism, namely "pessimillennialism," the amillennialist observes that the internal conflict now rising in postmillennial circles brings out a fundamental implication of the postmillennial understanding of the victory of Christ in future earthly history. Every human must be saved, and saved with perfect salvation. There may be no unbeliever and no sin at all in the postmillennial kingdom. Postmillennialism's "golden age" must in the end be heaven on earth, within history, prior to the coming of Christ. Anything else is pessimism, or to use postmillennialism's favorite slur, "pessimillennialism." On the thinking of "optimistic" postmillennialism, the victory of the kingdom of Christ in history also demands the resurrection of the dead saints to join in the "golden age" and the resurrection of the ungodly to be banished from the earth that is part of the dominion of the saints. This requires the final judgment prior to the return of Christ. Postmillennialism implies and longs for heaven on earth within history and the eternal state within time. No second, bodily coming of Christ is really necessary, or fervently longed for. A fundamental error of optimistic postmillennialism is the denial of the Christian hope: the second, bodily coming of Christ and the grand work of salvation that he is to accomplish at that coming. Postmillennialism has "optimism"; it minimizes or lacks the Christian hope.
7 Selbrede borrows this rampaging postmillennial optimism from the Presbyterian B. B. Warfield ("Reconstructing," 171). With regard to Warfield, "when great men err, they err greatly."

who are restrained by Revelation 20:7–10, which they see clearly prophesies a great falling away shortly before the return of Christ, Selbrede's version of the postmillennial victory of the kingdom of Christ within history must prevail among the advocates of a golden age for the church. The alternative consisting of a pessimistic postmillennialism must simply be anathema to the postmillennial champions of a carnal victory within history. No final defeat, as they view a final apostasy, can be acceptable. Exegetically, the preterist razor applied to Jesus' prophecy of the end in Matthew 24–25 cannot be withdrawn at chapter 24:35. Indeed, it cannot be withdrawn at chapter 25:30. On postmillennial principles, all of Matthew 24–25 must be applied exclusively to the destruction of Jerusalem in AD 70. Inherent in postmillennial principles and exegesis is full-scale, complete, consistent preterism. Jesus came, fully and finally, in AD 70. There is no hope of a second coming of Jesus and of a resurrection of the dead.

For postmillennialism in its milder, as yet undeveloped, inconsistent form, history tends toward a period of a thousand years or more before the coming of Christ in the body,[8] during which millennium Christians (read: Reconstructionists) will rule the world. This will be the golden age of the millennium of earthly peace, earthly prosperity, and earthly power of the church.

According to Ken Gentry, all the history of the new dispensation after AD 70 is the gradual realization of this millennial glory for the church. For this is the goal of history on the part of the exalted Jesus Christ. This postmillennial theology demands the rejection of the Christian tradition concerning the date of the writing of Revelation.

If, in fact, John wrote the book of Revelation after AD 70, that is, after Jerusalem fell, as the church has supposed, postmillennialism is exposed as an empty and fallacious dream. For in this case Revelation is forecasting tribulation for the church. Not the church but the antichristian kingdom will come to hold sway over all nations. The kingdom that comes to power at the end of history is not the church, but the kingdom of the beasts of Revelation 13. The church does not look forward to postmillennialism's golden age, but to amillennialism's

---

8 One of Gentry's colleagues is bold to predict a golden age of hundreds of thousands of years. His eschatological theology is post*multi*millennialism. Christian Reconstructionist, postmillennialist David Chilton rejoiced that history has "tens of thousands, perhaps hundreds of thousands of years of increasing godliness ahead of it, before the Second Coming of Christ" (*Paradise Restored* [Reconstruction Press, 1985], 221–22; cited in Engelsma, *Christ's Spiritual Kingdom: A Defense of Reformed Amillennialism* [Redlands, CA: The Reformed Witness, 2001], 11). That hundreds of thousands of years put the coming of Christ off virtually forever troubles this postmillennialist not at all. His heart is not fixed on the coming of Christ. It is set upon the golden age.

second coming of Christ Jesus, immediately preceded by the fiercest warfare that the kingdom of Christ has ever fought.

The solution for postmillennial Ken Gentry and his Christian Reconstructionist colleagues is to make the book of Revelation prophesy the persecution of the church by the Roman Empire under Caesar Nero, prior to AD 70. Then the whole of the book can be explained as referring to the Roman persecution of the church that, oddly for postmillennialism, culminated in the destruction of Jerusalem in AD 70. (I say "oddly" because the destruction of Jerusalem itself was not persecution of the church, but oppression of the Jews and of the unbelieving nation of Israel.) According to Gentry, John was exiled to the island of Patmos not during the reign of Emperor Domitian, about AD 95, as Irenaeus wrote and as the church has supposed in the past, but under Nero, about AD 65 or 66.

All of Revelation therefore refers to this oppression of the Jews, which is now safely in the past. Nothing of the book refers to the future, except of course the millennium of Revelation 20. This leaves the future open to the golden age of the church, as is essential to the eschatology of postmillennialism. That this doctrine of the last things drove Gentry's project of determining when Revelation was written, and why, comes out clearly at the book's end:

> On the one hand, if Christianity's eschatological expectation is that of an imminently portending and dismally precipitous decline and extinction of Christian influence in our day, as much of current Christian literature suggests, then our Christian endeavor will be powerfully bent in one direction. And it must necessarily be turned *away from* the implementation of long-term Christian cultural progress and dominion. If Revelation's judgments are yet to occur and lie in our future, then we must expect and prepare for the worst.
>
> On the other hand, if the expectation held by the Christian community is of a sure hope for progress and victory, then the focus of Christian enterprise will be of a constructive and future-oriented nature. Our cultural endeavor will not be in despite of our eschatology, but in light of it. In this regard, if Revelation's judgments lie in the past and punctuate the close of the old order in preparation for a divinely wrought *novus ordo seclorum* [new order of the world] in which God will be engaged in "reconciling the world to Himself" (2 Cor. 5:19) and "drawing all men" to Christ (John 12:31), then the Church can confidently seek to bring "every thought captive to the obedience of Christ" (2 Cor. 10:5).[9]

---

9 Gentry, *Before Jerusalem Fell*, 336–37.

This is the significance of the date of Revelation. The church must have a carnal victory in history. It must have this kind of victory in a golden age in order to dominate culture. This determines dating the book of Revelation before Jerusalem fell.

Gentry cannot refrain from taking a parting shot at the theology that, in his mind, is linked to the later date of Revelation: "cultural defeatism and retreatist pietism so influential in twentieth century Christianity."[10] Although this charge is not the main issue in the dating of Revelation—the issues are far more serious—it is so common on the part of postmillennialists, so serious in its own right, and so much a part of the dating of the last book of the Bible that a response is in order.

First, the charge is false on its very face. Even though Reformed Christianity, to restrict consideration to this branch of Christianity, is historically and in its creeds amillennial and therefore, according to Gentry, guilty of "cultural defeatism and retreatist pietism," the Reformed faith's belief and conduct regarding the life of Reformed Christians in God's world are not world flight. Rather, they are the belief and conduct expressed in the biblical injunction in the world, but not of the world (John 17:11, 16–17). If the Spirit of Christ intended the dominion envisioned by postmillennial Christian Reconstruction, he certainly could have, and would have, empowered the lives of Reformed Christians over the past five hundred years to this end, for they have been the kind of lives that might have had this result. That he has not done so makes plain either that he has no such intention with the active cultural lives of the members of the Reformed churches, or that he has been unable to realize his cultural purpose with the active Christian lives of his Reformed people. Gentry and his colleagues may take their choice.

Even secular historians virtually unanimously remark the aggressive nature of Calvinism regarding living according to Christian principles in every sphere of earthly life. These historians have many criticisms of the Reformed faith. Of one fault, they are agreed, it is not guilty: world flight.

Also, regarding the charge of "defeatism," in view of the fact that the amillennial understanding of Revelation is the right one, Gentry's harsh criticism falls in reality on the Holy Spirit, who inspired the book. According to Gentry, amillennialism is defeatist and results in retreating from the active Christian life that God calls his people to live. Who is to blame for this defeatism and retreatism? Why, the Holy Spirit who inspired, in the book of Revelation and elsewhere, an amillennial eschatology.

And then there is the truth that conclusively demonstrates that the

---

10 Gentry, *Before Jerusalem Fell*, 337.

amillennial understanding of Revelation does not, by anyone's standards, result in passivity, defeatism, and retreat. On the contrary, by the blessing of the Spirit who inspired the book, the book of Revelation has accomplished and accomplishes today the most vigorous activity known to humans, the most agonizing struggle, and the most glorious of victories. It is the activity of warfare on behalf of the kingdom of Christ against the kingdom of the antichrist, of struggle to defend oneself as a citizen in the kingdom of Christ and the kingdom itself against the assault of the kingdom of Satan, and the victory of oneself and of the true church in this warfare. This spiritual warfare and victory may not impress Ken Gentry. The only victory that impresses him would be one that catapults him into the White House as president, not only of the United States but also of all the nations on earth; that anoints Gary North as chief justice of the Supreme Court over all peoples; and that makes Gary DeMar head of a worldwide economic order.

But this spiritual warfare and victory impressed the apostle John, the elders of the church, and the Lamb himself:

13. One of the elders answered, saying unto me, What are these which are arrayed in white robes? and whence came they?
14. And I said unto him, Sir, thou knowest. And he said to me, These are they which came out of great tribulation, and have washed their robes, and made them white in the blood of the Lamb.
15. Therefore are they before the throne of God, and serve him day and night in his temple: and he that sitteth on the throne shall dwell among them…
17. The Lamb which is in the midst of the throne shall feed them, and shall lead them unto living fountains of waters: and God shall wipe away all tears from their eyes. (Rev. 7:13–15, 17)

The monotonous charge by the men of Christian Reconstruction that Reformed amillennialism is pessimistic defeatism and retreatism is factually and historically false on the face of it, to say nothing of its slander against the holy life enjoined upon believers in Scripture. We amillennialists reject the charge and denounce it as a mere canard on behalf of the pipe dream of the Christian Reconstructionists that they will bring about a carnal kingdom of Christ. The issue between Reformed amillennialism and the Christian Reconstructionists is not pessimism versus optimism. The issue is whether it is the will of God to establish a kingdom of earthly peace and earthly prosperity in history prior to the coming of Jesus Christ in the body.

But the implications of Gentry's analysis of the book of Revelation are far more serious than his demeaning of the faithful, holy lives of the people of God in the world as passive, defeatist, and retreatist. Gentry's analysis of the book is that, since the book was written before AD 70, all of the book, at least all of the warning of the forming of the kingdom of spiritual darkness, all of the struggle of Christians with this kingdom, all of the martyrdom, and all of the tribulation (which is far and away the bulk of the book) have no application to the church after AD 70, and certainly no application to the church of the twenty-first century.

According to Gentry and his colleagues, the book of Revelation is nothing more than the account of the history of the suffering mainly of Jews and of the destruction of their city in the past. Always with the exception of a few verses in chapter 20, the book of Revelation is of little or no interest to the Christian church. No minister will, or ought to, feel any attraction to the preaching of the book. He might as well preach Josephus' even more vivid account of the destruction of Jerusalem.

Why the Holy Spirit included the book in the canon is a puzzle, except, of course, for chapter 20.

Well may Gentry and his fellow preterists consider whether by consigning the book of Revelation, like Matthew 24, strictly to the past they are not guilty of the evil warned against in Revelation 22:19: taking "away from the words of the book of this prophecy." For one thing, this text identifies all of Revelation as prophecy, not merely as ancient history. In addition, to consign the book exclusively, or mainly, to the time of Nero in AD 66 is a kind of taking away from the words of the book. The words have lost their application to the church down the ages.

Then, very seriously indeed, Gentry commits himself to, and seduces his disciples with, full-scale preterism, even though he angrily rejects the charge. Full-scale, consistent preterism teaches that everything in the New Testament concerning the end (Greek: *telos*), or the last things, was fulfilled fully and finally in the destruction of Jerusalem in AD 70. Everything that the New Testament promises of a bodily resurrection, of a second, bodily coming of Jesus on the clouds, of a resurrection of the dead, of a final judgment, of a new creation, and of an eternal state in the new world was fulfilled finally in AD 70.

This heretical, ungodly doctrine is the denial of the coming of Jesus Christ, the hope of his church. This denial of the hope of the church is the inescapable implication of the theology that thrusts Matthew 24–25 and the book of Revelation into the past.[11] That Gentry himself is attracted to, or at least not

---

11 For the detailed proof that the inconsistent preterism of Gentry, DeMar, Chilton, and others of their eschatological school implies full-scale, consistent preterism that denies the bodily, second coming of Christ yet in the future, see Engelsma, *Christ's Spiritual Kingdom*, 129–58.

repulsed by, this denial of the second coming of Christ in the body is unmistakably evident. The father of the consistent preterism that openly denies a second, bodily coming of Christ is one J. Stuart Russell. Gentry refers to Russell some twelve times as an authority for Gentry's preterist interpretation of Revelation and of Matthew 24. Once he describes Russell's explanation of Revelation as "noteworthy and scholarly labors [that] merit a careful hearing."[12] Never does he so much as mention that Russell's book is a volume of eschatological unbelief, the heresy of Hymenaeus, who taught "that the resurrection is past already," thus overthrowing the faith of some (2 Tim. 2:17–18).

But things become even clearer concerning Gentry's attraction to full, consistent preterism. Having explicitly consigned every aspect of Christ's second coming, including the second coming itself, the resurrection of the dead, the final judgment, and the renewal of creation, to the destruction of Jerusalem in AD 70, Russell concluded:

> We are compelled…to conclude that the Parousia, or second coming of Christ, with its connected and concomitant events, did take place, according to the Saviour's own prediction, at the period when Jerusalem was destroyed, and before the passing away of 'that generation.'[13]

Russell himself draws the implication from this doctrine of eschatology, which is founded on the preterist explanation of Matthew 24 and the book of Revelation. He asks, "Whither are we tending? What is to be the end and consummation of human history?" Russell's answer to this fundamental question? "Scripture prophecy guides us no further…Where nothing has been revealed it would be the height of presumption to prognosticate the future."[14]

This book, which is the outright denial of the second, bodily coming of Jesus, features recommendation by Ken Gentry Jr.:

> I highly recommend this well-organized, carefully argued, and compellingly written defense of preterism to serious and mature students of the Bible. It is one of the most persuasive and challenging books I have read on the subject of eschatology and has had a great impact on my own thinking.[15]

This is the book that denies the bodily, second coming of Jesus Christ and every event related to this coming, and that does so on the basis of an

---

12 Gentry, *Before Jerusalem Fell*, 30.
13 James Stuart Russell, *The Parousia: A Critical Inquiry into the New Testament Doctrine of Our Lord's Second Coming* (Bradford, PA: Kingdom Publications, repr. 1996), 549.
14 Russell, *Parousia*, 549–50.
15 Gentry, back cover of Russell, *The Parousia*. See also https://www.truthaccordingtoscripture.com/documents/parousia/Parousia_Russell.pdf, accessed September 28, 2020.

explanation of Matthew 24–25 and of the book of Revelation that interprets the passages as referring exclusively to the fall of Jerusalem in AD 70. This is the book, by Gentry's own enthusiastic admission, that "has had a great impact on…[Gentry's] own thinking."

Indeed, it has had "great impact" on the thinking of Mr. Gentry with regard to eschatology.

Ken Gentry must not affect indignation when an amillennialist recoils from his preterist interpretation of the book of Revelation and finds in it at least the beginning—the principle—of the preterist heresy of a denial of the coming of Christ. Dutch Reformed theological thinking is committed to the truth of a familiar proverb, *beginselen werken door*, that is, translated freely, "principles work themselves out." With reference to the inconsistent preterism of Ken Gentry, his inconsistent preterism regarding Matthew 24–25 and the book of Revelation will inevitably become the consistent preterism that puts all of eschatology, including the second coming of Christ, into the past of the destruction of Jerusalem in AD 70. His inconsistent preterism is, in principle, the denial of the coming of Christ in the body in the future, and with this the denial of all the great events that are to take place at this coming.

The working out of the principle of inconsistent preterism has already taken place in one of the foremost champions of Christian Reconstruction, a colleague of Ken Gentry, David Chilton. Chilton's inconsistent preterism became consistent preterism. He has written, "Simply put, I now believe that Christ's Second Coming occurred in A. D. 70…I am convinced by Scripture that what Christ and the Apostles *meant* by His Second Coming occurred in A. D. 70."[16]

The first seriously erroneous implication of Gentry's early date of the fall of Rome, *as Gentry applies this early date in his doctrine of the last things*, then, is its threat to the essential biblical doctrine of the coming of Christ and, with this, to the hope of the church.

FUNDAMENTALLY UNIMPORTANT DATE

Gentry's second serious error is his conviction that it is of fundamental importance for a right understanding of Revelation and of the doctrine of the last things that Revelation be written before Jerusalem fell, that is, before AD 70. In fact, it makes no difference whether John wrote the book in AD 66, as Gentry insists, or in AD 95, as is the tradition in the church on the basis of the assertion

---

16 David Chilton, quoted in Vern Crisler, "The Eschatological *A Priori* of the New Testament: A Critique of Hyper-Preterism," *The Journal of Christian Reconstruction: Symposium on Eschatology*, no. 15 (Winter, 1998), 226; emphasis in the original.

of Irenaeus. Gentry supposes that establishing the date as the earlier AD 66 shuts the application of the book up to the fall of Jerusalem in AD 70, on behalf of the golden age of postmillennial glories thereafter. But the truth is that the book of Revelation in a highly figurative and symbolical manner prophesies the history of the church throughout the entire new dispensation, culminating in the second coming of Jesus Christ. This history is, and will be, the constant struggle of the kingdom of Christ with the kingdom of Satan. It is, and will be, the persecution of the church by the kingdom of Satan. This struggle will culminate in the great tribulation of Matthew 24:21, under the man of sin of 2 Thessalonians 2:3, whom Revelation 13 describes as the beast out of the sea.

The book of Revelation prophesies this history, as did Jesus in Matthew 24, under the figure, or type, of the persecution of the early church by the antichristian Roman Empire. What is on the foreground is not this particular emperor or that, but the godless Roman Empire, or kingdom, with all its antichristian emperors. John took his typology from the book of Daniel, especially chapters 7–12. In Daniel, the fourth beast, which is the persecuting Roman Empire, is a kingdom (7:23). Included are Nero, Domitian, and other emperors, or kings.

But this Roman Empire with its antichristian emperors was not the only beastly kingdom in view in Revelation. It was an early manifestation in the history of the church in the world of Satan's attempts to establish an antichristian world power that would eradicate the kingdom of Christ. Another obvious, worldwide, and more or less successful attempt by Satan in history to establish his beastly kingdom and to eradicate the church was the antichristian kingdoms of the West and the wholesale persecution of the church at the time of the Reformation of the church in the sixteenth and seventeenth centuries. Again and again in the history of the New Testament, there have been persecutions of the church by godless governments on a limited scale. All of these are the realities forecast by Matthew 24 and foretold in the book of Revelation. The "mystery of iniquity," that is, the man of sin of 2 Thessalonians, was working already in the days of the apostle but was restrained, so that he would be "revealed in his time" (2:6–7). Heads of these manifestations of the antichristian kingdom certainly include Nero and Domitian. But there are others as well.

The Roman Empire with its bloodthirsty emperors is certainly on the foreground in the book of Revelation, but it is on the foreground not as the full reality of the antichristian foe of the kingdom of Christ. Rather, it is the historical type of the beast out of the sea of Revelation 13. The reality is the antichristian world power with its beastly head that is yet to be revealed.

Whether John wrote Revelation in AD 66 or in AD 95 therefore makes no difference regarding Reformed amillennialism's expectation of the personal antichrist and his great tribulation of the church yet in the future. Christ prophesied, and John foretold, the last days under the type of the destruction of Jerusalem in AD 70. The full reality of the events of the last days—the false Christ and the tribulation for the church—is still before the church in the twenty-first century. The book of Revelation is not merely past and basically irrelevant history for the church of today, but prophecy of what lies before her. This is not the dream of postmillennial theology enabling Christian Reconstructionists to visualize their earthly kingdom, ignoring what everyone can see developing at the present time, but sober warning of the great conflict at the end between the kingdom of Satan under antichrist and the true church under Jesus Christ.

This warning rings true in light of the history of the church after AD 70 and in light of current developments in history. The history of the church from AD 70 to the present time has not been the carnal triumph of the church over all the nations of the world. Neither has it been the gradual development of a postmillennial kingdom of earthly peace, earthly power, and earthly prosperity. Postmillennialism is as mistaken a history as it is a theology. Rather the history of the church has been a spiritual struggle to maintain herself as a true church of Christ and, time and again, God's reformation of the church on account of apostasy. In this history, the church has not become numerically larger and culturally increasingly influential, but smaller and of lesser significance to an increasingly wicked world. The only ecclesiastical candidate that has approximated Reconstructionism's program for the victory of the kingdom of Christ is the Roman Catholic Church, and this church is, in reality, an aspect of the kingdom of antichrist.

Regarding the present, only the unfounded optimism of Christian Reconstruction can envision the earthly victory of the true church. The heathen nations remain sunken in their pagan religions. Islam is as hostile to Christianity as ever it has been, and it makes inroads into formerly "Christian nations." These formerly Christian nations cast off every vestige of whatever influence Christianity once had upon them. Their cultures degenerate into the extreme degradation of sodomy and lesbianism. This is God's hardening of them for their refusal to worship him as he has revealed himself to them both in creation and in the gospel, which gospel has shined brightly among them in the past (see Rom. 1:18–32). One effect of this hardening is that the nations of the once "Christian" West show themselves increasingly hostile to the Christian religion and church. Overt persecution is not far off. Those who forecast a gradual "Christianizing" of the world are as blind to present reality as they are to past history and to the doctrine of the last things in Scripture.

The reality of the old, godless Roman kingdom; of the fourth beast of Daniel 7; of the beasts from the sea and from the earth of Revelation 13; of the man of sin and lawless one of 2 Thessalonians 2; and therefore of the abomination of desolation and great tribulation of Matthew 24 is impending. Satan is finally being loosed (Rev. 20). The church and all Christians must be prepared for their last and greatest battle.

And quickened by the promise that the day of their redemption draws nigh in the coming—the *second, bodily* coming—of Jesus Christ the Lord!

3

THE SIGN OF THE PREACHING OF THE GOSPEL

INTRODUCTION

Before considering the sign of the end that consists of the antichrist, which usually dominates in any treatment of eschatology, it is fitting, if not demanded, that a study of the end devote attention to the closely related signs of the preaching of the gospel and apostasy. It would be a mistake to move immediately from the consideration of the idea and reality of signs of the coming of Christ to a treatment of antichrist, virtually overlooking the signs of preaching and of apostasy.

Especially the preaching of the gospel demands separate, prominent attention in any study of the Bible's revelation of the last things. It is of central importance in the time of the end, that is, with regard to time's attaining its goal. The gospel is of central importance for eschatology. Although antichrist tends to get more attention, the reality of antichrist is far less important for eschatology than the preaching of the gospel. Contrary to popular thinking, antichrist does not dominate the preaching of the gospel, but the preaching of the gospel controls antichrist.

Regarding apostasy, it is instrumental in the realizing of antichrist in the world (2 Thess. 2:3). It is fitting therefore to examine apostasy, in closest connection with preaching, prior to the consideration of antichrist.

Even though one cannot treat both preaching and apostasy in one chapter, because of the mass of material, it must be kept in mind that the two realities are inseparable in the history of the church in the last days. Apostasy accompanies the preaching of the gospel. They are always contending in a spiritual life-and-death struggle. Apostasy affixes itself to the preaching like a parasite on its host.

What follows in this chapter is not a theologically scientific, purely dogmatical study of preaching. Rather, it is an examination of preaching as a sign of the end. It is a study of preaching as a reality that brings about the coming of Christ. Our concern is the eschatological nature of the preaching of the gospel of Jesus Christ.

PREACHING AS THE SIGN

The unique importance of the preaching of the gospel for eschatology appears in the passage in which Jesus mentions preaching as a sign: "And this gospel of the kingdom shall be preached in all the world for a witness unto all nations; and then shall the end come" (Matt. 24:14). The parallel passage of Mark 13:10 reads: "And the gospel must first be published among all nations." Both the preceding and following context of the Mark passage make clear that "first" in the text has reference to the great tribulation of the church. Prior to the persecution of the church, with reference ultimately to the great tribulation under the antichrist, the gospel must be published among all nations.

Matthew 24:14 teaches that the worldwide preaching of the gospel is a sign that the end is at hand. It also teaches that the end of all things at the coming of Christ waits upon the preaching in all the world: "And *then* shall the end come." It is preaching, more than any other sign, that brings about the end.

This significance of preaching regarding the end is indicated also by another passage that concerns preaching as a sign. This is Revelation 6:1–2: "And I saw when the Lamb opened one of the seals, and I heard, as it were the noise of thunder, one of the four beasts saying, Come and see. And I saw, and behold a white horse: and he that sat on him had a bow; and a crown was given unto him: and he went forth conquering, and to conquer." The running of the white horse with its rider is the very first of the seven seals that represent the realizing of the counsel of God in history as that counsel is carried out by the exalted, risen Jesus Christ, who stands in the midst of the throne of God (Rev. 6). That the opening of this seal is first expresses not only that it is prominent in all the unfolding of the history, especially of the New Testament, but also that it governs everything else. The rest of the seals, the trumpets, and the vials represent all of history as concerns the church, and all is determined and governed by the first seal.

The white horse with its rider is the preaching of the gospel, which preaching, although instrumentally done by apostles and other human preachers, is essentially the work of Jesus Christ himself. And this work is mighty, indeed almighty and victorious, regardless of the opposition. The rider wears a crown given him by God. The rider goes forth "conquering, and to conquer."

As the first of the seals, and therefore first also regarding the trumpets and vials that unfold the seventh seal, the conquering preaching of the gospel is first in the execution of the counsel of God. All else—the content of the rest of the seals, all the trumpets, and all the vials—follows upon and serves the preaching of the gospel. Thus, the inspired book of the last things reveals that the preaching of the gospel is the reality that is decisive regarding the coming of Jesus Christ.

The importance of the preaching of the gospel for the end is, first, that by the preaching the elect are brought to salvation. Preaching is the primary means of grace,[1] and by this effectual means the elect are saved. The significance of the salvation of the elect for the end of all things is the testimony of the controversial text 2 Peter 3:9. This significance is often overlooked in the controversy whether the text teaches a universal will of God for salvation. The second part of the text declares that God is "longsuffering to us-ward, not willing that any should perish, but that all should come to repentance." In the doctrinal controversy it can be overlooked that the purpose of the text is to explain the apparent delay of the coming of Christ, occasioning the denial of that coming by scoffers. To this seeming delay of the coming of Christ, the first part of 2 Peter 3:9 refers: "The Lord is not slack concerning his promise, as some men count slackness." The explanation of the seeming delay—*the* explanation—is that the Lord "is longsuffering to us-ward, not willing that any [of us] should perish, but that all [of us] should come to repentance."

God has a certain, definite number of humans in all nations who are chosen unto salvation. All must be brought to salvation. Upon the salvation of all, the coming of Jesus waits. What determines the end, therefore, is the salvation of the elect church to the last member. Since humans are brought to faith and salvation by the preaching of the gospel, preaching is the primary sign of the end. Second Peter 3:9 is not mainly a text of soteriology, but a text of eschatology.

Article 37 of the Reformed creed the Belgic Confession echoes the main thought of 2 Peter 3:9 and by implication indicates the importance of the sign of preaching for the coming of Christ: "Finally, we believe, according to the Word of God, when the time appointed by the Lord (which is unknown to all creatures) is come, and the number of the elect complete, that our Lord Jesus

---

1   In answer to the question "whence comes this faith" by which we are made "partakers of Christ and all his benefits," the Heidelberg Catechism declares: "The Holy Ghost works it in our hearts by the preaching of the holy Gospel, and confirms it by the use of the holy Sacraments" (Q&A 65, in Philip Schaff, ed., *The Creeds of Christendom with a History and Critical Notes*, 6th ed., 3 vols. [New York: Harper and Row, 1931; repr., Grand Rapids, MI: Baker Books, 2007], 3:328).

Christ will come from heaven."[2] Christ will come again at the time appointed by the Lord God, and the Lord appointed this time mainly in view of the salvation of the last elect and thus the gathering unto Christ of the elect church in its entirety.

Second, the preaching of the gospel is decisively important for the coming of Christ because by the gospel the kingdom of God is established and extended in all the world. Matthew 24:14 significantly describes the gospel as the "gospel *of the kingdom.*" The gospel both has the kingdom as its theme and builds the kingdom. In the present new and last age, the kingdom established and advanced by Jesus Christ must *come*, must come *continuously*, and must come *victoriously*. This is the promise of the great Old Testament prophecy of the kingdom of Messiah, the book of Daniel: "The stone that smote the image became a great mountain, and filled the whole earth" (2:35). This stone represents the kingdom set up by God, and this kingdom must break in pieces all other kingdoms, and "it shall stand for ever" (v. 44). For the worldwide extension of the kingdom of God, every believer prays: "Thy kingdom come" (Matt. 6:10). First Corinthians 15:24–28 expressly makes the end dependent upon Christ's conquest of all enemies of the kingdom of God in order that he can deliver up the kingdom to God: "Then cometh the end, when he shall have delivered up the kingdom to God, even the Father" (v. 24).

This victorious coming of the kingdom of God takes place by the gospel, in the establishment of the kingdom in the hearts and lives of the elect, and in the gathering of the church. Throughout this present age, the spiritual reign of God in Christ by the Holy Spirit has been extended among all nations in all the world. The instrument has been the gospel. Even as faithful preaching is antithetical, the victory of the kingdom of God is accompanied by the overthrow of the kingdom of Satan. Exactly because "the weapons of our warfare are not carnal, but mighty through God to the pulling down of strong holds," by the word and Spirit the church casts down imaginations and every high thing that exalts itself against the knowledge of God, and brings into captivity every thought to the obedience of Christ (2 Cor. 10:3–6; see also 1 Cor. 15:24 and Matt. 12:25–29).

The mighty spiritual weapon consisting of the preaching of the gospel pulls down the stronghold of Satan in the establishment of a true church, in the conversion of every elect sinner, in the bringing to faith and obedience of every covenantal child, in the godly life of every saint, and in the good confession and defense of the faith on the part of every believer.

---

2 Belgic Confession 37, in Schaff, *Creeds of Christendom*, 3:433.

The preaching of the gospel pulls down the strongholds of the kingdom of Satan also by polemics. It exposes and condemns false doctrines and heretics. In the imagery of 2 Corinthians 10:3–6, the gospel does not only erect strongholds; it also pulls strongholds down. It does not only build up holy imaginations and high things that exalt the knowledge of God; it also casts down imaginations and every high thing that exalts itself *against* the knowledge of God. The preaching of the gospel is the *weapon of our warfare*.

According to Revelation 6:1–2, the figure of the preaching of the gospel has a "bow," not a powder puff. The white horse is a warhorse, not a plug for plowing. The preaching goes forth "conquering, and to conquer" (v. 2). The sphere in which the horse runs is that of battle. The victory of the gospel implies overcoming enemies in hard-fought war.

Church history substantiates this biblical conception of the preaching of the gospel. The victorious running of the white horse was Augustine's polemic against Pelagius; Luther's opposition to Erasmus' theology of free will, as well as his opposition to antinomianism; Calvin's struggle with innumerable heresies; and the maintenance of the gospel in every true church by hosts of unsung preachers whose sermons were antithetical.

The pernicious, popular view today that good preaching is only positive and that the good preacher is one always with a sweet smile on his face, as though a polemical preacher is unloving, is an attempt to cripple the white horse in its running and to strip the rider of his bow. Preaching that avoids controversy simply is not the running of the white horse of Revelation 6. Neither does it wear the crown of the passage. Churches overcome by such a philosophy of preaching and cursed by preaching that is only, ever, and always "sweetness and light" soon find themselves on the side of the adversary of the white horse and its rider of Revelation 6.

That adversary of the gospel is Satan, as Christ himself pointed out in his word in Luke 10:18. In the preaching of the gospel by his messengers, Christ saw "Satan as lightning fall from heaven," evidently soundly defeated (Luke 10:18). Calvin gives expression to the truth of the Lord's words by a lovely figure and sound interpretation:

> The thunder of the Gospel makes *Satan fall like lightning*; for it expresses the divine and astonishing power of the doctrine, which throws down, in a manner so sudden and violent, the prince of the world armed with such abundant forces.[3]

---

3   John Calvin, *Commentary on a Harmony of the Evangelists, Matthew, Mark, and Luke*, tr. William Pringle (Grand Rapids, MI: Eerdmans, 1949), 2:33; emphasis in the original.

There is yet a third way in which the preaching of the gospel determines the end of all things, or to speak more exactly, a third way in which God has determined the end in relation to the gospel. By the gospel, a witness must be given to all the world so that the reprobate ungodly are left without excuse, indeed are hardened in their unbelief, and thus are made ready for the end, particularly for the final judgment. Matthew 24:14 speaks of the gospel's being preached for a "*witness* unto all nations." A witness has a twofold effect, indeed a twofold purpose: not only does a witness effectually save some, it also testifies against others, leaving them inexcusable.

The parallel passage in Mark 13:9 has Jesus warning his disciples that they would be brought before rulers and kings for his sake, "for a *testimony against them*." Verses 10 and 11 make plain that it is the preaching of the gospel that occasions and constitutes this testimony against some. The gospel that must "first be published among all nations" (v. 10) serves to bring about the end, not only by its saving witness, but also by its condemning testimony.

HOW THE SIGN OF PREACHING APPEARS

This worldwide preaching of the gospel is realized as a sign to the believer gradually and steadily throughout the course of the present age, from the time of the apostles to the present. We must not expect some explosion of the gospel over all the earth at one time in the future. Nor does the preaching of the gospel have to reach every person. There is advance from Jerusalem to Samaria "and unto the uttermost part of the earth" (Acts 1:8). The gospel is satisfied with reaching all nations and peoples. It need not come to the attention of every individual.

There is also a finality about the gospel's having been proclaimed at one time in a certain nation. For the gospel once to have been witnessed to a nation, after which witness the nation has rejected or forsaken the gospel, means the loss of the gospel by that nation, or better, God's removal of the gospel from that nation forever. On one occasion, Martin Luther warned the German nation, whose national ear he had, that it pleased God that the nation and its people had the gospel at present, but that if they came to despise it God would take it away from them, never to be restored. This grave warning has become dreadful reality today, not only for Germany but also for all Europe. It is fast becoming a reality in North America.

Once the white horse with its rider has run through a nation and the nation has rejected the gospel, the white horse goes on its way, never to ride that way again. The church institute must be on guard that it does not banish the white horse by apostasy. The same holds true for a family. Luther's warning applies to families: God has given you the gospel of grace today; if you despise and reject it, he will take the gospel away, never to be returned. Do not reject, or take for granted, the white horse of Revelation 6:1–2. The sin of the grandparents is visited upon their grandchildren.

In AD 2022, the sign of preaching clearly shows the end. First, the very fact that there has been and still today is the worldwide preaching of the gospel assures that there will be an end, as Christ prophesied in Matthew 24:14. Who would have thought that the gospel of a crucified Jew in insignificant Palestine would have become a worldwide message forming a universal church? Second, by the present time, the gospel has overspread, or at least reached, almost all the inhabited world. Evidently, there are still more of us elect to be saved by the longsuffering Lord. Nevertheless, this all-important sign convinces the believer that the end is nigh.

The instituted church must be convinced of the importance of preaching for eschatology, so that she *preaches*, both in the congregation and on the mission field. Truly observing this sign, for the church, is not only noting that by this time the gospel has made great progress over all the world. But it is especially that the church is energetic and faithful in preaching the gospel everywhere that God opens a door. Eschatology puts missions high on the church's agenda: "The tie between eschatological expectation and mission call is essential and indissoluble."[4]

To this official witness must be added the unofficial (which is not to say ineffectual) witness to Christ Jesus of the holy life of the believer. Such a life, which is resonant of the mighty power of the gospel, is mighty through God to the pulling down of strongholds and thus subservient to the coming of Christ. Think only of the power of the witness of godly parents to their children and grandchildren. As an extension of the witness of godly parents, there is the witness of the good Christian school and, to borrow the wording of the original article 21 of the Reformed church order of Dordt, of the "good schoolmasters who shall…instruct the children…in godliness and in the Catechism."[5]

THE SIGN OF THE GOSPEL AND ANTICHRIST

Even though we reserve consideration of the sign consisting of antichrist until later, here it is fitting to take note of the fact that such is the fundamental importance of preaching for the end that the appearance of antichrist is strictly

---

4 G. C. Berkouwer, *The Return of Christ*, tr. James Van Oosterom, ed. Marlin J. Van Elderen (Grand Rapids, MI: Eerdmans, 1972), 132.
5 Martin Monsma and Idzerd Van Dellen, *The Church Order Commentary*, 3rd ed. (Grand Rapids, MI: Zondervan, 1954), 92–93.

determined by the gospel's having run its appointed course. The appearance of antichrist depends on the white horse of Revelation 6. The explanation of this dependence is that under antichrist no preaching of the gospel will be possible. This delay, or restraint, of antichrist in the interests of the gospel is implied by Matthew 24:14 and the parallel passage in Mark 13:10. In context, the latter passage teaches that before the great tribulation under antichrist can occur, the gospel must first be preached among all nations.

Two intriguing passages of Scripture teach that the preaching of the gospel determines when antichrist comes on the scene. The first is Revelation 11:7: when the two witnesses have "finished their testimony, the beast that ascendeth out of the bottomless pit shall make war against them, and shall overcome them, and kill them." The two witnesses symbolize the true, confessing church and her preachers. In verse 10, the two witnesses are called "these two prophets." Only when their work is brought to its God-ordained end does the beast conquer them and kill them. The verb translated "shall have finished" is in the Greek the verb form of the word that means *end* or *goal* (Greek: *teleoo*). It is the verb form of the noun translated *end* in Matthew 24:3, with reference to the end of the world, as God's goal with history and all things.

Revelation 11:7 is the first mention of the beast in the book of Revelation. The beast is antichrist, who is more fully described in chapter 13.

Antichrist comes to power only when the work of the church is finished. Only then may antichrist put an end to the church's preaching. Philip Edgcumbe Hughes comments, correctly:

> The witnesses cannot be killed before their witness has been completed. The Lord's witnesses have a course to finish, namely, "the ministry received from the Lord Jesus to testify to the gospel of the grace of God" (Acts 20:24).[6]

The sign of the preaching controls the sign of antichrist.

A second passage in the New Testament that teaches that antichrist is constrained to await the fulfillment of God's will regarding the preaching of the gospel and its accomplishments is 2 Thessalonians 2:6–8:

6. And now ye know what withholdeth that he might be revealed in his time.
7. For the mystery of iniquity doth already work: only he who now letteth will let, until he be taken out of the way.

---

6 Philip Edcumbe Hughes, *The Book of the Revelation: A Commentary* (Leicester, England: Inter-Varsity Press, 1990), 126.

> 8. And then shall that Wicked be revealed, whom the Lord shall consume with the spirit of his mouth, and shall destroy with the brightness of his coming.

The subject of the passage, the one called "that Wicked," literally "the Lawless One," is antichrist. In verse 3 he is referred to as "that man of sin…the son of perdition." Already in the apostle's time he was being withheld, or "let," so that he might be revealed in his time. In the original Greek the words translated *withheld* and *letteth* are the same word, referring to a restraining of antichrist so that he cannot be revealed in the world prior to the time that God has ordained for him. God has a special time (Greek: *kairos*) for him with regard to the history of salvation, and much as Satan desired the man of sin to appear already in Paul's day, God sovereignly controls the appearance of antichrist according to his own will, not according to the desire of Satan. Satan is in a hurry to establish his worldwide kingdom; God checks Satan's ambitions on behalf of the kingdom of his own dear Son.

Theologians have engaged in much speculation as to what, or who, the restraining power or person of 2 Thessalonians 2 might be. The theories include the Roman government with its emperors; civil government as such; the preaching of the gospel; indeed, Paul himself; a mighty angel; and others.

What the identity of the restraining person and power may be is not important. What is important is that antichrist strives to come in his full power ever since Christ ascended into heaven, already in the apostolic era. The apostle writes that in his day "the mystery of iniquity doth already work" (2 Thess. 2:7). Then already there was a power ("*what* withholdeth" v. 6) and a person ("*he who* now letteth" v. 7) restraining antichrist, with the purpose that antichrist be revealed in his own proper time, according to the timetable of God. Only when this power and person are taken out of the way will the lawless one be revealed: "*Then* [and only then] shall that Wicked be revealed" (v. 8).

Regardless of the identity of the restrainer, the meaning of the passage is plain. The sovereign Lord Jesus Christ controls the appearance of antichrist. Christ's timetable serves the preaching of the gospel and the gathering of the church. The restraint of antichrist in 2 Thessalonians 2 stands in close relation to the "free course" of the word of God for which the brothers are to pray in chapter 3:1.

The control of the appearance of antichrist by the preaching of the gospel is emphasized on a correct understanding of the "restrainer" and "restraining power" in 2 Thessalonians 2. The church knows the identity: "Ye know what withholdeth" (v. 6). Various theories are unsatisfactory on their very face. For example, the restraining power cannot be the Roman Empire, for that empire was itself the antichrist typically.

The restrainer is the Holy Spirit. He is the almighty power of God who governs all history by his providential might on behalf of the preaching of the gospel of Jesus Christ. He is personal: "*he* who now letteth" (v. 7). As to his power, it is impersonal: "*what* withholdeth" (v. 6). The Spirit of providential power over all things, including the rise of antichrist, governs all on behalf of the gospel of Jesus Christ, whose Spirit he is. Providence is governed by the interests of the gospel. The wicked world is made to be subservient to the church.

That the restrainer will be taken out of the way is offensive to some, if the restrainer is the Holy Spirit. The question is whether it is fitting to speak of God the Holy Spirit being taken out of the way. But the Spirit here is the Spirit of Jesus Christ, the Spirit who carries out the will of the Lord Jesus. Jesus sends the Spirit when and where it pleases him. Christ also takes him out of the way when it pleases him. When the last elect has been brought to salvation, so that the entire church has been gathered, and when it pleases God the Father that the wickedness of the world shall be consummated and that the church shall glorify him by engaging in the last battle of the kingdom of God in the world, then, and only then, does Christ take his Spirit of providence, who has been restraining antichrist, out of the way so that the lawless one is revealed.

It only remains to be noted that the preaching of the gospel has this importance as a sign of the coming of Christ because it is the living voice of the risen Christ himself (see John 10:27; Eph. 4:20, 21). Rightly, the Reformed creed the Second Helvetic Confession of 1566 declares about the preaching of the gospel that "the preaching of the Word of God is the Word of God."[7] So precious is the word of God that all, including antichrist, must wait on it. So powerful is the word of God that it compels all to wait on it.

---

7 The Second Helvetic Confession, 1566, in *Creeds of the Churches*, ed. John H. Leith, rev. ed. (Atlanta, GA: John Knox Press, 1973), 133.

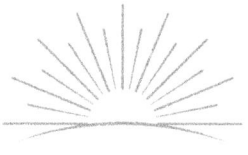

4

APOSTASY

INTRODUCTION

Apostasy is made a notable sign of the end in 2 Thessalonians 2:3: "Let no man deceive you by any means: for that day shall not come, except there come a falling away first, and that man of sin be revealed, the son of perdition." "Falling away" translates the one word *apostasia* in the original Greek, which means in English, as it sounds, *apostasy*. Verse 2 instructs the church of Paul's day that the day of Christ was not "at hand." That is, the day of Christ could not happen at any moment. Prior to the coming of Christ mentioned in verse 1, which is the main thought of the passage, there will be a falling away, or apostasy, first.

This apostasy will not be a phase of the more or less ordinary apostasy that is ongoing throughout the New Testament era. The apostle uses the definite article with *apostasy*, rather than the indefinite article found in the English translation of verse 3. Verse 3 speaks of *the* apostasy. The apostasy that will precede the coming of Christ and that will be an arresting sign of his coming will be a massive, unusual, unmistakable reality in the sphere of the church. No one will be able to overlook it, although in their spiritual blindness unbelievers, including unbelievers who are nominal members of nominal churches, will refuse to relate it to the coming of Christ.

Apostasy has this same prominence in Matthew 24. The immediate response of Jesus to the question of his disciples concerning the sign of his coming and of the end of the world is a warning against apostasy: "Take heed that no man deceive you. For many shall come in my name, saying, I am Christ; and shall deceive many" (vv. 4, 5). He repeats the warning in verse 11: "Many false prophets shall rise, and shall deceive many." Verse 24 relates the apostasy to "false prophets" and emphasizes its seductive power by adding the warning that "if it were possible, they [the false prophets] shall deceive the very elect."

Other passages in the New Testament predict the apostasy as a sign of the end. First Timothy 4:1 forewarns of apostasy in the "latter times": "In the latter times some shall depart from the faith, giving heed to seducing spirits, and doctrines of devils." *Depart* in the English translation is in the Greek the verb form of the noun *apostasy*. Literally the Holy Spirit inspired, "Some shall *apostatize* from the faith." That from which professing church members will apostatize is "the faith." "Faith" in the text is objective, that is, that which is believed and confessed by the church. The apostle predicts as a sign of the latter times that churches and their members will apostatize from the truth of the word of God, which ought to be believed.

Likewise, 2 Timothy 3:13 prophesies that "evil men and seducers shall wax worse and worse, deceiving, and being deceived." The ones who deceive are ministers and professors of theology. Those who are deceived are the members in the pews. Coming are "perilous times" for the churches, and these times will be "the last days" (v. 1). Obviously, these perilous times are a sign of the last days to the believer.

In 2 Timothy 4:3–4, the apostle returns to the sign of apostasy, with emphasis upon the fault of the people, who give ear to the apostate teachers:

3. For the time will come [the last days] when they will not endure sound doctrine; but after their own lusts shall they heap to themselves teachers, having itching ears;
4. And they shall turn away their ears from the truth, and shall be turned unto fables.

Apostasy is rooted in rejection of sound doctrine and in contempt for the truth.

The apostle John teaches apostasy as a sign of the end by warning against not abiding in the doctrine of Christ and by relating this unfaithfulness to the doctrine of Christ to the coming of antichrist (cf. 2 John 7–11).

THE NATURE OF APOSTASY

Apostasy is departure from Christ as he is revealed in the truth of his word and gospel by those who once by their profession held the truth and outwardly adhered to Christ in the truth. The full reality of apostasy is, on the one hand, that it is a fearful threat to the true church of Christ and, on the other hand, that it is impossible that any elect should be deceived and fall away from Christ into unbelief and damnation. Matthew 24:24 teaches both aspects of the reality of apostasy. On the one hand, so threatening is apostasy that if it were possible the very elect of God would be deceived. Nothing is more certain than the salvation of those whom God has elected unto salvation, *in the way of their steadfast belief of the truth*. Even to propose the deception of the elect *hypothetically*, as Jesus does in verse 24, is to indicate the power and danger of apostasy. At the same time, and in the same breath, Jesus proclaims that apostasy is impossible with regard to the elect: "*If* it were possible."

The apostle John explains both the fearful reality of the falling away of some who formerly confessed Jesus Christ and outwardly behaved as believers and the faithfulness to Christ of God's elect: "They went out from us, but they were not of us; for if they had been of us, they would no doubt have continued with us: but they went out, that they might be made manifest that they were not all of us" (1 John 2:19). Men and women who had been members of the apostolic churches abandoned the fellowship: "They went out from us." In their going out, the apostates denied Christ, whereas formerly they had confessed him as savior and lord. But this apostasy did not represent the falling away from Christ unto damnation of those who had truly believed on Christ unto salvation, that is, the falling away of saints. On the contrary, they had never been "of us," that is, true believers and living members of the church. The very fact that they apostatized was evidence of the falsity of their profession and outward membership in the church of which John was pastor. True believers persevere in the truth of the gospel and in holiness of life by God's electing grace.

The preceding context of 1 John 2:19 links apostasy closely to the sign of antichrist and identifies both as signs of "the last time": "whereby we know that it is the last time" (v. 18).

Apostasy is both individual and ecclesiastical. Individual members of the churches fall away. Hebrews 10:25 calls attention to individual apostasy: "Not forsaking the assembling of ourselves together, as the manner of some is." Noteworthy, first, is the close relation of apostasy and the forsaking of membership in a true church. The apostate member does not merely show his apostasy by forsaking the instituted church. His apostasy *consists of* forsaking the church. Second, this passage views apostasy as an important feature and therefore sign of the last days: "as ye see the day approaching." Also 1 John 2:19 addresses the apostasy of individual members of the church: "They went out from us."

This falling away of individuals has a covenantal aspect. That is, the departure from Christ on the part of parents takes with it their children and grandchildren in their generations. God visits the iniquity of the fathers upon the children. As the prophet put it in a vivid figure, "The fathers have eaten a sour grape, and the children's teeth are set on edge" (Jer. 31:29). More than once in my pastoral ministry, I have responded to the justification by parents of their forsaking a true church for one that had fallen away, or was in the process of falling away, or was by biblical, Reformed standards no church at all, in the words, "We will always remember what the truth of the gospel is." My warning was, "Perhaps you will, but what about your children and grandchildren?"

Apostasy is also ecclesiastical. Entire congregations and denominations of churches apostatize. They do this by the teaching of ministers, by the instruction in the seminary and writings of professors of theology, and by the false faith and corrupt confession of the members. Biblical examples of the falling away of entire churches prominently include the Galatian churches. They "removed from him that called [them] into the grace of Christ unto another gospel" (Gal. 1:6). They fell away under the influence of heretical preachers: "There be some that trouble you, and would pervert the gospel of Christ" (v. 7). For these instruments of the falling away of the churches, Paul had no tolerance. On the contrary, he leveled a double curse upon them (vv. 8, 9). His will regarding them was that "they were even cut off which trouble you" (5:12).

Several important aspects of apostasy are evident in the instance of the apostasy of the Galatian Christian churches. First, full-fledged apostasy can occur in a short time. The Galatian churches had been established by the apostle not long before he addressed the epistle to them charging them with having fallen away. Second, a good beginning and faithfulness over a period of years are no assurance of abiding in the truth. Every church must be on guard always against the threat of falling away. The watchmen on the walls of Zion must beware not only of enemies from without, but also of danger within. Third, the fundamental nature of apostasy always is departure from the gospel of salvation by grace alone through faith alone in Christ Jesus alone to the glory of God alone. The Galatian churches corrupted the gospel truth of justification by faith alone. They preached and confessed the heretical doctrine of justification by faith *and works*, thus compromising the gospel of salvation by the grace of God. The compromise itself took a seemingly innocuous form: "merely" adding the work of circumcision to the obedience of Christ as the way and basis of righteousness with God (see Gal. 5:1–4).

Another example of the apostasy of entire churches in Scripture is that of some of the seven churches of Revelation 2 and 3. These also had a good beginning in their establishment by the apostles and their coworkers but fell away already during the short time of the life and ministry of the apostle John. One important aspect of apostasy that some of these churches demonstrated was antinomianism. Antinomianism also is a corruption of the gospel of grace. This heresy denies that the gospel of grace always produces a holy life of thankfulness in the congregation, which holy life has the law of God as its standard or rule. In its extreme development and manifestation, the heresy of antinomianism preaches that the gospel of grace encourages—not merely *permits* but *encourages*—a life of deliberate disobedience to the law of God, so that the grace of salvation may be magnified. In keeping with this heresy, the antinomian church fails to exercise discipline, as though the exercise of the keys infringes upon the liberty of the gospel of grace. Especially the church at Thyatira had apostatized into grossest antinomianism. Its female preacher taught the congregation the false doctrine of knowing the "depths of Satan" as the way then to know the heights of gracious salvation (Rev. 2:18–29).

Despite the apparent difference between the heresy of works-righteousness as taught by the Galatian churches and the heresy of antinomianism as taught in the church at Thyatira, in the end the two false doctrines are the same in denying the gospel of grace. The former teaches the inability of the gospel of grace to save sinners in the fundamental saving act of justification; it needs the help of the works of the sinner. The latter also teaches the inability of the gospel of grace to save sinners: it is not able to sanctify them.

In the apostasy of individuals and churches the false prophet, or heretic, plays a powerful role. Already in the Old Testament, the false prophet was a danger against which Israel had to be on guard. In his instruction concerning the last days, Jesus emphasized the presence in the church, and destructive working upon the church *from within*, of false prophets: "For there shall arise…false prophets, and shall shew great signs and wonders; insomuch that, if it were possible, they shall deceive the very elect" (Matt. 24:24). False prophets were a threat to the apostolic churches: "But there were false prophets also among the people, even as there shall be false teachers among you, who privily shall bring in damnable heresies…And many shall follow their pernicious ways; by reason of whom the way of truth shall be evil spoken of" (2 Pet. 2:1–2).

Throughout the history of the church in the present age, heretics and their heresies prepare the way for the appearance and kingdom of antichrist. As Christ indicated in Matthew 24:24, false Christs and false prophets are related eschatological phenomena. Second Thessalonians 2:3 teaches the same: "That day [the day of the coming of Christ] shall not come, except there come a falling away first, and that man of sin be revealed, the son of perdition."

But the most explicit and vivid depiction of the close relation of false prophecy and antichrist is the thirteenth chapter of Revelation. Here the beast out of the sea, which is the antichristian world-kingdom of the end, headed by the personal man of sin of 2 Thessalonians 2:3, is significantly aided by a beast out of the earth, which is false prophecy, headed by a charismatic religious figure. This false prophecy, which is chiefly apostate Christianity, assists the antichrist in coming to power and in firmly establishing his rule over all the earth.

By heresy, the Reformed faith understands "stubborn and persistent error in fundamental doctrines." It distinguishes heresy from doubt and error.[1]

Scripture permits us to be more definite about the heresy that effects the falling away of churches and individuals, that is, the nature of this "stubborn and persistent error in fundamental doctrines." Heresy is always, in one form or another, a denial of Christ Jesus. It "confesseth not that Jesus Christ is come in the flesh" (1 John 4:3). It may deny Christ by corrupting the truth of his person, as was the case with those to whom John expressly referred. It may also deny Christ by corrupting the truth of his work, as was the case with those whom the apostle condemned in the epistle to the Galatians. The teaching that a sinner is justified by the law makes Christ "of no effect" regarding his work (Gal. 5:4). These denials of Jesus Christ accomplish apostasy: "Ye are fallen from grace" (v. 4).

Heresy is such a perversion of the gospel as results in a message that is no longer a means of saving grace but is, on the contrary, a damning lie. Not only does the book of Galatians curse the heretics, but it also pronounces judgment upon those who are seduced by the heretics into finding their righteousness with God partly in some work of their own: "If ye be circumcised, Christ shall profit you nothing…Christ is become of no effect unto you" (Gal. 5:2, 4).

With specific reference to the truth about Christ Jesus, the ecumenical Athanasian Creed affirms the necessity of orthodox doctrine for salvation: "Furthermore it is necessary to everlasting salvation: that he [who will be saved] also believe rightly the Incarnation of our Lord Jesus Christ." The creed concludes with the warning that heresy regarding the incarnation is damning: "This is the Catholic Faith: which except a man believe faithfully, he can not be saved."[2]

Inasmuch as Jesus Christ both in his person and in his work has as his outstanding purpose the glory of God his Father, it is the nature of heresy to rob God of his glory. The grievous sin of the heathen both in their idolatry and in their sexual perversion is that "they glorified him [God] not as God," but "worshipped and served the creature more than the Creator, who is blessed for ever" (Rom. 1:21, 25). The sin of those nominal Christians who proclaim and believe the heresy of salvation by the will and works of humans themselves is likewise the robbing of God of his glory in his great work of salvation. Heresy silences the grand doxology that resounds as the climax of the gospel of grace in Romans 11:36: "For of him, and through him, and to him, are all things: to whom be glory for ever. Amen."

---

[1] Cf. Herman Bavinck, "The Catholicity of Christianity and the Church," *Calvin Theological Journal* 27, no. 2 (November 1992): 240-41.
[2] The Athanasian Creed 29 and 44, in Schaff, *Creeds of Christendom*, 2:68, 70.

It is of the utmost importance regarding heresy that the way to detect and expose it is by the light and standard of holy Scripture. In the context of discovering heretics and warding off their heresies, one of the most important expressions of the doctrine of Scripture in all of the Bible appears in 2 Timothy 3:15–17. The passage is well-known. The Scriptures are holy. Scripture is a unity that is God-breathed, as is the literal translation of the King James Version's "given by inspiration of God." It is profitable unto salvation.

What is often overlooked is that the apostle stated such glorious truths about the Bible in the context of a warning against seducers in the sphere of the churches, who deceive and are themselves deceived, evidently concerning the truths of the Christian faith. These are heretics. The danger is that Timothy and others will not continue in the things that they have learned, that is, the sound doctrines of the Christian religion. This would be apostasy (2 Tim. 3:13–14). The sole safeguard for the members of the church is holy Scripture: "And that from a child thou hast known the holy scriptures" (v. 15). This passage concerning Scripture, one of the most clear and full in all the Bible, does not appear simply as a statement of the orthodox doctrine of Scripture. It presents Scripture as the defense against heresy and as the protection against falling away.

The church and her members must discover heretics and reject heresy by the standard of Scripture. They must not judge by the outward appearance of the false teachers—their friendliness and even their seeming piety. With explicit reference to "false apostles" and "deceitful workers" in the churches, Paul warns that "Satan himself is transformed into an angel of light" (2 Cor. 11:13, 14). It "is no great thing if his ministers also be transformed as the ministers of righteousness" (v. 15). The context of the entire chapter of 2 Corinthians 11 makes plain that Paul is addressing an actual situation in the Corinthian church: the congregation was welcoming false teachers because of their deceptive personal appearance, while rejecting Paul on account of his less winsome appearance. Paul calls such an all-too-common evil in the church "glory[ing] after the flesh" (v. 18).

Apostasy therefore is a sign of the end within the sphere of the churches. Lawlessness is "out there"; apostasy is "in here." Apostasy occurred already in apostolic times, as the books of Galatians, 1 John, and the opening chapters of Revelation indicate. With the apostle in Galatians 1:6, we "marvel" that churches founded by the apostles were "so soon removed from him that called [them] into the grace of Christ unto another gospel." As has been noted, apostolic churches apostatized during the ministry of the apostles themselves. Soon after the death of the last apostle, vast numbers of churches fell away into the heresy of salvation by the will and works of sinners themselves and became what today is the Roman Catholic Church.

Not long after God's restoration of true churches by the recovery of the gospel of grace in the Reformation of 1517 through the instrumentality of Martin Luther, many churches, not only in the Netherlands but also throughout Europe, fell away into the heresy of salvation by the will of the sinner under the influence of the heretic James Arminius. True churches were preserved by the defense of the gospel of grace in the Reformed creed the Canons of Dordt. This creed confesses that the grace of God is particular and sovereign, having its origin in God's unconditional election, founded upon the particular, definite, limited atonement of Christ, and preserving all the elect unto everlasting salvation. It condemns the "gospel" of a universal grace, dependent upon the will of the sinner and rooted in a death of Christ for all humans, as a "reviving of the Pelagian error out of hell."[3]

The biblical basis of the admittedly severe judgment that Arminianism is a heresy and that churches committed to Arminian theology are false churches is Romans 9:16: "It [salvation] is not of him that willeth, nor of him that runneth, but of God that sheweth mercy." The orthodox gospel is that salvation is of the mercy of God. Attributing salvation to the will of the sinner or to the works of the sinner are two forms of the heresy that salvation depends upon man, rather than upon God. And heresy renders churches apostate.

Apostasy is a massive reality in contemporary Protestantism, including Reformed and Presbyterian churches since approximately 1800. Protestantism is ravaged by theological modernism, which openly denies all the fundamental doctrines of the Christian faith from that of creation to the Godhead of Jesus. The churches espouse universalism, whether in the form of a sincere desire of God for the salvation of all humans, or in the form of a denial of eternal hell, or in the form of the final salvation of all. Syncretism is popular, that is, the doctrine that in the final analysis all religions are one and the same. This takes form in Christian churches' acceptance of Islam, Judaism, and other religions as essentially one with Christianity. One important expression of this repudiation of Jesus Christ as the only Savior and Lord and this utter rejection of the gospel of Scripture as the only way of salvation is the ecumenical movement that unites not only all nominally Christian churches, with complete disregard of their heterodoxy, but also all religions, regardless of their blatant rejection of Jesus Christ.

---

3 Canons of Dordt 2, error and rejection 3. The translation of the Latin original is mine. The Latin is: "*Pelagianum errorem ab inferis revocant*." Schaff does not give the rejection of errors sections of the Canons in English translation. Reformed orthodoxy condemns Arminian theology as a form of the ancient heresy of Pelagianism, condemned by the catholic church, and thus judges churches apostate that confess and proclaim the Arminian heresy.

This contemporary, massive, obvious apostasy does not leave reputedly conservative Reformed and Presbyterian churches untouched. In recent times, a doctrine that calls itself "federal [covenant] vision" finds a home in these churches. This "vision" openly denies the doctrines of grace confessed in the Canons of Dordt. It makes this denial on behalf of its doctrine of a conditional covenant. In view of the fundamental importance of the covenant of God with Christ and his people, the confession of a conditional covenant makes all of salvation conditional, that is, dependent upon the will and works of the sinner. The theology of the federal vision is a new form of the heresy of Pelagius and Arminius. It takes powerful hold upon churches that have long embraced the doctrine of a conditional covenant and the doctrine of salvation as the matter of a sinner's accepting God's well-meant, gracious, conditional offer to all to whom the gospel comes, especially to all baptized children.[4]

As is invariably the case, this apostasy in doctrine is accompanied by licentiousness in life. The young, unmarried members of the churches fornicate openly and freely, and "shacking up" is defended from the pulpits. There is divorce and remarriage on a scale that matches this adultery in the world. Sodomy and lesbianism are pronounced Christian conduct by ecclesiastical assemblies. Allegedly Christian officebearers approve the murder of the unborn and partially born. And this speaks only of sexual sins and sins against the sixth commandment.

The entirety of the holy life of obedience to the law of God is disregarded, if not despised, in contemporary Protestantism. This begins with disobedience to the first and second commandments, which forbid having any other object in which to trust than the one true God who has manifested himself in his word, worshiping God in any other way than he has commanded in his word, and teaching the people in any other way than the lively preaching of his word.[5]

The close relation of heresy with its effect of apostasy and the sound preaching of the gospel is noteworthy. They are not two entirely separate spiritual forces, moving side-by-side in history. But heresy feeds off and energizes itself from the gospel, as a parasite gets its life and vigor from the healthy host on which it has fastened itself. It creates its false Jesus from the true one. It fashions its theistic evolution from the biblical doctrine of theistic creation. It concocts its heresy of justification by faith and works from the biblical truth that the

---

4   For a thorough exposure of the heresy of the federal vision, cf. David J. Engelsma, *Federal Vision: Heresy at the Root* (Jenison, MI: RFPA, 2012).
5   See the explanation of these commandments by the Heidelberg Catechism in Schaff, *Creeds of Christendom*, 3:342–43.

justification that is by faith alone, apart from works, also works. Ultimately, it forms its idol god of exaggerated human love from the biblical revelation of God who is the divine love that demands righteousness. It is this aspect of heresy that makes it seductive and that enables it to create the idol that deceives many.

Heresy is Satan's most dangerous weapon against the means of the gathering and preservation of the church and the building and maintenance of the kingdom of Christ—the pure preaching of the gospel. Not persecution but heresy is the great threat to the church in all ages. Not the threat of the stake but apostasy is the appalling enemy of the church. Often believing members of churches, including ministers and elders, allow themselves to ignore this threat until it has well-nigh destroyed their denomination or congregation, and only a very few faithful remain.

But even this devilish evil of heresy with its concomitant apostasy serves the purpose of God. The gospel must make its victorious way in history by antithetical conflict within the sphere of the church herself. Heresy and apostasy manifest who are approved by God. They sharpen the knowledge of the truth in the faithful. And they realize God's sovereign purpose of reprobation, which serves to illumine and magnify the grace of election.

APOSTASY AND ANTICHRIST

In view of the nature of apostasy, it is not surprising that there is the closest relation between it and antichrist. Apostasy is an outstanding sign of the end time. The apostasy of the early twenty-first century signals the nearness of the antichrist and therefore that the day of Christ is at hand. Scripture teaches the close relation of apostasy and antichrist. It does so in 2 Thessalonians 2:3: "Let no man deceive you by any means: for that day [the day of Christ of verse 2 and the day of the coming of Christ of verse 1] shall not come, except there come a falling away first, and that man of sin be revealed, the son of perdition." Apostasy not only precedes the appearance of the man of sin, but also powerfully works to bring antichrist and his kingdom into existence. The falling away ushers in the man of sin, the son of perdition.

Revelation 13:11–17 teaches the same. The beast out of the earth exercises the power of the first beast before him. It causes all to worship the first beast. The fundamental issue at the end is, as always, *worship*. Then the precise issue will be worship of Christ Jesus or the worship of antichrist. The beast out of the earth, which is apostate religion headed by an impressive spiritual, papal individual, will accomplish worldwide worship of the beast out of the sea, which is the antichristian world kingdom headed by a charismatic, dominating, powerful individual—king, emperor, president, or prime minister. The beast out of the earth *deceives*, which is always the tactic of heresy and the engine of apostasy. The deception of the world employs miracles, as is typical of heresy and apostasy. When deception fails, the beast out of the earth resorts to persecution: all who will not worship the image of the beast will be killed. This too is characteristic of apostate Christianity and false religion. Behind the chapel of apostasy looms the stake.

This relation between apostasy and antichrist is foretold in the fundamental prophecy of antichrist in the Old Testament, Daniel 11. At the end, the king who magnifies himself above every god and speaks marvelous things against the God of gods comes to power by having intelligence with those who forsake the holy covenant and by deceptive flatteries. His apostate cohorts devastate the pure worship of God by establishing the abomination that desolates the right worship of God. In the end this will be the image of the beast out of the sea of Revelation 13 that all are required to worship. Where God formerly was worshiped, now the antichrist is worshiped.

G. C. Berkouwer is right in linking closely apostasy and antichrist: "In 2 Thessalonians 2, Paul is not writing about two separate and independent signs. The rebellion [antichrist] is closely connected with apostasy." He then adds: "a direct reference to the Daniel Apocalypse (cf. Dan. 11:31ff.)."[6]

It is not enough to state the fact of the close relation between apostasy and antichrist. The nature of the relation must also be brought to light. First, apostasy prepares the way for antichrist. This is the thought of 2 Thessalonians 2. The order of the two signs is important. Apostasy precedes the man of sin. Antichrist must have his seat of power in Christendom, indeed in the nominal Christian church. Verse 4 of 2 Thessalonians 2 seats antichrist in the "temple of God." This is not accidental. Satan's purpose is not merely to have the great opponent of Christ somewhere or other in the world. He will rear up his kingdom where Christ's kingdom has been established, so as to supplant and overshadow the kingdom of Christ. To this end, apostasy softens up nominal Christianity. At the very time of the revelation of antichrist, the apostate church will convince multitudes of professing Christians to hail antichrist as the real Christ of Scripture and of the Christian tradition. Geerhardus Vos expressed the relation of apostasy and antichrist this way: "In vs. 3 [of 2 Thess. 2], the sequence indicates that the apostasy comes first, and that on the waves of its tempest the Wicked One is lifted up and carried on to his ultimate destination."[7]

Apostasy is the means by which antichrist comes, as the gospel is the means

---

6 Berkouwer, *Return of Christ*, 282–83.
7 Geerhardus Vos, *The Pauline Eschatology* (Grand Rapids, MI: Eerdmans, 1972), 125.

by which Christ comes. According to the Greek original of 1 John 2:18, antichrist *comes*, not "*shall* come," as in the KJV. The verb is present tense, not future tense. Antichrist is always coming, and he comes constantly by means of the many heretics that rise up in the church and the apostasy that they cause, as the latter part of verse 18 and what follows in 1 John 2 make plain.

There is also this aspect of the relation between apostasy and antichrist: antichrist completes the apostasy. Apostasy in all its forms is the exaltation of man at the expense of God. Apostasy is the deifying of man. This is the essence of Roman Catholicism both in its theology of salvation by the works of man and in its glorifying of the pope. This is the doctrine of Protestant liberalism: man is the goal of the evolutionary process and the lord over all; man's will is divine law. This is the implication of Arminian theology: man is savior by his free will. This is also the underlying reality of the ethical apostasy of much of Protestantism: man decides what is right behavior regarding divorce, marriage, abortion, homosexuality, civil revolution, even suicide. The personal antichrist will be the epitome of man apart from God. The antichristian world power will be the kingdom of man.

The number of the beast will be 666, the number of man to the fullest extent, without God (Rev. 13:18). The KJV inserts the indefinite article, "*a* man," which the Greek lacks. The reference is not to an individual man but to man generally—man apart from God, to man falling short of communion with God, which would be represented numerically by the number 7.

Antichrist will bring to its complete development the sin of man in paradise in yielding to the temptation of the serpent, "Ye shall be as God" (Gen. 3:5).[8]

If it becomes increasingly evident that false religion, particularly apostate Christianity, is the beast out of the earth of Revelation 13, there ought equally to be recognition that the state more and more resembles the beast out of the sea. Godless man corrupts the state, which is as such the good institution of God, so that it becomes the embodiment of the autonomy, the sovereignty, and the glory of man—man apart from and against God. The state is the savior of mankind. The state is absolute lord. The state becomes beastly, in its murder of the babies, in its sanctioning of sodomite and lesbian "marriage", in its increasing hatred of Christian belief and precepts.

Even in this, the apostasy that brings in the antichrist, wicked mankind does not escape the sovereignty of God. The falling away in the churches and the revelation of antichrist in the state are divine judgment. "For this cause

---

8 This is the correct translation of the phrase that the KJV translates "as gods." The Hebrew original is "Elohim," a common name of God.

God shall send them strong delusion, that they should believe a lie: that they all might be damned who believed not the truth, but had pleasure in unrighteousness" (2 Thess. 2:11–12). The final apostasy is not only the unfaithfulness of the churches and their leaders. It is also God's punishment of previous failure to believe the truth and of their taking pleasure in unrighteousness. The sin of the churches at the end is especially that they do not receive "the *love* of the truth" (v. 10). This grievous sin of the apostates must be noticed: not *loving* the truth. This is the spiritual root of apostasy. Apostasy sets in within a true, orthodox church in this way: a generation arises that does not *love* the truth. This was the sin of Ephesus according to Revelation 2:4: "Thou hast left thy first love." "Leaving" is a term of apostasy, of falling away.

The sin of losing the love of the truth and leaving the first love of the truth is of the gravest seriousness. For this evil, the Lord threatens Ephesus with the removal of the candlestick (Rev. 2:5). For this evil, God sends strong delusions so that churches apostatize and thus become agents of the revelation of antichrist.

In their churches, pastors and elders must be concerned with symptoms such as indifference to sound doctrine, loss of interest in the truth, lethargic attendance at the services of worship, disregard of doctrinal error in the teaching ministry of the congregation, complaints about doctrinal preaching, and even opposition to polemics from the pulpit. Each of these symptoms, and usually all of them together, are apostasy in its beginnings.

Especially ministers are called of God to combat apostasy in its seemingly harmless, but actually malignant, beginning by preaching not only the truth but also the love of the truth, and by showing the love of the truth in their own ministries. A preacher who obviously is only "doing his job" will encourage formalism in his flock. A preacher who manifests an indifferent attitude himself toward sound doctrine, probably because his is a ministry of feeling, or of good works, to the detriment of sound doctrine, will inculcate this lack of love for the truth upon his congregation. The minister who is disparaging of sound doctrine, as though all that matters is the "practical" element of Christianity, and then only love, will drive his people straight into the bosom of the beast out of the earth.

APOSTASY AND THE PROVIDENCE OF GOD

Evil and damnable as it is, apostasy does not fall outside the providential government and purposes of God, specifically the purposes of God with regard to the coming of Christ. Apostasy serves the end, the *telos*, the goal, of God in the coming of Christ. This is the good news of one of the outstanding passages in all of Scripture concerning the antichrist, 1 John 2:18–19: the many antichrists in this "last time," which pave the way for the one, final antichrist, "went out from us…that they might be made manifest that they were not all of us." The last part of this text is a purpose clause. It should be read this way: "*in order that they might be made manifest.*" God's purpose with these preliminary antichrists applies also, and especially, to the ultimate antichrist. A purpose of God with the antichrist, both the political and the religious beasts, is that it may be manifest at the very end of the ages that many professing Christians are not "of us," that is, are not genuine believers at all; and by implication who are the genuine members of the kingdom of Christ will be made clear. Finally, at the end of the ages, there must be a clear separation between the citizens of the kingdom of Christ and the citizens of the kingdom of antichrist. By the apostasy, God will have cleansed his temple.

Ushering in the antichrist, and that within the sphere of the clearest revelation of the gospel—in the so-called "Christian West"—as it will do, apostasy must manifest the deepest depravity of fallen man, so that, against this darkest of all backgrounds, the light of the glory of God in Christ may shine most brightly. This light will shine in those days (or *these* days) in that, in the midst of the apostasy, the true church "stand[s] fast, and hold[s] the traditions" (2 Thess. 2:15). This standing fast and holding the traditions consists also of the faithfulness of the believers individually. Despite the seduction of the heretic and the threatening of the persecuting state, the believers in those (or *these*) days will confess, "Jesus Christ is Lord." In the climactic standing fast of the church and faithfulness of the believer, God will be glorified, as the climactic event in history.

This is the way the world ends
This is the way the world ends
This is the way the world ends[9]

Not with the triumph of evil, but with the victory of the kingdom of Christ, unto the glory of God.

APOSTASY AND FAITH

As a precursory sign, announced by Christ and known by the church, apostasy functions on behalf of the maintenance of faith in the last days. This sign guards against dismay and even despair over the fact—the *appalling* fact—of apostasy. In Matthew 24:25, Jesus declares, "Behold, I have told you before," immediately after he has forewarned in verse 24 that "there shall arise false Christs, and false

---

9 From "The Hollow Men," by T. S. Eliot, in *Poems 1909-1925* (London: Faber & Gwyer, 1926), 128.

prophets," who will, if it were possible, "deceive the very elect." Jesus' forewarning of the sign of apostasy must keep the true church from discouragement.

What an otherwise utterly discouraging reality is the apostasy of the present day! Although orthodox Protestants tend to take this for granted, it is, in fact, staggering that a billion professing Christians are apostate in the false church of Rome. Multitudes of professing Protestants have departed from Christ into the damning doctrines of liberalism. Millions of nominally evangelical Christians have departed from the gospel of grace into the heresy of Pelagianism and Arminianism—salvation by the will and works of the sinner—which is, according to the Reformed confessions, not a minor deviation from the gospel but a false gospel "out of hell"[10]—full-blown apostasy, therefore.

Of late, the apostasy of the end time extends its tentacles into churches that hitherto have been faithful, churches with a conservative reputation, churches Reformed and Presbyterian. The light of the gospel of grace that God lit in Germany at the Reformation is well-nigh extinguished by the darkness of a modernism that believes nothing of Scripture and of the Heidelberg Catechism. The Netherlands, which produced the Canons of Dordt and has in many ways been the mother of the Reformed faith in the world, is spiritually dead. The best of the churches ordain women to ecclesiastical office, which, although not by any means the worst of the sins of churches, is the dead giveaway that a church has succumbed to the world. The obituary of the Reformed churches in the Netherlands is the book *De Theologen Gingen Voorop*.[11]

In North America, which is always a few years behind developments in Europe, the sign of apostasy is also dishearteningly prominent. The evangelical churches are almost without exception Arminian. Reformed and Presbyterian churches with a name and history of rejecting modernism now embrace false gospels of salvation by the will or works of the sinner. This one teaches universal grace dependent for its efficacy on the accepting will of the sinner. That one now teaches a universal, ineffectual atonement of Christ. Yet another embraces or refuses to condemn the heresy that calls itself federal vision. This is a theology of justification by the good works of sinners, rooted in a covenantal doctrine that unites all baptized persons with Jesus Christ in a union, however, that depends for its continuance and final salvation upon conditions that the baptized person must fulfill. Thus in various ways, the gospel of salvation by grace,

---

10 Canons of Dordt 2, error and rejection 3. The translation of the Latin original is mine.
11 A. M. Lindeboom, *De Theologen Gingen Voorop* [The Theologians Led the Way]. The subtitle, in English translation, is: *A Simple Account of the Dismantling of the Reformed Churches*. Unfortunately, the book has not been translated into English. It is the gravest of warnings against developments now taking place also in Reformed churches in English-speaking countries.

as confessed in the Canons of Dordt, is compromised, to the spiritual death of the compromising churches. In many Reformed and Presbyterian churches, the doctrine of predestination, reprobation as well as election, as confessed in the Canons of Dordt and in the Westminster Confession of Faith, is buried under the message of a love of God for all humans and a sincere desire of God for the salvation of all.

As is the case always and everywhere, the apostasy shows its ugly self in ungodly behavior, especially in sordid sexual conduct. There is something significant about the expression of itself by apostasy in vile sexual sin. It is not merely a matter of the powerful appeal to humans of deviant sexual sin. There is a special, inherent connection between apostasy and sexual deviance. Apostasy is departure of churches and professing Christians from God their husband in a spiritual quasi-marital relation with other lovers, who have seduced these churches and nominal Christians. Apostasy is spiritual infidelity and whoredom. It is vile, sordid, extramarital relations. Fittingly, necessarily, the outstanding manifestation of this spiritual adultery and fornication is physical sexual sin.

The fornication of the young unmarried is tolerated and then approved by apostate churches. Divorce and remarriage, which the Bible condemns as adultery, is sanctioned by the churches. The last stage of sexual deviance is not a step too far in the apostate churches. They legitimize sodomite and lesbian sexual relations as a form of holy matrimony.

The appalling, frightening sign of apostasy alerts the church today that Christ's coming is near. The great falling away at the end is the sign that betokens the revelation of antichrist, and antichrist appears shortly before the coming of Christ on the clouds. This is where the church is in AD 2022. It witnesses and wars in the realization of the falling away of 2 Thessalonians 2. There is massive, dramatic, almost universal departure from Christ and the truth of the gospel.

Especially ministers of the gospel must take heed to this sign, and take heed in such a way that they respond to it rightly on behalf of both themselves and their churches. They must guard themselves against departure. They must examine themselves: Do I love the truth? Does my entire ministry demonstrate and express love of the truth?

Regarding their ministry, they must expose the false doctrines that are a threat to the church and expose the false teachers. This they are required to do in any case, according to article 55 of the Reformed Church Order of Dordt, which regulates their ministry:

> To ward off false doctrines and errors that multiply exceedingly through heretical writings, the Ministers and Elders shall use the means of teaching,

of refutation, or warning, and of admonition, as well as in the Ministry of the Word as in Christian teaching and family-visiting.[12]

The minister of the gospel must warn his congregation, urgently, against the very real and dreadful danger of falling away. God will preserve his church, and he will preserve it by the urgent warning in the preaching and teaching of ministers. How prominent and vehement are such warnings in the New Testament! Christ himself gave the warning in Matthew 24. Hebrews 10:26 intensifies the warning: "If we sin wilfully after that we have received the knowledge of the truth, there remaineth no more sacrifice for sins." Second Peter 2:1, 2 warns the New Testament church both of the threat of heretics and of the falling away of many in response to their heretical teachings: "There shall be false teachers among you, who privily shall bring in damnable heresies…And many shall follow their pernicious ways; by reason of whom the way of truth shall be evil spoken of."

The main calling of the minister in light of the sign of apostasy is that he redouble his efforts to teach sound doctrine. The protection of the brothers and sisters from heresy and falling away is, in the words of the apostle that immediately follow the warning of apostasy in 2 Thessalonians 2, the "belief of the truth," by which they "stand fast, and hold the traditions" (vv. 13, 15).

Also in 2 Timothy, the dark chapter on apostasy—chapter 3—is followed by the charge in chapter 4 to preach the word, being instant in season, out of season. The dreadful reality of apostasy does not permit discouragement or surrender, but demands energetic labor of faithful preachers.

---

12 The Church Order of Dordt article 55, in Monsma and Van Dellen, *The Church Order Commentary*, 227.

5

THE SIGN OF ANTICHRIST

INTRODUCTION

With the doctrine of antichrist, we come to one of the most fascinating aspects of eschatology, indeed one of the most fascinating aspects of all Scripture. It captures the attention even of secular writers and entertains, or frightens, millions of non-Christians. One thinks at once of C. S. Lewis, *The Last Battle* and *That Hideous Strength*; of George Orwell, *1984* and *Animal Farm*; of Aldous Huxley, *Brave New World*; and of V. Soloviev, *Short Story of the Antichrist*.

Among the passages in the New Testament that are especially important for the understanding of antichrist are Jesus' eschatological discourse in Matthew 24 and the parallel passage in Mark 13—the "false Christs"; 2 Thessalonians 2—the "man of sin" and "the son of perdition"; 1 and 2 John—the "antichrists" (plural) and "the antichrist" (singular); and Revelation 13, 17, and 19—"the beast."

Old Testament passages are of critical importance for the right understanding of antichrist in that the Holy Ghost developed the New Testament doctrine of antichrist from certain prophecies of the Old Testament. *The* Old Testament book on antichrist is the prophecy of Daniel. In Matthew 24:15, Christ himself locates the source of his prophecy of the "abomination of desolation" in "Daniel the prophet." Second Thessalonians 2 draws the characteristics of antichrist as the wicked, or lawless, one; as the great, blaspheming antagonist of God; and as the one who exalts himself into the place of God likewise from Daniel. And Revelation 13 obviously bases itself on Daniel 7 in presenting antichrist as the beast out of the sea. But also the association of antichrist with apostasy in 1 and 2 John derives from Daniel (cf. Dan. 11:30, 32).

The prophecy of Ezekiel also figures prominently in the doctrine of antichrist inasmuch as Revelation's teaching of Gog and Magog (20:8) has its source in Ezekiel 38–39, where a certain Gog, a prince of the land of Magog, comes up against God's people in the last days.

The truth of antichrist even directs the student into the apocryphal books and their history of the inter-testamentary period. Daniel's prophecy of antichrist in chapters 8 and 11 is typically fulfilled in one Antiochus Epiphanes, who persecuted the Jews during the four-hundred-year period between the testaments. This history is recorded especially in 1 and 2 Maccabees.

The truth of antichrist is the center of a cluster of related eschatological realities: the great apostasy, the abomination of desolation, the great tribulation, Gog and Magog, and the battle of Armageddon. The right understanding of all of these depends upon the right understanding of antichrist. As has been demonstrated in volume 1 of this set on eschatology, both premillennialism and postmillennialism err in their understanding of antichrist. They necessarily err also in their understanding of these related realities. Just as both millennial errors deny that the church in the future will be the object of the hatred and persecution of antichrist, so also do they deny that the church will experience these related realities. For the two millennial errors, antichrist is of no real interest to the church. Whatever interest the church might have is purely academic. For postmillennialism, antichrist is safely buried in past history. For premillennialism, antichrist is safely thrust into the future history of the nation of Israel. What this amounts to for both millennial errors, their theologians, and the members of their churches is that they cover their doctrinal eyes to a real and present, and especially future, danger to the people of God, thus leaving themselves unprepared for the greatest battle of the church in all her history.

THE NATURE OF ANTICHRIST

Antichrist is a future reality of opposition to God in Jesus Christ and therefore opposition also to the true church. The word "antichrist" (Greek: *antichristos*) expresses this opposition. The word itself is used in the Bible for this future opposition only in 1 and 2 John: 1 John 2:18, 1 John 2:22, 1 John 4:3, and 2 John 7—four passages, and five uses of the term. The Greek preposition *anti* has primarily the sense of opposition, so that *antichristos* means "against Christ," although it carries the sense as well of replacement, "in the stead of Christ."

In keeping with this latter sense of the preposition *anti*, antichrist displays marked similarities to Christ. This is necessary if antichrist is to be successful especially with nominal Christians in convincing men that he is the reality of the Christ of Scripture. Especially 2 Thessalonians 2 notes these formal similarities:

a revelation and a coming; sitting in the temple of God; showing himself that he is God; and supporting his claims with power, signs, and wonders. In addition, Revelation 13 describes him as head of an impressive, powerful world kingdom.

The determined, astounding antagonism of antichrist to Christ and thus to God comes out in every description of him and his deeds, even when the term *antichrist* is not used. This is true of the beast out of the sea of Revelation 13: "He opened his mouth in blasphemy against God, to blaspheme his name, and his tabernacle, and them that dwell in heaven" (v. 6). In this opposition to God, antichrist manifests himself as Satan's man, the embodiment, as much as Satan is able to imitate the incarnation of God in Jesus Christ, of Satan's antagonism against God in hatred of him. The name *Satan* means *adversary*. That the very essence of that spiritual creature is opposition to God and, in hatred of him, the determination to replace him is made known in such a passage as Isaiah 14:13–14:

13. For thou hast said in thine heart, I will ascend into heaven, I will exalt my throne above the stars of God: I will sit also upon the mount of the congregation, in the sides of the north:
14. I will ascend above the heights of the clouds; I will be like the most High.

Antichrist is this satanic spirit in human form.

But antichrist will not appear in the world out of the blue. He will be the culmination of the history-long opposition to God's Christ and the development to the fullest of opposition to God. The reality of antichrist is the warfare brought about in the human race by the word of God to the serpent in Genesis 3:15: "I will put enmity between thee and the woman, and between thy seed and her seed; it shall bruise thy head, and thou shalt bruise his heel." It is the fully developed expression of the antithesis between the two seeds: the serpent (of which the dragon of Revelation 13 is only a monstrous enlargement) versus the seed of the woman, who is Christ Jesus and his body, the church.

All denial, or weakening, of the reality of the antithesis—the spiritual separation and warfare between the holy church and the world of the ungodly—plays into the hand of antichrist by obscuring the reality of the assault on the church by an inveterate foe and by hindering the resistance to this assault on the part of the church and her members.

This basic characteristic of antagonism to Christ as the revelation of God identifies antichrist as the creature, the front, the manifestation, the power, and, speaking loosely, the embodiment of Satan. Scripture stresses this close relation of antichrist and Satan. According to 2 Thessalonians 2:9, the coming of antichrist is "after the working of Satan." *Working* in the KJV translates the Greek word for *energy*. Just as the coming into the world of Jesus Christ was accomplished by the extraordinary energy of God, so also the coming of antichrist will be due to the extraordinary energy of Satan. Satanic energy will have prepared the world to receive antichrist. In fact, inasmuch as the full reality of antichrist is the entire world as a godless realm, Satanic energy will have *made* the entire world antichrist.

Satanic power will energize the individual antichrist, in an extraordinary way. He will not be an incarnation of Satan, that is, Satan and man in one person. Incarnation lies beyond even Satan's extraordinary powers. Only God can accomplish the wonder of incarnation. But Satan can infuse into his man mighty gifts and powers—*demonic* gifts and powers. Second Thessalonians adds that the working of Satan in effecting the coming of antichrist bestows "all power and signs and [as the original Greek has it, wonders of the lie]" (2:9). Satan will endow the antichrist with supernatural powers. In an extraordinary way, antichrist will be devilish.

Also Revelation 13 teaches the close relation of antichrist and Satan. The dragon of chapter 12, which is Satan, gives the beast out of the sea his power, seat, and great authority (13:2). The beast out of the sea, which is antichrist, strikingly resembles the dragon, its progenitor: it is a monstrous wild animal, red in color, with seven heads and ten horns, which horns are crowned (v. 1). Both the dragon and the beast are blasphemous. It belongs to the similarity also that both are unnatural: a dragon, which is not found in nature, and a beast unlike any animal created by God. Satan corrupted himself, thus becoming a demon, who had been an angel, the lovely Lucifer of Isaiah 14. He then perverted mankind in the fall of Adam so as to produce from the glorious man who came forth from the hand of God the depraved, ugly man of sin.

Because of the close relation of antichrist and Satan, to deny Satan, or merely to ignore this enemy of God and his church, is to weaken the church regarding its powerful seduction by and great conflict with antichrist at the end of the ages. If there is no Satan, neither is there an antichrist. If Satan need not be taken seriously, neither is antichrist an existential threat. It is preferable with Luther to throw ink bottles at an apparition of the devil than with modern Christianity to smile indulgently at ministers who evidently take the great dragon seriously.

THE FUTURITY OF ANTICHRIST

Antichrist is a *future* reality. This is not to say that there have not been manifestations of antichrist in the past. The prophecy of Daniel (in chapters 7–12) reveals that various heathen kingdoms with their persecuting kings were workings of the mystery of iniquity already in the time of the old covenant (cf. 2 Thess. 2:7).

Christ's application of Daniel's mention of the abomination of desolation to the time of his own generation makes plain that the Roman Empire with its emperors was the antichrist in type (Matt. 24:15). But no past realization of antichrist fulfilled this eschatological reality exhaustively. The former appearances were merely typical. "That man of sin" of 2 Thessalonians 2:3 has yet to be revealed.

With its teaching that antichrist is still future, the Reformed faith differs significantly from postmillennialism, which without any certainty identifies the man of sin with some figure in the past and makes of the reality of antichrist some relatively minor event in the past. Two things are incontestably true of antichrist in light of the biblical prophecy, both in the Old and in the New Testaments: when he has come, there will be no doubt whatever concerning his identity, and he and his kingdom will be a worldwide assault on the church of Jesus Christ and on Jesus Christ himself in his church. Postmillennial theories about antichrist fail to meet both of these criteria.[1]

Contrary to the theology of dispensational premillennialism, antichrist is a future reality for the church. The church will be on the earth when antichrist is revealed. The object of his persecuting hatred will be the church. Antichrist will oppose Christ in his church, his body. The church will suffer his severe persecution. It is the church, therefore, that is in need of the apostle's instruction about antichrist in 2 Thessalonians 2. The perfectly plain implication of 2 Thessalonians 2 is that all the instruction concerning the revelation of antichrist is instruction that the church needs to receive. Antichrist concerns the church, not the nation of Israel.

Apart now from the fundamental truth that the church is the New Testament fulfillment of Israel, the apostle does not at all reassure the church at Thessalonica, in verses 3–12, that the man of sin will not threaten the church, because the church will have been removed from the arena of earthly history when antichrist shall be revealed. On the contrary, the entire passage is instruction and encouragement for a church that must enter the lists against antichrist and suffer his onslaughts. The comfort of the church regarding antichrist, in

---

1 The antichrist of postmillennial, Christian Reconstructionist Gary DeMar fails on both counts. According to DeMar, the man of sin of 2 Thessalonians 2 was some Jewish high priest or other at the time of the destruction of Jerusalem in AD 70. His identity is forever unknown. His opposition to Christ was merely the prevention of the worship of God in the localized temple in the localized city of Jerusalem in the localized country of Palestine. The rest of the world hardly knew, or ever knows, of his wickedness (cf. Gary DeMar, *Last Days Madness* [Atlanta, GA: American Vision, 1994], 343–44). Why Scripture in 2 Thessalonians 2 and in the book of Revelation makes so much of the antichrist of the end times is a mystery for postmillennialism. For postmillennialism, antichrist is a (weak) tempest in a (very small) teapot. And for the church, the tempest bubbled only for a few years in the earliest days of the church.

verses 13–17, is not: "But we are bound to give thanks alway to God for you, brethren beloved of the Lord, because God will rapture you out of the world before antichrist comes on the scene, so that everything I have written you about antichrist in the preceding verses is of no application to you, and is of no interest to you, whatsoever. In fact, when I was yet with you and told you these things about antichrist (v. 5), I wasted my breath. I might as well have been speaking those things about antichrist to the cattle in the barnyard."

But the comfort and assurance of the church concerning the revelation of antichrist is that God has elected the church to the obtaining of the glory of our Lord Jesus Christ (2 Thess. 2:12–14). Though antichrist will do his damnedest in both seduction and persecution, the church and all her members are perfectly secure. Nor is the calling of the church, in view of the coming of antichrist, "Be looking eagerly for the rapture, like so many cowards, pathetically determined to escape the contest of the kingdom of Christ with the kingdom of Satan." But her calling is: "Therefore, brethren, stand fast, and hold the traditions," like men and women of courage (v. 15).[2]

SEEING THE SIGN

Antichrist is a precursory sign for the true church and the believer. First, antichrist *is* a sign of the coming of Christ. It is a sign, if we may distinguish among all the signs, that the coming of Christ is "at hand," to use the language and express the thought of the apostle in 2 Thessalonians 2:2. The apostle John taught that the last, real "antichrist" in the future, preceded by many "antichrists" in the present, makes known to the church that "it is the last time" (1 John 2:18). And it is the overwhelming testimony of the book of Revelation that the beast from the sea with his great war against Christ as Christ is present in his church will loom large at the very end, and that those who will be the object of his war will be those whose names are written in the book of life of the Lamb, which is a description of the believing church (Rev. 13).

The early church father was correct both in viewing antichrist as a future sign of the coming of Christ and in portraying antichrist as the imitation of Christ: "The hour of the Lord's appearing is uncertain, but it will be heralded by the manifestation of Antichrist disguised as God's Son."[3]

---

2 Here, the Reformed faith opposes the premillennial, dispensational doctrine of antichrist. For premillennialism, antichrist is future, but future for the Jews, the church having been raptured out of the world. See volume 1 of this set for an extended critique of this heresy with regard to its eschatology.

3 Hermas, in J. N. D. Kelly, *Early Christian Doctrines*, 4th ed. (London: Adam & Charles Black, 1968), 462.

Second, antichrist is a sign of practical importance and urgency for the believers. Antichrist means trial and conflict for them—the supreme trial and conflict. There have been many trials and conflicts for the church in past history. Those under antichrist will surpass them all in severity. The trial very much includes the seduction of the apostasy that tempts all to acknowledge antichrist as the true Christ and the impressive kingdom of antichrist as the kingdom of Christ. Those churches that increasingly make the salvation of Christianity deliverance from earthly evils, for example, relief from poverty, racial justice, rescue of females from sexual inequality, and such like, minimizing and even ignoring spiritual deliverance from sin against God, will be deceived into heralding antichrist as the genuine Christ.

The trial and conflict that antichrist will bring about for believers also include the great tribulation for all those who refuse to take the mark of the beast of Revelation 13.

In view of the coming of antichrist, therefore, the believer ought to prepare himself, as Paul enjoins in 2 Thessalonians 2:13–17. He ought to stand fast and hold the traditions. Preparation for the coming of the man of sin is implied by the warnings in verses 10–12. The believer must receive the love of the truth. He ought to believe the truth. He ought to examine himself whether he now has pleasure in unrighteousness.

Then, knowing that antichrist is the sign of the soon coming of Christ, when antichrist appears and is raging the believer will not be surprised or disheartened. Rather, he will be encouraged that his hope, the day of Christ, is now "at hand," in the very sense Paul spoke of it in 2 Thessalonians 2:2. Within time, times, and half a time from the first appearing of the man of sin, the Lord will return in the second coming to consume "that Wicked…with the spirit of his mouth, and…destroy [him] with the brightness of his coming" (v. 8).

The time of the antichrist is very brief.

And, with regard to the elect church, futile.

6

IDENTITY OF ANTICHRIST

INTRODUCTION

The subject of the identity of the biblical antichrist is rife with theories, many of them frivolous, if not absurd. Already the millennial controversy raises differences of opinion. Postmillennialism is compelled to suggest Caesar Nero or some other Roman emperor in the distant past. Dispensational premillennialism puts forward an unnamed political anti-Semite in the Jewish future.

More or less serious candidates for the ignoble position have included Martin Luther (by the intensely biased Roman Catholics),[1] Napoleon, Hitler, Stalin, Mussolini, Henry Kissinger, Ronald Reagan, and others. It would be surprising if his religious and political foes did not nominate Donald Trump. In view of the feminist movement, a contemporary writer suggests a female.[2] Protestants, of course, have identified the antichrist as the papacy of Rome,

---

1   The Jesuit scholar Vincent P. Miceli has dared to resurrect the old Roman Catholic charge that Luther was "without a doubt the last precursor of the greatest and cruelest Antichrist" as evidenced by the fact that he was a monk who "eloped with a nun" (Vincent P. Miceli, S.J., *The Antichrist* [West Hanover, MA: Christopher Publishing House, 1981], 126). The Roman Catholic Church raised this charge already during Luther's life. Luther shut the mouths of his foes with the observation that if antichrist was to be the result of the sexual relations of a monk and a nun, antichrist had been born thousands of times before the marriage of Luther and Katie. And Luther and Katie *married*—in a public ceremony. They did not "elope."
2   Peter Jones, *The Gnostic Empire Strikes Back* (Phillipsburg, NJ: P&R, 1992), 48: "The ultimate incarnation of antichrist may well be a woman!"

including some particular pope in the future.[3] This identification is creedal for Presbyterians.[4]

All these theories transgress the biblical principle concerning the revelation of such truths as that of the identity of antichrist. Scripture does not identify antichrist with definiteness. Rather, it paints the reality of antichrist with a broad brush, describing him according to his fundamental spiritual features. It leaves the definite identification for the appearance itself of the man of sin. Therefore, all specific identifications beforehand go beyond and outside the revelation of the Bible. Such identifications of antichrist are as foolish as speculation of the precise date of the end of the world.

By no means does this imply that the church knows nothing at all about the identity of antichrist or that this knowledge is unimportant to the church. Scripture does reveal much about the identity of antichrist, and the knowledge of this identity is of vital importance to the church and believer. The identity of antichrist is threefold. Antichrist is a worldwide political power, a religious entity, and an individual—a *male* individual. More than this the church does not know or need to know. Antichrist is an extraordinarily wicked man, who heads an awesome kingdom, and whose rise to power is aided and abetted by false religion.

To this identity of antichrist, we now turn in our consideration of the coming of Jesus Christ.

A KINGDOM

Antichrist will be a political power, a *universal* world power, or, to use the biblical term, a kingdom. This is the identification of antichrist in Daniel and Revelation. Daniel reveals the victorious realizing of God's purpose in the Messiah as the establishing of a world kingdom against the efforts of man to establish a world kingdom devoted to man. The four beasts out of the sea of Daniel 7 are

---

3   It is well known that Luther held that the antichrist is the Roman Catholic papacy. Not so well known is that this identification was not merely the visceral expression of his detestation of the Roman Catholic Church. On the contrary, it was the conclusion of Luther's carefully thought out eschatology. "Luther's position was eschatologically actual—something to be watchful for—and not futuristic. Luther felt himself surrounded by great eschatological tensions, and part of this for him included the role played by the antichrist. For Luther the antichrist was not a remote figure of some future 'end-time' but a threatening and dangerous possibility each and every day. Given this kind of expectation of the future…the contours of world and church history become extremely important. Luther concentrated his attention on *the last hour*" (Berkouwer, *Return of Christ*, 262–63).

4   The Westminster Confession of Faith (1646), 25:6, in *Creeds of the Churches*, ed. John H. Leith (Atlanta, GA: John Knox Press, 1973), 222: "The Pope of Rome…is that Antichrist."

four great kingdoms (v. 23), just as that which the Ancient of Days gives to the Son of Man, in opposition to these beasts, is "dominion, and glory, and a kingdom" (v. 14). The fourth beast is the Roman Empire and the source of antichrist. The little horn that comes up among the ten horns of the fourth beast with the eyes of man and a mouth speaking great things is antichrist. The fourth beast that produces antichrist is "the fourth *kingdom* upon earth" (v. 23).

In Daniel 8, the "rough goat," out of one of whose horns comes "a little horn" which symbolizes antichrist according to verses 8–12, is the world power of Greece and Macedonia (v. 21). The four horns are "four kingdoms" (v. 22).

That antichrist is a kingdom is also the meaning of Nebuchadnezzar's dream in Daniel 2. The four parts of the great image were four kingdoms (vv. 36–43). The fourth, the iron kingdom, was the Roman Empire, the source of the antichristian kingdom. The little stone that destroyed the four kingdoms by its demolition of the iron kingdom, is God's kingdom (v. 44). Even as Christ is, in an important sense, a kingdom, so also is antichrist.

The identification of antichrist by the book of Revelation is the same. The beast out of the sea of Revelation 13 and 17 is a political entity. It is a composite of the beasts of Daniel 7, which are kingdoms (Rev. 13:2). Its power is the kind that subdues "kindreds, and tongues, and nations" (v. 7). It is the power of the material sword (v. 7). The beast out of the sea is formed in part by the ten horns giving their kingdoms over to it (17:17). The ten horns are earthly kingdoms (vv. 12–13).

There is coming a one-world government. One nation will achieve supremacy and dominance by deceit and by dint of superior physical might. It will overawe and fascinate all the nations of the world. Thus, it will unite all nations under itself. This wondrous union of all nations and peoples under one government will be antichrist. This will be the beast out of the sea of Revelation 13. This will be the fourth kingdom of Daniel 7:7–8, 19–25.

The nation that realizes this union of all the nations and will therefore be the core and power of the world kingdom will arise out of the (formerly "Christian") West, not out of the heathen East. It will represent the revival of the Roman Empire of the time of Christ and the apostles. Thus will be fulfilled the prophecy of Daniel that the "exceeding dreadful" fourth beast takes final form in the little horn (Dan. 7:19), which little horn is antichrist, as chapter 7:25 makes unmistakably plain: the little horn that comes out of the fourth kingdom will "speak great words against the most High, and shall wear out the saints of the most High, and think to change times and laws: and they shall be given into his hand until a time and times and the dividing of time." This will be antichrist, and antichrist will be a kingdom.

Daniel and Revelation identify antichrist also regarding its spiritual nature. Thoroughly, it will be a kingdom of man. Man will be all in this kingdom. Although in reality its origin, power, and end will be the great dragon, which is Satan (Rev. 13:2), in the thinking of humans themselves man is the be-all and end-all of the kingdom. Man erects the kingdom; man is the law of the kingdom; and man is honored and worshiped in the kingdom.

This is the meaning of the declaration of 2 Thessalonians 2:4, that antichrist "opposeth and exalteth himself above all that is called God, or that is worshipped; so that he as God sitteth in the temple of God, shewing himself that he is God." While noting in passing that the text identifies antichrist as an individual, the passage discloses the spiritual nature of the entire kingdom of antichrist. It denies any and all divinity other than man. It allows no worship other than the worship of man. The main doctrine of this kingdom is that man is God.

What may not be overlooked in any explanation of the dream of Nebuchadnezzar in Daniel 2 is that the four elements of the image were parts of a *man*. The image as a whole was the image of a man. In the dream, the image was "great," and its "brightness was excellent…and the form thereof was terrible" (v. 31). Such is man in the thinking and entire culture of the fallen human race.

This deification of man is the explanation of the "number of the beast" in Revelation 13:18, the number "six hundred threescore and six." The original Greek reads not "the number of *a* man," but simply "the number of man." The idea is that the number of man, of humanity, without God is 666. As the number that represents man in covenantal fellowship with God is seven, so the number of man apart from God is six. The number 666, therefore, describes antichrist as humanity without God striving to attain to the glory and bliss that attend humanity's being in communion with God, but never, in spite of all its striving, attaining to what is symbolized by the number seven. The number 666 is not some arbitrarily selected individual, for example, Caesar Nero, but man without God.

The number 666 is mankind without God striving itself to be God in the utmost attempt of this futile effort. It is mankind without God, always coming short of the deity to which it aspires. It is mankind on its own, apart from the covenant of grace in Jesus Christ. It is therefore mankind under God's curse, subject to death under God's curse, doomed to fail in its grandiose ambition to establish an everlasting kingdom of peace, prosperity, and power. The implication of 666 is the battle of Armageddon of Revelation 16:16 (about which more later). After only a very short time, the antichristian kingdom is destroyed in a world war. The reason is that its number is 666. Only the kingdom whose number is seven is everlasting.

That the antichristian kingdom is the kingdom of man explains its lawlessness and persecution of the saints. "Iniquity shall abound" in the antichristian kingdom (Matt. 24:12), where *iniquity* is literally *lawlessness*. This lawlessness will not be disorder. On the contrary, the antichristian kingdom will be a kingdom of rigorous "law and order," the like of which the human race has never before seen. But the law will be the will of man. And the order will be the worship and service of man, as decreed and enforced by the antichristian authorities and as will be the universal will of the people, except for those who are written in the book of life of the Lamb. For example, the law will be the right of abortion as desired by mothers and as authorized by the state. The order will be the punishment of every church and every Christian that condemn abortion as murder.

As the kingdom of man, the antichristian kingdom will be a persecuting kingdom. Christ prophesied "the tribulation of those days" (Matt. 24:29). Divine man cannot tolerate the confession and worship of another God, that is, the one, true God who is revealed in Jesus Christ. The number six rages against the number seven. This is an important truth of biblical mathematics: six hates seven. This truth about numbers should be part of the instruction in math in the good Christian school. History demonstrated this truth in the persecution of the nation of Israel by Antiochus Epiphanes in the inter-testamentary period; in the persecution of the saints in Jerusalem by the Roman Empire in AD 70; in the persecution of the Reformed by the Roman Catholic Church in the sixteenth and seventeenth centuries; and in all lesser persecutions of the church by her enemies throughout all ages. It will come to its most intense expression in the great tribulation of the church by antichrist in the future. In the rage of spiritual numerology, 666 will persecute seven.

The spiritual nature of the antichristian kingdom is also that it will be satanic. It will be the creature of Satan; it will serve Satan; it will worship Satan. Regarding the personal head of the kingdom, 2 Thessalonians 2:9 states that his "coming is after the working of Satan." But it is especially Revelation 13 that describes the kingdom of antichrist as satanic. The beast that is the antichristian world power has its power, seat, and great authority from the dragon (v. 2). The dragon is the great, red dragon of the preceding chapter, chapter 12. And this chapter identifies the dragon as the "old serpent, called the Devil, and Satan," who was cast out of heaven into the earth (12:9) upon his revolt. In his great poem *Paradise Lost*, John Milton persuasively suggests that Satan, who as Lucifer was originally the splendid head of the entire host of angels, rebelled against God over the matter of God's decree to glorify himself not by means of the angel who became Satan, but by means of the woman's child, who is Jesus.

> Satan, so call him now, his former name
> Is heard no more in Heav'n; he of the first,
> If not the first Arch-Angel, great in Power,
> In favour and preeminence, yet fraught
> With envy against the Son of God, that day
> Honour'd by his great Father, and proclaim'd
> Messiah King anointed, could not bear
> Through pride that sight, and thought himself impair'd.
> Deep malice thence conceiving and disdain,
> Soon as midnight brought on the dusky hour
> Friendliest to sleep and silence, he resolv'd
> With all his Legions to dislodge, and leave
> Unworshipt, unobey'd the Throne supreme
> Contemptuous.[5]

Revelation 13 also describes the antichristian kingdom as satanic in that the kingdom and its citizens worship "the dragon which gave power unto the beast" (v. 4). Among all the features of the kingdom of antichrist, this is fundamental: it worships the devil. This is the essence of the kingdom: not its physical power, not its earthly glory, not its material prosperity, not its worldly peace, but its worship, and this is the worship of Satan.

One must not misconceive this worship. It will not be the weird chanting of witches, a bowing down of a bewitched congregation before a terrifying image of a red-eyed, black-cloaked demon, and the sacrificing of goats. But it will be the cultured, if enthusiastic, worship of an image of the personal antichrist, as representative of the antichristian kingdom, by a confession that antichrist is god and by the bowing down to the image. All this worship will be explained as the rightful acknowledgment that man is god and as the public declaration that one is a sincere and grateful citizen of the kingdom of man. And religion is the best means of unifying an empire.

> 1. Nebuchadnezzar the king made an image of gold, whose height was threescore [60] cubits, and the breadth thereof six cubits: he set it up in the plain of Dura, in the province of Babylon...
>
> 4. Then an herald cried aloud, To you it is commanded, O people, nations, and languages,

---

5 John Milton, *Paradise Lost*, in *Paradise Lost* and *Paradise Regained*, ed. Christopher Ricks (New York: New American Library, 1968), 167.

5. That at what time ye hear the sound of…all kinds of musick, ye fall down and worship the golden image that Nebuchadnezzar the king hath set up:
6. And whoso falleth not down and worshippeth shall the same hour be cast into the midst of burning fiery furnace (Dan. 3:1, 4–6).

This satanic nature of the kingdom will be the deepest cause of the antagonism of antichrist to God, that is, the true God revealed in Jesus Christ. Satan is the adversary of God. The dragon is "wroth with the woman" and goes to "make war with the remnant of her seed," because the woman and her seed "keep the commandments of God, and have the testimony of Jesus Christ" (Rev. 12:17).

It is not at all difficult in AD 2022 to envision the kingdom of antichrist, uniting all the nations and peoples of the world. All nations are self-consciously secular and increasingly culturally antichristian, including the West, which once was strongly influenced by Christianity. The only problem at this stage in history is to accommodate Islam. Everywhere are longing and striving, clandestinely as well as openly, for the uniting of nations as one world of humanity. More and more, the nations become interdependent economically. "Globalization" is on the lips of the movers and shakers of the world. "Nationality" fast becomes an obscenity. And the removal of borders is the beginning of the realization of the oneness of all nations and peoples in hard fact. All that is necessary yet is the charismatic head of a mighty nation with the dream of truly united nations and the will to bring it about.

THE FALSE CHURCH

Antichrist will also be a religious entity—chiefly the apostate, nominally Christian church. Especially two passages of Scripture identify antichrist as false religion, particularly apostate Christianity. One of the passages is the first and second epistles of John. These epistles are the only passages in Scripture that use the term *antichrist*. Both describe antichrist as a religious reality. According to 1 John 2:18–19, although the one consummate antichrist is still future, there were in John's own day "many antichrists." These were men who were once members of the visible church but "went out from us." That John has heretics in mind is evident in chapter 2:22, where John identifies an antichrist as one who denies the Father and the Son (cf. also chapter 4:1–3). Likewise, 2 John 7 identifies an antichrist as a doctrinal deceiver, whose deceit is that he denies that "Jesus Christ is come in the flesh."

John's instruction regarding antichrist is not only that there are many antichrists who precede and pave the way for the one final antichrist at the end.

But it is also his doctrine that the full reality of antichrist is religious as well as political. This full reality is, mainly, apostate Christianity and the false church. In all kinds of ways, beginning already in the time of the apostles, the religious antichrist denies that Jesus is the Christ. The "gospel" of antichrist is that he, mankind, is the Christ and that his carnal world kingdom is the true kingdom of Christ. Antichrist opposes Christ, and he opposes Christ by replacing him. Man is God as the true savior of the human race.

The second passage is Revelation 13:11–18. The beast out of the sea of verses 1–10 is not the complete reality of antichrist. There is also a beast out of the earth (vv. 11–18). This beast is allied with the beast out of the sea. The idea of the two beasts is that together they make up the one whole reality of antichrist. Antichrist is twofold: primarily political, but also religious. That antichrist is primarily political—a kingdom—is evident in that the second beast exercises "all the power of the first beast before him, and causeth the earth and them which dwell therein to worship the first beast" (v. 12). The second beast serves the first beast by proclaiming him as god and causing the entire world to worship the first beast.

Thus, the second beast displays that it shares in the beastly nature of the first beast, which is that of the dragon. The second beast exercises the power of the dragon by speaking dragon language: "He spake as a dragon" (v. 11). If the power of the first beast is the sword, the power of the second beast is speech—*dragon* speech; *religious* dragon speech; *lamblike*, religious dragon speech.

The second beast of Revelation 13 is apostate religion, specifically, the apostate Christian church. Although it speaks like a dragon, it resembles a lamb (v. 11). The lamb everywhere in Revelation is Jesus Christ (cf. 5:6, 8, 12–13; 6:1; 17:14; 19:7; 21:9, 22–23, 27; 22:1–3). In chapter 19:20, the beast out of the earth is called "the false prophet." This description of the beast out of the earth confirms the identification of this beast as the false church. The outstanding function of the true church is that it speaks the word of God, or prophesies. The *false* prophet is the false church. This church's prophecy will be that the political antichrist, headed by its powerful, charismatic leader, is god. By this prophecy, accompanied and confirmed by great wonders, which the false church will be able to perform by supernatural powers derived from the dragon, the apostate church will function as the effectual means by which the political antichrist comes to power.

Humanity is incurably religious. The only power, therefore, that can finally convince the human race that the political antichrist is the realization of the biblical kingdom of Christ and that the personal antichrist is the reality of the mythical Christ of Scripture (such will be the message of the false church) is religion, specifically, apostate Christianity. Only when the false church throws its weight behind the claims of antichrist, that is, itself becomes part of the full reality of antichrist, does the beast out of the sea prevail.

It is not difficult to see the religious antichrist developing in our day. Many nominally Christian churches deny that Jesus is Christ, with all the truths this implies, particularly that salvation is redemption from sin by the atoning sacrifice of the crucified Jesus. The churches come together as one in the ecumenical organization that calls itself the World Council of Churches. This council is active behind the scenes in uniting all the nations on earth. The Roman Catholic Church, which has always worked at bringing the nations together under her dominion, is today as influential a power for the uniting of churches and nations as she has ever been. Her fundamental doctrine of justification by works gains the day in all the supposedly conservative Presbyterian and Reformed churches that approve or are open to the heresy of the federal vision. The ecumenical movement known as Evangelicals and Catholics Together (ECT) recognizes Rome as a true church and strives for church union with Rome by ignoring, and thus denying, the fundamental doctrines of the Protestant Reformation and of the Reformed creeds. Such a popular and influential churchman as N. T. Wright openly advertises that the purpose of his ministry is the reunion of Protestantism and Rome, which ought never, according to Wright, have been separated.

Ominously, the Christian Reformed Church in North America, which by its institutional impressiveness, its reputation for Reformed orthodoxy, its missionary activities, and its academic fame has great influence in North America, if not in all the world, has recently repudiated question and answer 80 of the Reformed creed the Heidelberg Catechism, that is, that part of question and answer 80 that condemns the Roman Catholic mass. Question and answer 80 of the catechism charges that "the Mass at bottom is nothing else than a denial of the one sacrifice and passion of Jesus Christ [and an accursed idolatry]."[6] The mass being at the heart of the Roman Catholic Church, this charge condemns Rome as a false church.

The 2004 synod of the Christian Reformed Church declared that "Q. and A. 80 can no longer be held in its current form as part of our confession."[7] The 2006 synod of that denomination decided that the entire section of answer 80

---

6 Heidelberg Catechism Q&A 80, in Schaff, *Creeds of Christendom*, 3:336.
7 "Acts of Synod 2004," Christian Reformed Church in North America, 629.

of the catechism that condemns the Roman Catholic mass and thus the Roman Catholic Church is "no longer confessionally binding on members of the CRC."[8]

Whether question and answer 80 was part of the creed in its original form does not detract in the slightest from the ominous significance of the repudiation *at this time* of the catechism's condemnation of Rome. If a church were determined to be and remain a true church of Christ in view of the well-nigh irresistible seduction and deception of apostasy in these last days, in which deception Rome plays the leading role, the church would strengthen question and answer 80 rather than elide it. Repudiation of question and answer 80 of the catechism is a step toward recognition of Rome as a true church of Christ and thus toward the existence of the beast out of the earth and its service of the beast out of the sea, which is antichrist.

Inasmuch as Islam must be brought into the sphere of the religious beast that is antichrist, it is worthy of note that the pope is presently engaged in high-powered discussions with the leaders of Islam, in order to bring about an understanding and some kind of union between that false religion and apostate Christianity. One may be sure that in effecting this ecumenical oneness with Islam the pope is working on behalf of apostate Protestantism as well.

Yet another spiritual force that is presently in operation to unify not only all Christian churches but also all religions is syncretism. This is the religious philosophy that contends that all religions are basically one. There are a few fundamental elements that are the same for all religions, including the fatherhood of God, the brotherhood of man, and the calling to love one another.

---

8 "Acts of Synod 2006," Christian Reformed Church in North America, 710–11. Hilarious, were not the matter so deadly serious, is a ground for thus eliding the catechism's condemnation of the Roman mass, namely, that in a consultation of a Christian Reformed delegation with Roman Catholic bishops and other theologians, the Roman Catholic prelates informed the Christian Reformed clergy that the mass is not, in fact, what question and answer 80 charges. Rome denies that its mass is a denial of the one sacrifice and sufferings of Jesus Christ and an accursed idolatry, and therefore a Reformed church must elide the charge! Not far-fetched, in view of the Reformation's judgment of the Roman Catholic Church as antichrist, is a similar consultation of a delegation with antichrist when he appears. When he denies that he is in fact the antichrist, despite all the evidence to the contrary, including that he demands worship in the stead of Jesus, the Christian Reformed synod will reject the churches' judgment of him as the antichrist, on the ground that the antichrist denies this. Regardless of the denial by the Roman Catholic bishops and theologians, "the Mass teaches that the living and the dead have not forgiveness of sins through the sufferings of Christ unless Christ is still daily offered for them by the priests" (Heidelberg Catechism A 80, in Schaff, *Creeds of Christendom*, 3:335). Sobering is the remembrance that thousands of Reformed believers have been put to death by Rome for confessing what the synod of the Christian Reformed Church so lightly—and *falsely*—stripped from the confession.

Whether Jesus is the Son of God and whether Muhammad is the special prophet of God are incidental and, in ecumenical deliberations, negotiable. It is possible therefore and necessary for mankind's welfare, threatened as it is by world wars, widespread poverty, atomic weapons, and mistreatment of females, that religions come together on the basis of the few religious fundamentals. This is happening. Then whoever refuses to become part of this beast from the earth is the real heretic, and heretics ought once again, as in past times, to be excommunicated from human society and burned. A mark will distinguish true believers from the divisive unbelievers, and as many as will not join the one, true, recognized religion of the beast will be excommunicated from the beastly church, which is the society of all the world, and "should be killed" (Rev. 13:15).

An aggressive, outspoken, and popular (but by no means rare) exponent of syncretism is the Roman Catholic theologian Hans Kung. For Kung, all the great religions of the world, including Buddhism, Hinduism, Islam, and Christianity, are essentially one. "The other religions…complete, correct, and enrich the Christian religion."[9] When all the extraneous beliefs are stripped from them, their oneness is their deep concern for the earthly welfare of humans. Obvious is Kung's omission from this oneness of the sole authority of Scripture and of Jesus Christ as the only savior as God in human flesh. The authority for all the religions is not an inspired book, that is, the Bible, but the contemporary culture of all nations. As for a unique savior, "even *after* Christ…[there are] prophets…outside the Church as well, among whom the prophet Muhammad and the Buddha should no doubt be included *par excellence*."[10]

With all this approval of false prophets, salvation by works, and idolatry, and with all this denial of Jesus as the Son of God, the one and only savior from sin, salvation by faith alone, and the triune God as the only deity, the purpose of Kung is ecumenicity. The ecumenicity of Kung's syncretism involves not only all Christian churches, very much including Rome, but also all religions. There can, and must, be "an ecumenical community of all Christians." This ecumenicity will then become "a future ecumene of [all] religions and cultures."[11]

Truth plays no part in this ecumenicity. Christianity is not *the* truth. It is merely truth for the Christian, as Buddhism is truth for the Buddhist. "This one religion [Christianity] is *for me the true religion*…This (for me, for us Christians)

---

9 Hans Kung, *Theology for the Third Millennium: An Ecumenical View*, tr. Peter Heinegg (New York: Doubleday, 1988), 254.
10 Kung, *Theology*, 251.
11 Kung, *Theology*, 179.

one true religion in no way excludes the truth in *other religions,* but lets them have a positive validity."[12]

Any Protestant explanation of antichrist as a religious entity must take into account the contention of the reformers that antichrist is the papacy of Rome. All the reformers were of this conviction. The Westminster Confession of Faith made this conviction creedal for Presbyterians in chapter 25:6: "The Pope of Rome…is that Antichrist, that man of sin and son of perdition."[13] The reformers were right insofar as the Roman Catholic Church is the basic element of the full reality of antichrist—the *religious* element, that is, the beast out of the earth of Revelation 13. As question and answer 80 of the Heidelberg Catechism clearly implies, Rome is a false church. In view of Rome's size and ecclesiastical and political influence, Rome undoubtedly will be the driving force of the beast out of the earth, the organization that actually brings together all the churches and religions and that exercises "all the power of the first beast before him, and causeth the earth and them which dwell therein to worship the first beast" (Rev. 13:12). The Roman Catholic Church, which has hardened itself against the gospel of grace since the sixteenth-century Reformation of the church, perfectly fits the description of the beast out of the earth as resembling the lamb but speaking as a dragon.

A future pope, revered and worshiped as a religious icon—as virtually a god—by a billion humans in all nations, skilled in ecumenical diplomacy, and practiced in political wizardry, will represent and direct the beast out of the earth in this beast's service of the beast out of the sea. No doubt, the purpose of the Roman Catholic Church in all this collaboration with the political power that heads the beast out of the sea will be to seize the reins of power from the beast out of the sea at an advantageous time, so that Rome herself will be the dominant power in the world. Single-mindedly, Rome always plots her own primacy.

---

12 Kung, *Theology,* 250, 254; emphasis in the original. In light of 1 Thessalonians 1:9–10 and chapter 2, one imagines Kung's sermon at Thessalonica. It would have gone something like this. "Hans, to the church at Thessalonica. I am thankful to have found you worshiping Zeus, when I came to you preaching my god. Mine is the same as yours. Therefore, I did not try to convert you. But I introduced to you a man named Jesus, with the allure that he would improve your relations with each other, especially your poor treatment of the women among you. Above all else, Jesus came to save humans from the mistreatment of females. The church that I established among you (with some embarrassment in that I may have offended you as though your religious organizations were evil) is holding its sacrament of the Lord's supper next Sunday. I suggest that you invite your pagan relatives and friends to participate. Tell them that their gods and your god will rejoice to see us worshiping together. All the gods want us to become one, as they are. (Just ignore the meaning of the broken bread and the poured-out wine; by all means ignore this.)"
13 Westminster Confession of Faith 25.6, in Schaff, *Creeds of Christendom,* 3:658–59.

This critique of the tenuous relation of the beast out of the earth, which is primarily the Roman Catholic Church, and the beast out of the sea directs every study of antichrist to Revelation 17, John's vision of the whore sitting upon a scarlet-colored beast (v. 3). There can be no doubt that the beast is the beast out of the sea of Revelation 13. The beast has seven heads and ten horns and is characterized by blasphemy against God. It is antichrist as the worldwide union of nations under one mighty ruler.

Sitting upon the beast, as though reigning over the confederation of nations that comprise antichrist, is a whore who has by her whoredoms become wealthy and impressive. As a whore is a woman who is unfaithful to her husband, so is this harlot the church, or union of churches, that once was married to Jesus Christ and still by the name of church professes to be married to Christ, but that has gone after lovers. This whore is especially attracted to, and used by, the beast on which she sits, which is the political antichrist. The whore is apostate Christianity, or the false church, of which the Roman Catholic Church is the dominant part.

Although the Roman Catholic Church will be the main component of the religious aspect of antichrist and although as such it will be closely allied with the political antichrist, as the beast out of the earth of Revelation 13 is closely allied with the beast out of the sea, the reformers were mistaken in their identification of the antichrist as the papacy. This was mistaken, first, because it failed to do justice to the truth that antichrist must be identified as an individual. Antichrist is not only an office, that is, the papacy. Second, and more importantly, antichrist is mainly a *political* entity, not a religious reality. It is mainly a kingdom, not a church. The personal antichrist is a political figure, not an ecclesiastical figure—a president, or king, or emperor, not a pope.

Further, the personal antichrist is irreligious, anti-supernatural, and thoroughly secular. He is a person who openly repudiates God and who bluntly exalts man as the only deity. This is the conclusive testimony of 2 Thessalonians 2. Antichrist opposes and exalts himself above all that is called God or that is worshiped. He unceremoniously evicts God from his temple, replacing him with himself, declaring himself to be God, and demanding that he himself, and he alone, be worshiped as God (v. 4). These cannot be the pretensions and actions of the Roman Catholic Church and its pope. Rome claims the honors and saving acts of God. It claims to represent God. It cannot deny God—the God revealed in Scripture. It cannot, without jeopardizing the adherence of its faithful, deny that God exists and banish God altogether, thus denying itself. Rome is a false religion. It is not, and cannot be, irreligious, as is the son of perdition of 2 Thessalonians 2.

The prophecy of Daniel 11 also identifies antichrist in such a way as makes it impossible that he be a pope or the papacy. Verses 36 and 37 state that the king, who is antichrist, "shall exalt himself, and magnify himself above every god, and shall speak marvellous things against the God of gods…Neither shall he regard the God of his fathers…nor regard any god: for he shall magnify himself above all." Verse 38 adds that "in his estate shall he honor the God of forces." The passage identifies antichrist as an avowed atheist, a political figure, and one who rules by means of physical arms.

The identification of antichrist as political and the identification of the whore as false religion, primarily as the Roman Catholic Church, harmonize with the end of the whore at the hands of the kings that make up the beast, as related in Revelation 17:16. The ten horns of the beast "hate the whore, and shall make her desolate and naked, and shall eat her flesh, and burn her with fire." This description of the end of the whore maintains the figure. When a man has finished using the whore, he is disgusted with her, to the point of willing her destruction. The reality of the passage is that after the political antichrist has used the false church to solidify his dominance over all the world, he destroys the false church, or false religion. Antichrist brooks no opposition or challenge to his own absolute sway over all. The whore is a threat. She aspires to dominance herself. For a time she rides the beast. Besides, although the god she worships is a false god, she does confess it to be God. As long as the whore exists, she negates antichrist's claim to be God, the one and only God. Antichrist brooks no opposition to his claim to sole deity.

The understanding of antichrist as mainly political exposes the identification of antichrist as "the pope of Rome" by the Westminster Confession of Faith (WCF) as mistaken: "The Pope of Rome…is that Antichrist, that man of sin and son of perdition, that exalteth himself in the Church against Christ, and all that is called God."[14]

It ought to be noted about this declaration that, at bottom, it is not a concern to identify antichrist, but a concern to identify the pope. The article does not occur in a chapter on eschatology, but on ecclesiology. The creed does not affirm that antichrist is the pope, but that the pope is antichrist. The real concern of the article is to deny that the pope is head of the church. And then, regarding its assertion that the pope is antichrist, the meaning is not that a particular pope will be the antichrist, but that the papacy—the papal office itself—is antichrist.

Nevertheless, the WCF does identify the antichrist of 2 Thessalonians 2 as

---

14 Westminster Confession of Faith 25.6, in *Creeds of the Churches*, 222.

the pope. There is, however, no such definite identification of antichrist in the Reformed three forms of unity. Abraham Kuyper explains why there is not, and should not be, any such confessional identification of antichrist.

> That the Antichrist would come thus in the papal hierarchy can not be adopted as dogma and is then also never confessed by the Dutch Reformed churches…It indeed belongs to the confession that Antichrist comes and how he will be, but not the realization thereof, for example, the designation of the pope at Rome as such; for this is not indicated in Scripture and is merely fruit of a personal conviction. That therefore can never be a dogma.[15]

THE MAN

The biblical antichrist is both a political power and an ecclesiastical organization. It is also a certain, particular, individual human. This has been debated, but the biblical evidence is conclusive. Second Thessalonians 2 speaks of "that man of sin"; "the son of perdition"; and of "that Wicked [one]" (vv. 3, 8). It has one sitting in the temple of God and showing himself that he is God (v. 4). "He" will be revealed in "his" time (v. 6). Likewise, Daniel 7 describes the little horn of the fourth beast as a king, who (masculine singular) speaks great things against the Most High and wears out the saints of the Most High (vv. 24–26). Also the description of the coming antichrist in Daniel 11:36–39 makes clear beyond all doubt or contradiction that antichrist is a political *person*: he is a king, who does according to his will, he magnifies himself above every god, etc.

That antichrist is an individual man is virtually demanded by its being a political power, a kingdom. Every great kingdom not only *has* its mighty king, but also *is* itself the extension of the king who is its head. The king does not take over an existing kingdom, but the kingdom comes into existence by virtue of the mind, will, and strength of the king. So it is with the kingdom of God. It is the creation of King Jesus. So it has been with regard to all the great kingdoms of man in history. Babylon was Nebuchadnezzar; Persia was Cyrus; Greece was Alexander the Great. Recent history confirms this. Nazi Germany was Hitler; the Soviet Union was Stalin; China was Mao.

There was truth in the declaration attributed to Louis XIV of France, the "Sun King": *L`etat C`est Moi* (The state is me).

The world power of Satan at the end will be the body of which the personal antichrist is head.

---

15 Abraham Kuyper, *Dictaten Dogmatik* [*Dictated Dogmatics*], 5 vols. (Grand Rapids, MI: J. B. Hulst, n.d.), 5:231–32. The translation of the Dutch is mine; the work has not been translated.

Concerning this man, he will be Satan's astonishing, formal imitation of God's Christ. This similarity, as depicted in 2 Thessalonians 2, is remarkable. As was the case with Christ, antichrist will have his revelation (v. 3). He will, like Christ, claim deity (v. 4). He has his own, definite "time" (v. 6). He has a "coming" (v. 9, where the Greek is *parousia*). Indeed, the Greek original of verse 9 has "*the* coming," with reference to a singular, notable coming on behalf of the human race. This coming, like the coming of Christ, will be attended with, and commended by, supernatural deeds (v. 9). And then antichrist will be the head of a world power, uniting in himself state and church. Thus, he will provide (a certain kind of) salvation for (nearly) all humans.

Because of this formal similarity of antichrist to Christ Jesus, the medieval church referred to antichrist as *simia Christi*, that is, "ape of Christ." As noted earlier, the church father described antichrist as "disguised as God's Son."[16]

This remarkable formal similarity to Christ supports the antichristian claim of antichrist. He does not claim to be the preferable substitute for the biblical Christ. But he claims to be the reality toward which the biblical Christ pointed, indeed, what the biblical Christ *is*, whether the biblical Christ actually lived or was merely a lovely myth. Or, to say it differently, antichrist is the truth of which the biblical Christ was merely a symbol. In the strange little work that only a Russian could have written, Soloviev analyzes antichrist's claim in relation to the biblical Christ correctly:

> He [the personal antichrist] considered himself to be what Christ in reality was…"I am the final savior of the world, and Christ is my precursor. His mission was to precede and prepare for my coming." Thinking thus, the superman of the twenty-first century [the personal antichrist] applied to himself everything that was said in the Gospels about the second coming, explaining the latter not as a return of the same Christ, but as a replacing of the preliminary Christ by the final one—that is, by himself.[17]

Although a creature, and only a creature, antichrist will be specially and wondrously empowered by Satan with extraordinary abilities. Every revelation of antichrist in Scripture calls attention to the fact that his claim to be the reality of the Christ of Scripture will be supported by his, or his advocates', performance of miracles. According to Jesus himself in the fundamental New Testament prophecy of antichrist, the false Christs and false prophets will show

---

16 Cf. Kelly, *Early Christian Doctrines*, 462.
17 Vladimir Sergaevitch Soloviev, *A Story of Anti-Christ* (Monee, IL: Kassock Bros., reprint 2012 [first published 1900]), 7–8.

"great signs and wonders." It will especially be this performance of miracles that will "deceive the very elect," if this were a possibility (Matt. 24:24). In keeping with this warning of Jesus, 2 Thessalonians 2:9 describes the coming of the personal antichrist as a coming "with all power and signs and lying wonders." It attributes these supernatural deeds to "the working of Satan" in the antichrist.

Revelation 13 emphasizes the miraculous powers of the antichrist. Operating through the ecclesiastical aspect of the full reality of antichrist, he "doeth great wonders, so that he maketh fire come down from heaven on the earth in the sight of men" (v. 13). Verse 14 speaks of "those miracles which he had power to do." The epitome of the miracles is that he "[gives] life unto the image of the [first] beast, that the image of the beast should both speak, and cause that as many as would not worship the image of the beast should be killed" (v. 15).

It is the result especially of the wonders that antichrist can perform that he "deceiveth them that dwell on the earth," to worship him as God's Christ, indeed as God himself (v. 14).

These wonders are not mere tricks, a magician's sleight of hand. They are deeds of superhuman power. "Lying wonders," in 2 Thessalonians 2:9, is literally "wonders of the lie," that is, real wonders performed on behalf of the lie. The only way to distinguish these wonders from miracles performed by Christ and his apostles is by their being performed on behalf of the lie that antichrist is God. The distinction is not in the power and splendor of the deeds in the eyes of the beholder, but in the message they intend to confirm. What will save the believer from deception in the time of these "lying wonders" will be the conviction of faith that the Jesus Christ of holy Scripture, and not antichrist, is God in the flesh. The explanation of the miraculous deeds of antichrist is that the ability to perform them is the power in him of the (superhuman) dragon (Rev. 13:2).

What is truly appalling about the personal antichrist is his wickedness. This is the emphasis of 2 Thessalonians 2. Antichrist is the "man of sin" (v. 3). All of the manifold malignancy of the mysterious power of sin is fulfilled in him, just as all the mysterious reality of holiness is fulfilled in Jesus Christ. Because sin is hatred of God, antichrist is the embodiment of hatred of God. What explains his being the man of sin is that he is the "son of perdition" (v. 3), that is, the child born of hell, so that the very nature of hell as the proper abode and atmosphere of Satan is his. Satan plays an extraordinary role in the conception and birth of the personal antichrist. Although Satan is incapable of uniting the child to himself personally, as by demonic incarnation, he can infuse into the child in a unique manner and measure his own demonic hatred of God and his Christ. Sharing as he does the very nature of his spiritual father to the fullest extent possible for a human, antichrist rages against God and everything reflecting or testifying to the Godhead of God. This makes certain his persecution of the true church.

That which more than anything else identifies antichrist as the spiritual offspring of Satan is that he revolts against God himself, purposing to overthrow God and replace him: "he as God sitteth in the temple of God, shewing himself that he is God" (2 Thess. 2:4). This, of course, was the sin of antichrist's spiritual father, the devil. As a high-ranking angel, he attempted the overthrow of God himself, in order that he—Satan—might be God, certainly the expression of pride, rage, and revolt bordering on madness. Like father, like son.

Daniel 7:25 specifies a mysterious expression of antichrist's aspiring to godhead: "[He] think[s] to change times and laws." Exactly what form this godlike action will take awaits the event. But already the spirit of antichrist, which is in the world, changes the fundamental law of male and female and, with this, the basic law of marriage. One is reminded that the French Revolution of the late eighteenth and early nineteenth centuries, a precursor of the antichristian revolution, changed the week and the calendar for no other reason than to demonstrate, in God's face, that the revolutionaries occupied the throne of God and wielded divine powers.

THE END OF ANTICHRIST

As the full reality of antichrist is threefold—political, ecclesiastical, and individual—so also is antichrist's end. Prior to the coming of Christ, after the false church has been useful to the political antichrist in uniting all nations and peoples under it, the political antichrist will turn on the false church to destroy it. One uses a whore; he does not marry her or permit her to interfere with his life. The political antichrist brooks no rivals, including a religious rival. Revelation 17:16 has the ten horns that cast in their lot with the beast out of the sea to form the one world government of antichrist turn at the end on the whore that rides the beast: "And the ten horns which thou sawest upon the beast, these shall hate the whore, and shall make her desolate and naked, and shall eat her flesh, and burn her with fire." Both the motivation of the nations and the sovereignty of God in the event are explained in verse 17: "For God hath put in their hearts to fulfil his will, and to agree, and give their kingdom unto the beast, until the words of God shall be fulfilled."

As for the world kingdom that is the political antichrist, shortly before the coming of Christ it breaks up in world war. This is the battle of Armageddon of Revelation 16:12–21 (about which more in the next chapter).

At his bodily coming, Jesus Christ himself personally confronts the individual antichrist. According to 2 Thessalonians 2:8, the Lord Jesus will "consume [the man of sin, the son of perdition, of verses 3–8] with the spirit of his mouth, and shall destroy [him] with the brightness of his coming." There is a dramatic, personal confrontation: Christ versus antichrist; God's man versus Satan's man; the personification of God versus the "embodiment" of Satan. It is no contest. Nor is there any possibility of a later revival of antichrist and a resumption of his wicked designs. The Lord Jesus shall consume the man of sin and will do so simply by the spirit of his mouth. On the basis of the cross, in the power of his resurrection and ascension, by the might of the Spirit who has been given him, and on behalf of God his Father, Christ Jesus utterly destroys the final champion of Satan and the cause of evil in God's world forever. The Savior and Lord of the church is victor, by his own personal act.

Evident in this threefold defeat of antichrist is that God shortens the time of the sway of antichrist. Whereas the power of antichrist appears to be so great, indeed unassailable, that the false church has the upper hand, the one world government has dominion, and the personal antichrist reigns for many years, if not in some respects forever, abruptly the entire, vast, magnificent, powerful, satanic enterprise collapses and is destroyed. Exactly this is the prophecy of Scripture in various enigmatic descriptions. In the foundational, New Testament prophecy of Jesus, "Those days [shall] be shortened" (Matt. 24:22). Obviously derivative of Jesus' word is the judgment of John upon the time of antichrist: "He must continue a short space" (Rev. 17:10).

As with so many aspects of the truth about antichrist, the shortened duration of antichrist originates in the prophecy of Daniel in the Old Testament. Daniel 7:25 describes this shortening as "a time and times and the dividing of time." Corresponding to Daniel's time, times, and the dividing of time are the 1,260 days of Revelation 12:6 (one year, two years, and half a year); the time, times, and half a time of chapter 12:14; and the forty-two months of chapter 13:5 (again one year, two years, and half a year).

In the highly symbolical books of Daniel and Revelation, the time, times, and half a time, the 1,260 days, and the forty-two months are not to be taken literally, as though the reign of antichrist and the duration of the antichristian empire are to last three and a half years. But the thought is rather that after the time of antichrist's coming to power (a time) and the longer time of his full exertion of his godless reign (times), when it seems that he and his kingdom are omnipotent and will endure forever, suddenly the antichristian kingdom is overthrown and cut off (half a time).

The final, all-important word about antichrist is "half a time." This should be the warning about the kingdom of the beast for the ungodly, who are awed and seduced by antichrist and therefore pledge their allegiance to him and cast in their lot with it: "half a time." This is the encouragement of the saints in their suffering on account of their refusing the carrot of seduction and their enduring the stick of persecution: "half a time."

Fearful as the beast is, faith's attitude regarding antichrist is neither terror nor apprehension. It is not terror, because the Lamb who sits at God's right hand has said to faith, "Fear not…for it is your Father's good pleasure to give you the kingdom" (Luke 12:32), and "In the world ye shall have tribulation: but be of good cheer; I have overcome the world" (John 16:33). Faith's attitude is not apprehension, because every believer is confident that his name is written in the book of life of the Lamb, so that he will not worship the beast (Rev. 13:8).

Faith is fully aware of the coming of the beast out of the sea—a coming in conflict with the church, accompanied by the beast out of the earth. It entertains no foolish notions about an escape of the church from antichrist and his tribulation. It examines current events in light of the coming of antichrist, for example, the lawlessness of the times, the apostasy of the churches, and the uniting of the nations.

Faith prepares itself for the coming of the beast. It roots itself ever more deeply and thoroughly in the doctrines of the gospel of Jesus Christ. By the word and Spirit of Christ, it strengthens itself for the impending war, that it may stand in that evil day. It is instant in prayer that it may work by the love for Jesus in resisting the plea to love antichrist and the antichristian kingdom, which will have their appeal to the natural love of humans.

Faith has its desire for the coming, spiritual battle against antichrist. To be the church and the citizen of the kingdom of Christ who are privileged to confess that Jesus Christ is Lord in the greatest battle of this kingdom in history, indeed in the greatest battle of all of human history, appeals to faith. Faith's "come, Lord Jesus" includes a challenge to the antichrist to have his coming, so that the host of Christ's army may overcome him, be it by martyrdom.

And then, above all, faith's attitude toward antichrist is that his appearing signals the nearness of the coming of Jesus Christ. Faith looks through and beyond the beast to the Lamb. Revelation 12–13 and 17, concerning the beast, are followed by Revelation 19 about the coming of Jesus:

11. And I saw heaven opened, and behold a white horse; and he that sat upon him was called Faithful and True, and in righteousness he doth judge and make war.
12. His eyes were as a flame of fire, and on his head were many crowns; and he had a name written, that no man knew, but he himself…

15. And out of his mouth goeth a sharp sword, that with it he should smite the nations: and he shall rule them with a rod of iron: and he treadeth the winepress of the fierceness and wrath of Almighty God.
16. And he hath on his vesture and on his thigh a name written, KING OF KINGS, AND LORD OF LORDS…

19. And I saw the beast, and the kings of the earth, and their armies, gathered together to make war against him that sat on the horse, and against his army.
20. And the beast was taken, and with him the false prophet that wrought miracles before him, with which he deceived them that had received the mark of the beast, and them that worshipped his image. These both were cast alive into a lake of fire burning with brimstone (Rev. 19:11–12, 15–16, 19–20).

7

ANTICHRIST-RELATED EVENTS

INTRODUCTION

Antichrist is a massive reality in the history of the church and particularly in the history of the coming of Christ. The coming of antichrist therefore involves a number of events that, although closely related to the antichrist itself/himself and aspects of the reality of antichrist, are significant eschatological happenings in their own right. Therefore, although they are aspects of the sign of antichrist that believers ought to see in their waiting for Christ's coming, they deserve separate treatment.

Two of these monumental events are part of the fundamental instruction of Jesus in Matthew 24 concerning the last days, culminating in his coming. In verse 15, he forewarns of a mysterious "abomination of desolation." Verse 21 foretells a "great tribulation." A third event is taught in Revelation 16:12–16. The passage speaks of the battle of "Armageddon" in the context of the very end of history, immediately before the destruction of the world by the pouring out of the seventh vial of the wrath of God upon the earth.

With a brief explanation of these three events, all of which, I repeat, are closely related to the sign of antichrist if not part of this sign, I conclude the exposition of the eschatological sign of antichrist.

Intimately related to the abomination of desolation is the brooding, Old Testament figure of Antiochus Epiphanes. Any treatment of the abomination of desolation therefore finds it necessary to say something about this heathen ruler and his assault upon the covenantal people in the period between the testaments.

THE ABOMINATION OF DESOLATION

The phrase itself, "abomination of desolation," occurs only in Jesus' eschatological discourse in Matthew 24:15 and the parallel passage in Mark 13:14. Matthew 24:15 has the abomination standing "in the holy place." Mark 13:14 locates it "where it ought not [be]." An *abomination* is a detestable idol. The sense of *desolation* in the Greek original of Matthew 24 and Mark 13 is a *making desolate*. The abomination of desolation therefore is an idol that desolates the place where it stands. It desolates the place first in the sense that no worship of God is possible in that place, and second in the sense that now that place is polluted by the worship of an idol. What makes this desolation truly appalling is that the place that is thus desolated is, according to Matthew, "the holy place," the place where God was once worshiped and the place where he ought to be worshiped. Originally, this place was the temple in Jerusalem.

Jesus derives the phrase, and its eschatological idea, from the prophecy of Daniel. The "abomination of desolation" of which he speaks and that will be an event in the last days leading up to his second coming was "spoken of by Daniel the prophet" (Matt. 24:15). The phrase itself is found in Daniel 11:31 and 12:11.[1] In both passages, it is translated as "the abomination that maketh desolate." In the Hebrew original, *abomination* is a detestable thing, with reference to an idol. The word that is translated *maketh desolate* combines the ideas of *causing horror* and *desolating*. The abomination of desolation in the prophecy of Daniel, which is foundational for the use of the abomination in the eschatological doctrine of the New Testament, is the installment and worship of an idol in the place where God ought to be worshiped. The result is not only that the worship of God is made impossible, but also that there is the appalling worship of an idol in its place. The holy place is not only devoid of the worship of God that ought to take place there. This is desolation. But it has also been made the place of the worship of an idol. This is appalling.

This prophecy of Daniel has several fulfillments, two of them typical, and a third the reality in the days of antichrist. The first fulfillment is the history of Antiochus Epiphanes in the time between the testaments. Antiochus IV Epiphanes was a Syrian king who reigned over the region east of the Mediterranean Sea, including Palestine, from 175 to 164 BC. His blasphemous presumption was evident in the title he adopted for himself, "Epiphanes," which means "the god who reveals himself." His avowed purpose was utterly to destroy the worship of Jehovah God by the Jews—the people of God still at that time—as

---

1 Although the phrase is not used, the same reality is found in Daniel 8:11–14, where the corrupting of the "sanctuary" is described as "the transgression of desolation."

well as to exterminate the Scriptures and to forbid obedience to all the laws of God upon his people, for example, circumcision. It was the policy of Antiochus to eradicate everything that made up the worship and service of Jehovah as revealed in the Old Testament and to replace it with the idolatrous worship of the pagan Greeks.

The deed of opposition to the worship of God that especially concerns us here is Antiochus' devotion of the entire temple in Jerusalem to the worship of the Greek god Zeus. One aspect of this desecration of the temple was his placing of a small altar dedicated to sacrificing to Zeus atop the great altar of burnt offering in the temple and then actually offering sacrifices to Zeus on this altar. The apocryphal book of 1 Maccabees describes this abomination: "Now the fifteenth day of the month Casleu…they set up the abomination of desolation upon the altar, and builded idol altars throughout the cities of Judah, on every side" (1 Maccabees 1:54). Verse 59 adds, "Now the five and twentieth day of the month, they did sacrifice upon the idol altar, which was upon the altar of God."

In light of the claim to deity on the part of antichrist, according to 2 Thessalonians 2:4, which is the fulfillment of the Old Testament type of Antiochus, it should be observed that Antiochus did indeed show himself that he was God. Antiochus "thought he might command the waves of the sea, (so proud was he beyond the condition of man) and weigh the high mountains in a balance" (2 Maccabees 9:8). He "thought…he could reach to the stars of heaven" (v. 10). He "proudly [thought] of himself if he were God" (v. 12).

Antiochus also typified antichrist regarding antichrist's dreadful persecution of the church in the great tribulation. He slaughtered thousands of Jews, men, women, and children (2 Maccabees 5). His cruelty knew no bounds. He tortured to death seven brothers in the presence of their mother for keeping the law of God (chapter 7).[2]

To this historical event (of Antiochus), Daniel refers in the first place as a type of the abomination of desolation of the last days. But this event did not exhaust the prophecy of Daniel. We know this because, in his explanation of the abomination of desolation prophesied by Daniel, Jesus spoke of the abomination as a *future* event: "When ye therefore *shall* see the abomination of desolation" (Matt. 24:15). There was yet another historical fulfillment of Daniel's prophecy as also another type of the fulfillment at the end. This is evident

---

2   In his study of eschatology, the Reformed believer might well heed the implied advice of the Belgic Confession, that he "read and take instruction from" the books of 1 and 2 Maccabees regarding antichrist, the abomination of desolation, and the great tribulation as typically revealed in the history of Antiochus Epiphanes (Belgic Confession 6, in Schaff, *Creeds of Christendom*, 3:387).

from what Jesus went on to say about the abomination in verses 16–20. When the Jewish believers in Jerusalem would see the abomination of desolation stand in the holy place, they must flee into the mountains without taking anything with them. They should pray that their flight not be on the sabbath day.

The historical realization of the abomination of which Jesus spoke was the invasion into the temple by the Roman soldiers with their idolatrous paraphernalia as part of the destruction of Jerusalem in AD 70. This too was the abomination of desolation: the defiling of the place of the worship of God and the rendering impossible of any worship of God there.

But this historical event also was only a type of the prophesied abomination of desolation. The reality lay yet in the future, in the days shortly before the coming of Christ, in the time of the coming of antichrist. AD 70 did not exhaust the prophecy. AD 70 was not the real abomination. AD 70 was merely a shadow, a shadow cast by the future reality.

That the reality of the abomination of desolation is still future to AD 70 is evident from two conclusive biblical testimonies. First, all of Matthew 24 finds its reality in the future of the coming of Christ. In Matthew 24, Jesus is not answering the question, "What shall be the sign of the destruction of Jerusalem?" But he is answering the question, "What shall be the sign of thy coming, and of the end of the world?" (v. 3). In Matthew 24, the tribulation of the last days, which is part of the sign of the antichrist with his false prophet, is immediately followed by convulsions in creation, upon the occurrence of which Christ appears (vv. 29, 30).

To the sign of the coming of Christ and of the end of the world belongs the abomination of desolation. To the sign *of the coming of Christ and of the end of the world!*

Second, Scripture puts beyond all question or doubt that the abomination of desolation is still future, as part of the coming of antichrist immediately before the coming of Christ, in its teaching about the desolation in 2 Thessalonians 2. This chapter is revelation about the second, bodily coming of Christ. The great truth made known in the chapter by the Holy Spirit is the "day of Christ" and its timing, specifically whether this day is "at hand" (v. 2). Just prior to this coming of Christ, the individual, personal antichrist will be revealed and finally have his coming (vv. 3–12).

Although the phrase "abomination of desolation" does not appear in the passage, with an eye on the prophecies of the abomination by Daniel and Christ the apostle nevertheless refers to the abomination. He speaks of it in 2 Thessalonians 2:4: "who [the personal antichrist] opposeth and exalteth himself above all that is called God, or that is worshipped; so that he as God sitteth in the temple of God, shewing himself that he is God." An idol will invade the holy place, where God ought to be worshiped. Men will worship this idol, desolating the place where God formerly was, and still ought to be, worshiped. This is the abomination of desolation, of which Daniel and Christ spoke in prophecy. This is the final, full reality of the abomination.

The idol in the case of the real abomination of 2 Thessalonians 2 is the personal antichrist himself. He shows himself that he is God. The temple in which he locates himself is no earthly building, including a material temple in Jerusalem, which will have been demolished centuries earlier. It is rather the sphere in which the New Testament church worships God. It is any and every gathering of believers and their children. Antichrist forbids any gathering for the worship of the one, true God. Instead, he commands gatherings, undoubtedly advertised as gatherings for the worship of God in Christ, that are devoted to antichrist, and at which services the congregations worship the image of him that has been constructed by the beast out of the earth (see Rev. 13:11–17). This future event will desolate the worship of God and will appall the saints.

THE GREAT TRIBULATION

Refusal to participate in the abominable, idolatrous worship of antichrist will occasion the "great tribulation" of the elect believers. Revelation 13 warns that "as many as would not worship the image of the beast should be killed" (v. 15). In fact, the persecution of the holy people of God at the end is a main theme of the book of Revelation. Persecution, although not expressly stated in 2 Thessalonians 2, is implied. Refusal to give worship to God is punishable, and antichrist shows "himself that he is God" (v. 4). Matthew 24 speaks expressly of the "great tribulation" and links it closely to the abomination of desolation: "For then shall be great tribulation, such as was not since the beginning of the world to this time, no, nor ever shall be" (v. 21).

Also the prophet Daniel warns of the great tribulation: "There shall be a time of trouble, such as never was since there was a nation even to that same time" (Dan. 12:1). This prophecy also gives clear instruction regarding exactly when this tribulation takes place relative to other events in the last days. It occurs during the heyday of antichrist, whose reign Daniel has been describing in chapter 11. "At that time…shall be a time of trouble" (12:1). It takes place immediately before the deliverance of the church by the coming of Christ: "At that time thy people shall be delivered" (v. 1). And the great tribulation is immediately followed by the resurrection of all the elect from the dead: "Thy people shall be delivered, every one that shall be found written in the book [the elect]. And many of them that sleep in the dust of the earth shall awake, some to everlasting life, and some to shame and everlasting contempt" (vv. 1–2).

That this tribulation is the result of the antichrist's exaltation of himself as the sole object of worship is evident from Daniel's description of the cause of the persecution as the setting up of the "abomination that maketh desolate" (Dan. 12:11) and from the prophet's description of the time of the tribulation as "a time, times, and an half" (v. 7).

In light of all the biblical prophecy of the event, the great tribulation will be the intense persecution of the church by antichrist at the very end of history. It will be great in that it will be the worst persecution that has ever taken place. It will be the most determined, inasmuch as the earthly persecutor is Satan's man, extraordinarily motivated by furious hatred of Christ and therefore of those who confess Christ. It will be worldwide, in that the personal antichrist and his minions hold sway over all the world. It will be the most effective in that the instituted church over all the earth will be destroyed.

Here the truth of the two witnesses of Revelation 11 comes to the fore. These are two prophets, according to verse 10. They represent in this symbolical identification the instituted church that officially witnesses to the truth that Jesus is Christ. With the very first reference to the beast in the book of Revelation, verse 7 foretells that when the work of the church has been completed, the beast, which is antichrist, will kill the witnesses. The great tribulation of the last days will put an end to the instituted church and her public worship of God worldwide, something that has never happened before: "The beast…shall make war against them [the two witnesses], and shall overcome them, and kill them" (v. 7).[3] The coming tribulation will be great, indeed. It will finally "overcome" the church, if only seemingly and for a very short time.

Antichrist's overcoming of the church will be only apparent, first, because a real overcoming would not be the physical prevention of public worship and the killing of the members of the church, but the denial of Christ by the church and her members. This, antichrist will not be able to accomplish. The doors of the church will close upon the congregation's singing from the psalms that Jesus is the Messiah. And the members will go to the stake confessing aloud that the triune God and Father of Jesus the Christ is God. Second, despite the destruction of all public worship, there will remain in the world a number of believers who

---

3   After a short period of time, the witnesses are raised from the dead and in a noisy event ascend into heaven at the coming of Christ. For a complete explanation of the two witnesses and their life, work, death, and resurrection, see David J. Engelsma, "The Two Witnesses of Revelation 11," in *Behold, I Come Quickly: The Reformed, Biblical Truth of the End* (Ballymena, N. Ireland: British Reformed Fellowship, 2018), 74–88.

will be believing the gospel and confessing that Jesus is the Christ. They will be the church, not the institute of the church, but the living church.

The prospect of great tribulation calls for great encouragement of the church that faces this tribulation, and faces the tribulation in the near future, as all the biblical signs forecast. On the basis of Scripture, the Reformed faith gives this encouragement to the church. Encouragement is radically different from the false (and cowardly) hope that both dispensational premillennialism and postmillennialism give to their adherents in these last days. This hope, as has been shown in volume 1 of this study of the last things, is that the church and the believers will escape the tribulation altogether, premillennialism by a future rapture out of the battlefield, and postmillennialism by a kind of past rapture out of the battlefield.

Reformed amillennialism stands and fights for God, for Christ, and for the kingdom of which Reformed Christians are citizens and soldiers and whose banner they fly. No craven cowardice for them. Indeed, they can find it in themselves, cowardly as they also are by nature, to anticipate the last, great battle. To confess that Jesus is Christ when all the world denies him, and to do so under the threat of the stake and flame, why, this will be the highest honor. This will carry out the purpose of God, to show the power of his grace in his elect, who will do valiantly, sealing by suffering and death their witness to the truth in a world of the lie. And likely, at the stake or in the den of the wild, ravenous beasts, they will be privileged, like Deacon Stephen, to see heaven opened for them and the Son of man standing for their help and soon reception at God's right hand (Acts 7:56).

No mere looking down upon the great tribulation, like so many idle spectators, from heavenly heights, as is the (fallacious) prospect of premillennialism, for the Reformed faith. Nor a merely academic interest in the tribulation as an event in the distant past, like some spiritual battle of Gettysburg, now only a matter of (safe) historical curiosity, as is the (fallacious) attitude of postmillennialism. But the Reformed amillennialist marches onward to the fray in which he or she must fight, singing the militant psalms, armed with the sword of the truth, protected by the armor of faith and hope, and led by the captain of his or her salvation. He or she will hardly dare to believe that God has counted him or her worthy of such privilege.

The battle of the great tribulation concerns Christ and his coming. In the great tribulation, the church of the elect fills up the measure of Christ's sufferings (Col. 1:24; Rev. 6:11). When the martyrs in heaven cry out for the day of Christ's coming to the earth for judgment upon the wicked, the reply of heaven to them is "that they should rest yet for a little season, until their fellowservants also and their brethren, that should be killed as they were, should be fulfilled" (Rev. 6:11). The privilege of martyrdom belongs to others besides only themselves.

Although Christ's redemptive sufferings were accomplished by him alone and have been fulfilled in him by himself alone, there is another kind of suffering that he graciously shares with his church. This is the suffering that demonstrates the love of the head and of the body of the church for God. This is the suffering that prepares the entire church for the glory that God has prepared for her. Paul speaks of this kind of suffering in Colossians 1:24. His own intense sufferings, he assures the Colossians, "fill up that which is behind of the afflictions of Christ in my flesh for his body's sake, which is the church." All of the suffering of the apostle in his ministry (and it was much, manifold, and massive) was, in fact, part of the afflictions of Christ. It was Christ's own suffering, but that part of it that he deliberately reserved for Paul and for the members of his church. It was suffering that was beneficial for the church: "for his body's sake." This is why, contrary to every natural human response to suffering, Paul rejoiced in these sufferings (v. 24). Both premillennialism and postmillennialism would rob the church in the last days of sharing in these sufferings of Christ.

According to Colossians 1:24, the great tribulation serves the coming of Christ in that it completes the non-redemptive sufferings of Christ. It also serves the coming of Christ in that it fills up the measure of the cup of iniquity of the reprobate wicked world so that Christ may be just when he judges this world at his coming. He comes not only for the salvation of his church, but also for the punishment of the ungodly world. This punishment may be administered only in justice. And justice requires that the ungodly have made themselves worthy of the punishment, which is severe—eternal hell. This, the world will do by the great tribulation. The Belgic Confession bases the awful, eternal punishment of the ungodly world on the world's dreadful persecution of the church, such as will climax in the great tribulation: "They [the elect] shall see the terrible vengeance which God shall execute on the wicked, who most cruelly persecuted, oppressed, and tormented them in this world."[4]

BATTLE OF ARMAGEDDON

Yet one other highly significant and gripping event belongs to the full reality of antichrist. This is the battle of Armageddon. This battle is named in Revelation 16:16: "And he gathered them together into a place called in the Hebrew tongue Armaggedon." Those who will be so gathered are "the kings of the earth and of the whole world" (v. 14). That the coming Armageddon will be a battle is also taught in verse 14: "to gather them [all the nations of the whole world] to the battle of that great day of God Almighty."

---

4 Belgic Confession 37, in Schaff, *Creeds of Christendom*, 3:435.

This battle occurs at the very close of human history. It is the sixth of the seven vials of Revelation 16. The vials are all the judgments of God upon the kingdom of antichrist and upon those who have the "mark of the beast, and upon them which worshipped his image" (v. 2). These "vials of the wrath of God" (v. 1), which include the battle of Armageddon, fall upon the kingdom of the beast, to bring about the end of that kingdom, already before the coming of Christ. Like the last of the ten plagues of the Old Testament, the vials make distinction between the antichristian kingdom and its citizens, on the one hand, and the saints who remain alive, on the other hand. As verse 2 expresses concerning the first vial, all these outpourings of the fierce wrath of God fall "upon the men which had the mark of the beast, and upon them which worshipped his image." Although some believers are still to be found in the world, the special providence of God spares them from the vials and their intense miseries. The vials are a foretaste for the reprobate, ungodly citizens of the kingdom of antichrist of the hell that is shortly to follow.

As Revelation 16:16 itself expresses ("in the Hebrew tongue"), the word itself, *Armageddon*, is the transliteration in Greek and English of the Hebrew phrase *Har Megiddo*, which means *Mt. Megiddo*. The reference is to an area in Old Testament Israel in the plain of Esdraelon, known as Jezreel, where important battles were fought. These battles were decisive for the delivery of the Old Testament people of God. In Armageddon, Deborah and Barak defeated the Canaanites (Judges 5:19). In that territory, called Jezreel in the text, the Spirit of Jehovah gave a great victory over Israel's multitudinous enemies, the Midianites, the Amalekites, and the children of the east (6:33).

Armageddon, in Revelation 16, is not literally the site of the great battle to which the chapter refers, as though the battle will be fought in Palestine in the erstwhile territory of the tribe of Issachar, at the same place in which Deborah fought and defeated the Canaanites. As is the case with the book of Revelation generally, the name is symbolical. Armageddon describes a coming war as having the same significance as the battles fought in the area that bore that name in the time of the Old Testament.

Immediately prior to the coming of Jesus Christ and as one of the fearsome judgments of God upon the antichristian kingdom that break up and destroy that kingdom already before the appearance of Christ on the clouds (one of the seven vials of the wrath of God), there will be a battle. This will be a physical battle. It will be the last, greatest, and genuine world war. The combatants will be the heathen nations of the East, which for a time have allied themselves with the antichrist to form the antichristian world kingdom, and the formerly nominally Christian nations of the West—the seat of the power of antichrist.

The sixth vial that brings about this world war dries up the Euphrates River to enable the nations of the East to advance on Israel at Armageddon. Historically, the Euphrates separated the heathen nations from Israel. In modern times, of course, no river separates the fighting forces of eastern nations from nations in the west. The thought is simply that the kingdom of antichrist breaks up into its two main constituent parts: the heathen nations of the East, for example, China, Japan, and the Islamic nations, and the nominally Christian nations of the West, for example, the nations of Europe and North America.

The meaning of this war is that the kingdom of antichrist breaks up already before the coming of Christ. Christ returns on the clouds to a world engaged in war, war that involves all nations, and war that employs all the destructive weapons that modernity has developed. Christ comes as the savior of humanity, in the elect among all nations, when all nations are engaged in destroying humanity.

The significance of the battle of Armageddon is that it demonstrates that humanity is not able to erect a kingdom of universal peace and prosperity that endures. The supreme effort of the dragon and his gifted beast fails. It fails within history. It fails not by its defeat at the hands of Christ at his coming, but by virtue of its own inherent weakness—the weakness of man's hatred of man because of its hatred of God. Only the kingdom of God, established, maintained, and perfected by Jesus Christ, is solidly founded and everlasting. Satan himself must confess at the coming of Christ his inability to establish for humans a kingdom of lasting peace and prosperity. His "finest" effort goes down in the flames of a world war.

The error of some makes it necessary to observe that the battle of Armageddon is a different battle than the battle of Revelation 20:8 involving Gog and Magog. Drawing on the prophecy of Ezekiel 38 and 39, Revelation 20:7–9 has the nations of all the world, called Gog and Magog, after the heathen nation Magog under its prince, Gog, in Ezekiel, attacking the saints of God and the beloved city. In Revelation 20, this war is the assault of Satan, by means of antichrist, against the church of Christ. When the millennium in which Satan is bound comes to an end, all the nations of the world, under the personal antichrist, attack, persecute, and attempt utterly to destroy the church of Christ. This is expressed symbolically in verse 9 as Gog and Magog's compassing the camp of the saints. This attack culminates in the great tribulation of chapter 16.

The battle of Gog and Magog in Revelation 20 is the war of antichrist against the church. The battle of Armageddon in chapter 16 is the internal war of the antichristian kingdom, the ungodly nations of the world fighting themselves, as the kingdom of antichrist breaks up.

8

THE *PAROUSIA*

INTRODUCTION

Such is the significance of the second coming of Jesus Christ, or as it might well be called, the full reality of the coming of Jesus Christ, that it is the purpose of God not only with all the work of salvation, but also with the work of creation and providence. This is to say that the coming of Christ is the purpose, or goal, of God with all his works and ways.

The second coming may rightly be called the full reality of the coming of Christ because there is a sense in which Jesus' coming to the world is one, with two distinct aspects. For the church at the beginning of the twenty-first century, these two aspects are past and future. The past aspect was his coming as a baby in Bethlehem. The future aspect will be his coming on the world's last day to all the world. These two comings in Scripture, for example in Philippians 2, are a coming in humiliation and a coming in glory. But these two aspects, distinct though they are, comprise one coming, chiefly for the glorifying of God in the saving of the elect human race.

The oneness of the coming explains why the Old Testament does not clearly and sharply distinguish the twofold coming of Christ, but simply directed the hope of the saints to the one coming of the Savior. It does this, for instance, in Psalm 72, which prophesies the coming of the Messiah as one coming. Although the emphasis is on the victory and glory of this coming, and therefore on what the New Testament believer would refer to as the second coming, there is also in the prophecy distinct allusions to what the New Testament believer would call the first coming. There is no deliverance of the needy (v. 12) or sparing of the poor and needy apart from the humiliation and suffering of the Messiah himself in his first coming. Verse 14 expressly promises the redemption of his needy people by the coming savior, which redemption is surely that of the cross.

Although the church concentrates—rightly—on the first coming of Christ in her understanding of the prophecy of the Messiah in Isaiah 53, there are definite references in the passage also to what we view as the second coming. "The pleasure of the Lord shall prosper in his hand" (v. 10). As a reward of the Messiah for his obedient suffering, God "will…divide him a portion with the great, and he [the Messiah, the suffering servant of the Lord] shall divide the spoil with the strong" (v. 12).

Likewise, Micah 5:2–7 prophesies the coming of Israel's savior as one coming, without any delineation of that coming as a first coming in humiliation and as a second coming in glory. In fact, it describes the one coming in terms of its final victory and glory.

The explanation of the Old Testament's viewing the coming of Christ as one coming is not only that the vision of the Old Testament was not as full and clear as that of the New Testament. But the explanation is that, in fact, the future coming of the Messiah, from the viewpoint of the Old Testament, would be one, with two phases or aspects. The first phase would be his coming in lowliness for the redemption of his own, the second would be his coming in glory for the perfecting of this redemption.

That this twofold coming of the Christ is the goal of all the ways and works of God with his world and its history is the teaching of Colossians 1:17, 18: "And he [Christ Jesus, God's 'dear Son: in whom we have redemption through his blood' (vv. 13, 14)] is before all things, and by him all things consist. And he is the head of the body, the church: who is the beginning, the firstborn from the dead; that in all things he might have the preeminence."

The coming of Christ is not only eschatological (having to do with the last things) therefore, although it is this, but also cosmological (having to do with the world, or everything). It is the goal and meaning of the cosmos. Although last in dogmatics and in history, the coming of Christ is first in the counsel of God.

WHAT IT WILL BE

Herman Hoeksema offers a definition of the *parousia* that expresses the Reformed, creedal consensus:

> [The *parousia* will be] the final, sudden, personal, and visible coming of our Lord Jesus Christ on or with the clouds of heaven, for the purpose of raising the dead and executing judgment, to give everyone according as his work shall be and to make all things new.[1]

---

1 Hoeksema, *Reformed Dogmatics*, 2:570.

One might make explicit what is implicit in the definition in the adjective *visible*. The coming of Jesus will be a *bodily* coming. He will come in the body—the body of his birth; the body in which he was cruelly and shamefully put to death; the body that was raised on the third day; and the body that ascended into heaven and now sits at the right hand of God.

The *parousia*, or coming, will be final, because it culminates his previous comings—the first consisting of his birth and another having been his coming in the outpouring of the Spirit on Pentecost. The *parousia* will result in his abiding with the church in the new world. There will never again be any departure from the church. That the *parousia* will be his final coming implies the error of premillennialism in teaching that Christ's coming for the church in the rapture will be followed by yet another coming a thousand years later at the end of history. Scripture teaches one, final coming of Christ in the future.

The *parousia* will be sudden in two important respects. It will be unexpected by the wicked world of the ungodly. Christ taught this suddenness of his coming in the application of his eschatological instruction in Matthew 24:36–51. Just as the ungodly of Noah's day were living in complete oblivion of the flood, although Noah had warned them, "so shall also the coming of the Son of man be" (v. 37). Christ will come when the ungodly "looketh not for him, and in an hour that he is not aware of" (v. 50). Also the parable of the wise and foolish virgins, which is part of Jesus' instruction concerning the end, stresses this suddenness of Jesus' coming (25:1–13).

This aspect of the suddenness of the coming is also the meaning of Scripture's warning that Jesus will come "as a thief." This is the warning of 1 Thessalonians 5:2, 3: "The day of the Lord so cometh as a thief in the night. For when they shall say, Peace and safety; then sudden destruction cometh upon them, as travail upon a woman with child; and they shall not escape." Contrary to a common misconception, this suddenness of the coming of Christ is not applicable to the believing church as well as to the ungodly. The text itself makes plain that Christ comes as a thief only to the ungodly. It takes them by surprise and is their everlasting destruction. They are not living in expectation of his coming, as are his people, who see the signs and are watching for him.

There is, however, a sense in which the coming is sudden also for the saints. This is the sense implied in Scripture's description of the duration of the reign of antichrist as time, times, and half a time (Dan. 12:7). When it seems as though antichrist has so solidified his reign that it will go on for many years, if not forever ("times,") suddenly the reign is broken up ("the dividing of time," 7:25) by the mighty judgments of God upon that kingdom, including the battle of

Armageddon (see Rev. 16). The time of antichrist shall suddenly be shortened (Matt. 24:22).

The coming of Christ will be personal and visible in that it will be a coming in the resurrection body of Christ, which all mankind will actually behold. "Behold, he cometh with clouds; and every eye shall see him, and they also which pierced him: and all kindreds of the earth shall wail because of him. Even so, Amen" (Rev. 1:7). Every clever effort to spiritualize the coming of Christ, or in any other way to deny the genuinely bodily nature of the coming, is in fact the denial of the *parousia* of Christ. Such will be the very nature of that coming that the question of the bodily nature of the coming will not arise in the mind of anyone. But if the question did arise in the mind of a believer, the response of Christ could be that which he gave to doubting Thomas: "Reach hither thy finger, and behold my hands; and reach hither thy hand, and thrust it into my side" (John 20:27).

That Jesus will return on or with the clouds (Matt. 24:30; 26:64; Rev. 1:7) is often misunderstood, as though this were a general description of the manifestation of his glory at his return. The clouds then are more or less ordinary clouds. The reference, however, is to a special cloud, thus signifying a particular glory. The clouds are the effulgence of the special cloud that in the Old Testament rested upon the tabernacle (Ex. 40:34–38); that led Israel through the desert (13:21); and that rested upon the mercy seat in the tabernacle (Lev. 16:2). It is the bright cloud that overshadowed Jesus, Moses, and Elijah on the mountain and out of which the voice of God sounded, "This is my beloved Son, in whom I am well pleased; hear ye him" (Matt. 17:5).

This cloud is special. It is the cloud that is the shining forth of the glorious being of God himself. It is the presence of God with his people in the most visible manifestation of this awesome being possible for humans, other than his presence in Jesus, of course. As named by an extra-biblical source, it is the "Shekinah-cloud."[2] That Jesus comes in the clouds of heaven therefore signifies, as Jesus himself explained, that he comes "with power and great glory" (Matt. 24:30). That power and great glory will be the power and glory of God himself in the fullest manifestation of the divine power and glory possible to humans. Jesus' coming is a coming *with* this power and glory; *on* this power and glory; *attended by* this power and glory.

---

2 Calvin explains that in the cloud God "familiarly presented Himself before their [the Israelites'] eyes." The cloud was "His visible presence." This was true, the reformer quickly adds, in a "sacramental mode of speaking" (cf. John Calvin, *Commentaries on the Four Last Books of Moses*, tr. Charles William Bingham, 4 vols. [Grand Rapids, MI: Eerdmans, 1950], 1:236).

The day of Jesus' coming will be the day of his exaltation, as the first stage of his coming was the day of his humiliation. Believers will rejoice in his coming, not only on account of its accomplishment of their perfect salvation, but also on account of its magnifying of their Savior and Lord by the entire human race, many of whom had denied and mocked him. "Every knee [shall] bow…and…every tongue [shall] confess that Jesus Christ is Lord, to the glory of God the Father," on and with whose cloud he comes (Phil. 2:10–11).

Altogether apart from the hosts of mighty angels, who accompany Jesus at his coming, the sheer power and glory of Jesus, as signified by the cloud on which he comes, expose as utter nonsense that explanation of Revelation 20:7–9 that has the wicked opposing Christ with physical arms at his coming, at the end of the millennium as they conceive it. Such is his power and glory as evident—and *present*—in the cloud of his coming that were there millions of heavily armed troops in opposition to him and though a foe had his finger on a button that would detonate a million hydrogen bombs against Jesus descending from heaven, nothing of all this weaponry would avail against this Jesus with his power and glory. Indeed, no enemy would so much as dare to entertain the thought of entering into combat against him. Every knee will bow. All his adversaries will immediately cry out "to the mountains and rocks, Fall on us, and hide us from the face of him that sitteth on the throne, and from the wrath of the Lamb: for the great day of his wrath is come; and who shall be able to stand?" (Rev. 6:16–17).

Scripture adds that Jesus will come surrounded by the hosts of angels and by the saints. Second Thessalonians 1:7 enhances the power and glory of Jesus' coming by stating that "the Lord Jesus shall be revealed from heaven with his mighty angels." First Thessalonians 4:14 promises that God will bring with Jesus at his coming those who now "sleep in Jesus," that is, all elect believers who have died prior to his coming. Verses 16 and 17 add that we believers who are alive at his coming will "be caught up together" with those who have been raised from the dead "to meet the Lord in the air." Both the angels and the elect church, therefore, will share in the glory of the coming Christ. Not only does Christ share his glory with his body the church, but also he unites the angel world and the world of humans at the end.

However, the significance of the "Shekinah-cloud" with which Jesus comes at the end is not exhausted by the explanation that Jesus comes in the power and glory of God himself, who reveals himself in the cloud. The root meaning of the Hebrew word that describes the presence of that fiery cloud over Israel is *dwelling* and *resting*.³ According to Numbers 9:17, the cloud "abode," or dwelt, with Israel above the tabernacle. According to chapter 10:12, this dwelling of the cloud above the tabernacle was its resting with the Old Testament people of God. And when the cloud rested, Israel rested with it.

The significance of the cloud was covenantal. In the cloud, the awesome Jehovah dwelt, or abode, with his people in the fellowship of the covenant. The coming of Jesus with the clouds, therefore, proclaims that Jesus comes on behalf of God's resting upon his people in the friendship of the covenant of grace. The coming of Jesus will be the reality of the restful dwelling of God with his people in the Shekinah-cloud. Not only is there nothing to fear for the saints in the glory of Jesus, attended though he will be by the fiery cloud, but also he comes to give them rest by his dwelling with them and even to share in his glory. The saints will be called up to meet Jesus in the air on the cloud and then to descend to the earth with Jesus on the cloud.

BIBLICAL TERMINOLOGY

The full truth of the second coming of Christ is brought out by the several Greek words for that coming in the New Testament. The main word is *parousia*, which has the meaning not so much of *coming* as of *presence*, by virtue of his "arrival." This is the word translated *coming* in 2 Thessalonians 2:8: "the brightness of his coming." In his second coming Jesus will finally be fully present to his church. He will be present in the body, not only by his word and Spirit. In the body, he was "taken up from [us] into heaven" in the ascension. In the future, he "shall so come [in the body] in like manner as ye have seen him go into heaven" (Acts 1:11).

This bodily and full presence of Jesus will also be the full enjoyment of complete salvation. As long as Jesus is not present (*parousia*), the members of the church lack the fullness of the salvation that his presence brings. There is only a beginning of the enjoyment of eternal life. There is yet the suffering of sorrows and of death. His presence brings with it complete deliverance from sin and death, the fullness of eternal life, and the resurrection of the dead. All of the fullness of salvation awaits the full presence (*parousia*) of the Savior.

Another Greek word for the second coming of Jesus is *epiphaneia*, which translates best as *manifestation*. This is the word used of his coming in 1 Timothy 6:14, where it is translated *appearing* in the KJV: "That thou keep this

---

3   The Hebrew root is *shchn*, which Gesenius explains as "settling down" in the sense of "resting," "dwelling," and "abiding," with reference to "the pillar of fire and cloud" in Numbers 9:17, 22; 10:12; and Exodus 24:16.

commandment without spot, unrebukeable, until the appearing of our Lord Jesus Christ." The word is used of the second coming of Christ also in Titus 2:13, where again the KJV translates as *appearing*: "the glorious appearing of the great God and our Saviour Jesus Christ." This word in the Greek language has the meaning of Christ's becoming visible at his coming by piercing through that which obscures him from sight, as the sun finally pierces through clouds that were hiding it. The thought is not so much that Christ will break through the physical heavens to show himself to all in the sphere of the earthly creation. Rather, at the end he will personally pierce through all the dark clouds of the denial of himself by the ungodly, all the opposition to himself in the attacks of the wicked upon the confessing church, all the obscuring of him by heresies, all the struggles of the faithful church in the world, and all the sorrows of the believer in his discipleship after Christ. The reference is also to the dark clouds of the sinful nature of the believer.

Calvin explains the appearing:

> How many things does Satan constantly present to our eyes, which, but for this [the "appearing" of Christ, in 1 Tim. 6:14], would a thousand times draw us aside from the right course! I say nothing about fires, and swords, and banishments, and all the furious attacks of enemies. I say nothing about slanders and other vexations. How many things are within, that are far worse! Ambitious men openly attack us…impudent men provoke us, hypocrites murmur at us, they who are wise after the flesh secretly bite us, we are harassed by various methods in every direction…The only remedy for all these difficulties is, to cast our eyes towards the appearing [Greek: *epiphaneia*] of Christ, and to keep them fixed on it continually.[4]

Yet a third word in the Greek of the New Testament for the second coming of Christ is *apokalupsis*. This word occurs of the second coming of Christ in 1 Peter 1:13: "hope to the end for the grace that is to be brought unto you at the revelation of Jesus Christ." The idea of this word is similar to that of the preceding, *manifestation*. But *revelation* has the distinct meaning of uncovering or disclosing what heretofore has been veiled, or covered, or hidden from sight. Whereas the ungodly could ignore and deny Jesus before, at his coming he will be disclosed so that every knee must bow and every tongue must confess. Whereas now even the saints, indeed Paul himself, "see through a glass, darkly," so that we know only "in part," by the revelation of Jesus Christ at

---

[4] John Calvin, *Commentary on the Epistle to Timothy*, tr. William Pringle (Grand Rapids, MI: Eerdmans, 1948), 165–66.

his coming we will see "face to face," so that we will know even as also we are known (1 Cor. 13:12).

And *revelation* expresses that the coming of Jesus Christ is the miraculous act of God, which is not so forcefully brought out by the other two words in the New Testament for the coming of Christ. As revelation, Christ's coming will be the triune God's making known of the Lord Jesus. God sends him on the clouds. As his conception and birth were God's act, so also his coming will be, and will be seen to be, the marvelous doing of God.

Combining the senses of these three words for the second coming of Christ in the New Testament, we arrive at the understanding of this coming as Christ's full and final presence to his church with the manifestation of himself as lord and savior before the sight of all the human race, and this as the wonderful act of God in making Jesus known to all, but especially to the elect in the perfection of their salvation.

This understanding of the second coming indicates that the truth that Christ's coming is one reality with two aspects does not intend to deny that the future bodily coming of Christ is a distinctly *second* coming. Scripture speaks of Christ's future coming as a second coming. "Unto them that look for him shall he appear the second time without sin unto salvation" (Heb. 9:28). The text distinguishes this "second time" from the first time, when he was "offered to bear the sins of many" (v. 28). The text also suggests that the difference between the two comings is the difference between the humiliation of the first coming and the glory of the second coming. That the second coming will be "without sin" certainly does not imply that he came the first time with sin of his own. But he came the first time in the lowliness of bearing the sin of his people. He will come the second time without the burden of sin, since he has atoned for their sin. Implied is that he will come in all the glory of God's reward of him with a name above every name. The first coming was in shame; the second will be in glory.

CONFESSIONAL STATEMENTS

The ecumenical creeds are content to affirm the future, bodily coming again of Jesus, linking it closely with the resurrection of the dead and the judgment of all humans. The Apostles' Creed is the confession of the orthodox Christian church that Jesus Christ shall come from his present position at the right hand of God the Father Almighty to judge humans. The Athanasian Creed says the same, adding that "at his coming all men shall rise again with their bodies."[5] The Nicene Creed adds that his future coming will be "with glory" and that

---

5 Athanasian Creed 41, in Schaff, *Creeds of Christendom*, 2:69.

his kingdom, which evidently he establishes perfectly at his coming, "shall have no end."[6] "His kingdom" is unquestionably the kingdom of Jesus the Messiah, or the messianic kingdom. That this kingdom shall have no end condemns the popular notion that the kingdom of Jesus Christ will come to an end upon his coming and that the distinctly different kingdom of the triune God will replace it. The truth is that Jesus the Christ is an everlasting king and that his kingdom, the church, will be an everlasting kingdom. The triune God will reign in and over this kingdom, but he will reign by means of the man Jesus Christ forever. As the Belgic Confession declares in the article on the church, "Christ is an eternal king."[7]

Of the three Reformed confessions, the Heidelberg Catechism and the Belgic Confession have the most to say about the return of Christ. Both make the reality of Jesus' bodily return to earth the confession of the Reformed, Christian church. Answer 46 of the catechism confesses the second coming by its explanation of the ascension of Christ into heaven: "in our behalf there continues, until he shall come again to judge the living and the dead."[8]

Question 52 of the catechism asks directly about the coming again of Christ. As the question directs, the answer regards the truth of the second coming not as a fearful reality, but as comfort. The comfort is that at his return Christ will "cast all his and my enemies into everlasting condemnation, but shall take me, with all his chosen ones, to himself, into heavenly joy and glory." The circumstances in which the Christian looks for this deliverance at Christ's coming are "sorrows and persecutions." Always in the time between Christ's ascension and his return the church suffers sorrows and persecutions. There is no millennium of earthly victory over the enemies. The attitude of the believer regarding the second coming is a looking for Christ "with uplifted head." The possibility of such an attitude regarding the coming of the awesome "Judge from heaven" is that the Christ who comes is "the self-same One who has before offered himself for me to the judgment of God, and removed from me all curse."[9]

The Belgic Confession treats of the coming of Christ in the last article, article 37, under the heading "Of the Last Judgment." The confession adds to that which is found in the catechism that Christ will come from heaven "when… the number of the elect [is] complete." Contrary to the contemporary effort to shove election into the deep background of the gospel, if not to deny the decree

---

6 Nicene Creed, in Schaff, *Creeds of Christendom*, 2:59.
7 Belgic Confession 27, in Schaff, *Creeds of Christendom*, 3:417.
8 Heidelberg Catechism A 46, in Schaff, *Creeds of Christendom*, 3:322.
9 Heidelberg Catechism A 52, in Schaff, *Creeds of Christendom*, 3:324.

altogether, the Reformed confession has it determining the second coming of Christ and the end of history and this present world. So important is election to the church and to God. The confession makes explicit that the coming will be "corporally and visibly" and "with great glory and majesty." As all the creeds make clear, the main purpose of the coming will be conducting the final judgment. The outcome of the coming, by way of the judgment, will be that "the faithful and elect shall be crowned with glory and honor." The attitude of the believer and of the church toward the coming of Christ is that "we expect that great day with a most ardent desire, to the end that we may fully enjoy the promises of God in Christ Jesus our Lord."[10]

The "ardent desire" with which the believer looks forward to the coming of Christ contrasts both with the terror of the ungodly whenever he anticipates that coming and with the complete unconcern of many regarding the coming of Christ because they are wrapped up in earthly life, its pleasures, and its demands. Witness to an unbeliever of the coming, and his response is that of the ungodly at the actual appearing of Christ on the clouds: "Fall on us [mountains and rocks], and hide us…from the wrath of the Lamb" (Rev. 6:16). As for many professing Christians, their attitude toward the second coming is that described—and *warned against*—by Jesus in Matthew 24:48–49: "That evil servant shall say in his heart, My lord delayeth his coming; and shall begin to smite his fellowservants, and to eat and drink with the drunken."

The believer is to live, work, play, eat and drink, act and rest in the ardent desire for and eager expectation of the coming of Christ. Every morning he rises and every evening he retires in the consciousness of the coming of Christ. Upon awakening in the morning, he greets the day with the prayer, "Come, Lord Jesus." With this petition upon his soul, he closes his eyes in sleep every evening.

THE PURPOSE AND NATURE OF THE COMING

The purpose of Jesus in his coming again will be the same as it was in his first coming: the glorifying of God in the salvation of elect sinners, as magnified in the condemnation of the reprobate ungodly. At his second coming, Jesus will accomplish this purpose fully by the final judgment of all humans, which judgment demands the resurrection of the dead (about this, more in the next chapter).

Something of the purpose of Christ with his coming, something that makes that coming overwhelmingly desirable to the church and to every believer, is the nature of the coming as the consummation of the marriage of Christ and the

---

10 Belgic Confession 37, in Schaff, *Creeds of Christendom*, 3:433–36.

church. Now the church is engaged to be married to Christ Jesus. At his coming, the marriage will be realized, celebrated, and consummated.

Again and again, Scripture describes the coming of Christ as his marriage to the church. The coming is not simply the coming of the savior for the salvation of elect sinners. It is also the coming of the husband for his bride. With reference to the second coming of Christ, which is impending, the voice of a great multitude announces the nature of the coming as "the marriage of the Lamb" (Rev. 19:7). The celebration of the coming is "the marriage supper of the Lamb" (v. 9). Strikingly, the honorable marriage of Christ to the church is accompanied by the judgment of the "great whore," the false and faithless church, which, in despite of her vow of engagement to Christ, gave herself to the antichrist (v. 2).

Explaining the saving work of Jesus Christ at his coming, the angel showed John "the bride, the Lamb's wife" (Rev. 21:9). The nature of the coming of Christ is not simply that a multitude of elect sinners are perfectly saved. Rather, a marriage is realized, consummated, and celebrated. In the light of Ephesians 5:22–33 and many other passages, this bride of Christ is the church. But the emphasis falls now on the nature of the coming of Christ as a marriage—the real marriage, of which the earthly institution is merely a faint, though suggestive, symbol.

Proclaiming the coming of Christ as a marriage ceremony and celebration, Scripture teaches that the essential nature of the coming is covenantal. Christ comes again to fulfill the covenant of God with his people. In Christ, at his coming, God has the deepest, richest fellowship with his chosen people. This is the fullness of salvation. God is their God, and they are his people, in the covenant of grace. This is the heights of joy for the church and each member of the church. This is delight both for God in Christ and for them.[11]

The nature of the coming of Christ as the full realization of the covenant explains the ardent desire for that coming both on the part of Christ and on the part of the church. Christ comes quickly because he desires to embrace his bride. Like the woman who longs for the wedding to her lover, so the church longs for the coming of Christ. Not a day goes by that she does not yearn for the

---

11 Viewing the return of Christ as the fulfillment of the covenant is not unknown in the Reformed tradition. In his magisterial presentation of historic Reformed orthodoxy, Heinrich Heppe explains the "day of this reappearance of Christ on earth" as the day "when all the elect are introduced to the enjoyments of the covenant of grace." It will be "the day of consummation…for the covenant of grace" (Heinrich Heppe, *Reformed Dogmatics*, tr. G. T. Thomson, rev. and ed. Ernst Bizer [London: George Allen & Unwin, 1950], 696–97). Not so clear in the tradition is that this fulfillment of the covenant is essentially the realization of the intimate fellowship of Christ with the church. All of Heppe's "enjoyments of the covenant of grace" are aspects of the bliss of the covenant as communion.

approaching wedding. Then he will be hers, and she will be his. "Come, Lord Jesus; come quickly!"

THE NEARNESS OF THE COMING

The question that always comes up in response to the promise and exposition of the blessedness for the church of the coming of Christ is "when?" As the bride-to-be has the date of the wedding fixed in her mind and on her calendar, so the church has the "day of Christ" (2 Thess. 2:2), which is the day of her wedding, always before her mind. It was fitting that the question of the disciples concerning the sign of Christ's coming began with the request regarding the *time* of the coming: "Tell us, *when* shall these things be?" (Matt. 24:3). Nor did Christ condemn the question concerning the time of his coming. On the contrary, he answered the question. He answered it differently than the disciples intended. He answered it differently than the way in which believers would like, but he answered the question about the time of the coming. And he answered the question in the way that is necessary and profitable for the expectancy of the church down the ages.

Neither directly nor by his apostles did Jesus disclose the day, the year, or even the millennium of his coming. Making known that he was not answering his disciples' "when" by indicating a calendar date, and forbidding all such speculation not only as foolish but also as presumption on the prerogatives of God, Jesus warned, "But of that day and hour knoweth no man, no, not the angels of heaven, but my Father only" (Matt. 24:36). Again and again, self-styled elite experts in biblical prophecy forecast the date of the coming of Christ. Again and again, they gain a following, usually a large following. And again and again, the event, or lack thereof, proves the prophet false and his followers fools.

Today also, increasingly clear and convincing as the signs become, it does not behoove ministers to forecast the coming of Christ "in the lifetime of the younger members of the congregation." Well do I remember the impressive statement, by a minister who was obviously convinced himself, at a worship service of the church on New Year's Eve that we teenagers would likely witness the coming of Christ. "Likely" saved him from sinful false prophecy. But the thrust of the statement bordered on transgression of the warning of Christ in Matthew 24:36. There is a deep-seated weakness in the church to know the day and the hour.

But the church does know what is necessary for her to know concerning the time of the coming. The coming is "at hand," or near (Phil. 4:5). It is "before the door" (James 5:9). "The end of all things is at hand" (1 Pet. 4:7). These revelations of the time of the coming can be summed up as the proclamation that the coming of Christ is *near*. This was the explanation of the time of the coming already during the ministry of the apostles, within a few years after the departure of Christ in the ascension.

But the apostles themselves explained that this time of the coming did not mean that Christ could come at any moment, or even that he could come during the time of the apostles' ministry. Paul condemned the thinking that "the day of Christ is at hand" in the sense that he might come at any moment and in the sense that he might come before two great events took place. These events are the "falling away first" and the revelation of the "man of sin," the "son of perdition," that is, the antichrist (2 Thess. 2:1–3). These events had not yet taken place at the time of the ministry of Paul. And these events demand the passage of a long period of time.

Misunderstanding the apostolic timing of the coming of Christ as near, theologians have erred in two serious ways regarding the time of the coming. The older liberals have concluded that the apostles erred with respect to the time of Christ's coming. They say the apostles expected the return in their own lifetime, and they taught this in their preaching, as well as in their writing of the books that are now New Testament Scripture. It is obvious that this charge against the apostles both criticizes their preaching ministry and denies the inspiration of Scripture. If the apostolic teaching about the coming of Christ is in error in Philippians 4, in James 5, and in 1 Peter 4, Scripture is not inspired and authoritative. Liberalism can live with this charge against the apostles and against the Bible. The church of Christ cannot.

The other error occasioned by misunderstanding of Scripture's teaching that the coming of Christ is near is called *preterism*, from a Latin word that means *past*. The error, which appears in Reformed and Presbyterian circles, indeed in supposedly conservative Reformed and Presbyterian circles, argues that the second coming of Christ is past. It happened in AD 70 in the judgment of Israel and the liberation of the church from all the shadowy entanglements of the laws of the Old Testament.

Some preterists are consistent. They contend that Jesus came in AD 70 with the full and final coming foretold in the New Testament in all the passages that speak of his return. Specifically, Matthew 24 was fulfilled in AD 70. There is no coming of Jesus to be expected in the future, after AD 70. This obviously is a form of the heresy of Hymenaeus and Philetus, "who concerning the truth have erred, saying that the resurrection is past already" (2 Tim. 2:17–18). Here the apostle condemns preterism as "profane and vain babblings" and admonishes believers to "shun" such teachings (v. 16).

Contemporary teachers of this full-fledged, consistent preterism include R. C. Leonard and J. E. Leonard. These deniers of the Christian hope—the second coming of Christ—have written:

Since the coming of Christ, as predicted in the New Testament documents, has already taken place, little scriptural basis exists for perpetuating the doctrine that it still lies in the future...The destruction of Jerusalem in AD 70 represents the fulfillment of what the apostolic church knew as the promise of Jesus' coming and the end of the age...For today's Christians, the last days to which the New Testament refers lie in the past.[12]

As the Leonards themselves acknowledge, they depend heavily upon the nineteenth-century Congregational theologian James Stuart Russell. Russell contended that every prophecy in the New Testament of the coming of Christ and the events attending this coming was fulfilled in its entirety in AD 70 in the destruction of Jerusalem:

We are compelled...to conclude that the Parousia, or second coming of Christ, with its connected and concomitant events, did take place, according to the Saviour's own prediction, at the period when Jerusalem was destroyed, and before the passing away of 'that generation.'[13]

Lest the incredulous Christian reader of this blatant denial of the Christian hope fails to take this denial to heart, Russell adds that he imagines the Christian to be responding, "Whither are we tending? What is to be the end and consummation of human history?" Indeed! Russell's answer to the question is: "Scripture prophecy guides us no further." That is, there is no coming of Christ after AD 70.[14]

There are also inconsistent preterists. Influenced strongly by the consistent preterists, as they themselves admit, they find such eschatological events as lawlessness, apostasy, antichrist, and the great tribulation in the past, in the destruction of Jerusalem, but draw back from denying the second coming itself as a future event. These are the men of Christian Reconstruction, including Gary DeMar, Kenneth L. Gentry Jr., Gary North, Andrew Sandlin, and David Chilton.

Christian Reconstructionist Gary DeMar betrayed the yielding of his inconsistent preterism to the irresistible pressure of consistent preterism in his hearty recommendation of James Stuart Russell's grossly heretical book of eschatology:

Russell's *Parousia* takes the Bible seriously when it tells us of the nearness of Christ's return. Those who claim to interpret the Bible literally often trip

---

12 R. C. Leonard and J. E. Leonard, *The Promise of His Coming: Interpreting New Testament Statements concerning the Time of Christ's Appearance* (Chicago, IL: Laudemont Press, 1996), 216–20).
13 Russell, *Parousia*, 549.
14 Russell, *Parousia*, 549–50.

over the obvious meaning of these time texts by making Scripture mean the opposite of what it unequivocally declares. Reading Russell is a breath of fresh air in a room filled with smoke and mirror hermeneutics.[15]

Regardless whether he identified himself with the school of Christian Reconstruction, also R. C. Sproul gave a glowing recommendation of Russell's book denying a future coming of Christ: "Russell's work is one of the most important treatments on Biblical eschatology that is available to the church today."[16] In a recent book of his own on eschatology, Sproul is far too concessive in his critique of Russell's blatantly heretical doctrine of the coming of Jesus. He interacts with it at length as though it were a debatable theology of the end. Never does he condemn it as the grossest of heresies. With reference to Russell's doctrine that the coming of Christ occurred fully and finally in AD 70, as taught by another, Sproul concedes that "the substance of the Olivet Discourse was fulfilled in A. D. 70 and that the bulk of Revelation was likewise fulfilled in that time-frame."[17]

Despite their vehement objection to being charged with the doctrinal sin of preterism when they are called to account, these inconsistent preterists are, in fact, guilty of preterism, which is a form of the denial of the second coming of Christ. Inconsistent preterism is preterism. It denies fundamental aspects of the truth of the coming of Christ. These include lawlessness, the great apostasy, antichrist, and the great tribulation. All these realities are linked inseparably in Scripture with the second coming, so that the denial of these realities as future precursors of Christ's coming is the denial of the second coming in its full truth. One example will make this clear. According to the men of Christian Reconstruction, the coming of Jesus announced in Philippians 4:5 as "at hand" was his coming in AD 70 in the destruction of Jerusalem. But the coming of Philippians 4 is the coming that, according to chapter 3:20, is the object of the church's one and only looking for the Savior. And this coming of the Savior, according to verse 21, is the coming that raises our body. Biblically, the preterism of Christian

---

15 Gary DeMar, in Russell, *Parousia*, back cover. Russell's book, let the reader remember, denies the bodily, second coming of Jesus Christ, the (future) resurrection of the dead, a (future) final judgment, the (future) re-creation of the heavens and the earth, and an eternal life. This theology is DeMar's "breath of fresh air."
16 R. C. Sproul, in Russell, *Parousia*, back cover.
17 R. C. Sproul, *Last Days according to Jesus* (Grand Rapids, MI: Baker, 1998), 158. The truth is that merely the type was fulfilled in AD 70, as also the eschatology of the book of Revelation. The substance of Matthew 24–25 awaits the coming of Christ in the future, as also the "bulk" of Revelation. What is telling is that this language is Sproul's assessment of the full, radical preterism of Russell and his disciples.

Reconstruction is necessarily a preterism that consigns the one, entire coming of Christ to the past. Biblically as well as logically, it is impossible to maintain an "inconsistent preterism."[18]

In addition, an inconsistent false doctrine invariably develops into the consistent form of the heresy. The principle that applies to doctrinal errors, as to all others, is "Resist the beginnings." With regard to physical health, no one ignores, much less welcomes and promotes, the beginning of cancer in the body. Inconsistent preterism at best is the beginning of doctrinal cancer in the body of the truth.

The explanation of the Bible's teaching that the coming of Christ is near, already in AD 50 or 60, is first that the return of Christ is the next and final wonder work of God in the history of the church. Second, the risen Christ, who is governing all history, directs all things to the goal of his coming, and that as rapidly as possible. Third, by all the events in history, and especially the events in the history of his church, he is coming continually. "Surely," he exclaimed, "I *come* [not: *will* come, but am coming] quickly" (Rev. 22:20). Fourth, there is also the explanation of the nearness of the coming that the death of the believer is a coming of Christ for him personally. This coming is near.

This understanding of the nearness of the coming of Christ is the understanding of Reformed orthodoxy and of the great father of the Christian church Augustine, as Francis Turretin makes plain in his explanation of the nearness of the coming of Christ.

> "The end of all things is at hand," says Peter…(1 Pet. 4:7)…the coming of the Lord draweth nigh" (Jam. 5:8). Not that in fact in the time of the apostles he was to come, for many things were to happen beforehand and especially the apostasy…and the revelation of the mystery of iniquity, of which the apostle speaks (2 Thess. 2:7). But because we ought both to be ready at all times to receive Christ and so to live as if every day he was to come, lest we be found asleep. "In what condition his own last day shall find anyone, in that the last day will meet him because such as each one dies in the former day, such in the latter day he will be judged," as Augustine expresses it…Also because it was much nearer than before, since the time of the New Testament is the last, after which no other dispensation is to be expected; and on account of the shortness of time, which has the relation of a moment when compared with eternity. And if even in the time of

---

18 For a more thorough examination of the preterism of Russell and the men of Christian Reconstruction, with particular reference to the postmillennialism of the men of Christian Reconstruction, see Engelsma, *Christ's Spiritual Kingdom*.

the apostles the end of all things drew on, how much more now when we see every day the signs of that advent being fulfilled.[19]

His coming was near in AD 95. It is near, much nearer, in AD 2022. After AD 70, the Lord Jesus says, "Surely I come quickly."

And the church responds, in hope: "Even so, come, Lord Jesus"—not an illusory millennium, but "Lord Jesus" (Rev. 22:20).

---

[19] Francis Turretin, *Institutes of Elenctic Theology*, tr. George Musgrave Giger, ed. James T. Dennison Jr., 3 vols. (Phillipsburg, NJ: P&R Publishing, 1997), 3:585.

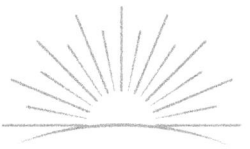

9

THE RESURRECTION OF THE DEAD

INTRODUCTION

At his coming, Jesus Christ will perform two wonders. He will raise the dead and conduct the final judgment. With the judgment, the resurrection of the dead, as a constituent element of the coming of Christ, is the goal (Greek: *telos*) of all things. First, it is the goal of all inasmuch as this is the great hope of the child of God and of the church. It is the perfection of salvation. Resurrection was the hope of Israel in the Old Testament. "That God should raise the dead" was "the hope of the promise made of God unto our fathers: unto which promise our twelve tribes, instantly serving God day and night, hope to come" (Acts 26:6–8).

The resurrection is also the ultimate hope of the New Testament Christian. "If in this life only we have hope in Christ, we are of all men most miserable. But now is Christ risen from the dead, and become the firstfruits of them that slept…For as in Adam all die, even so in Christ shall all be made alive" (1 Cor. 15:19–20, 22). "We ourselves groan within ourselves, waiting for the adoption, to wit, the redemption of our body. For we are saved by hope" (Rom. 8:23–24).

Resurrection is the goal of all, second, because in the resurrection of the saints is perfected the body of Christ, so that Christ and his body, the church, are glorified.

Also, in the resurrection Jesus Christ conquers the last enemy, thus revealing the greatness of his grace in the perfecting of the salvation of his people.

25. For he must reign, till he hath put all enemies under his feet.
26. The last enemy *that* shall be destroyed *is* death.

54. So when this corruptible shall have put on incorruption, and this mortal shall have put on immortality, then shall be brought to pass the saying that is written, Death is swallowed up in victory.

WHAT IT IS

Herman Hoeksema defines the resurrection as "the wonder of grace whereby the God of our salvation calls our mortal bodies out of the dust of death through the resurrection of Jesus Christ, in order to make them like unto the glorious body of our risen Lord."[1] Resurrection is a wonder. Not only is it a work of God of surpassing power, which the child of God believes on the testimony of Scripture and in light of the resurrection of Jesus in his body, so that all the natural impossibility of it does not weigh with him. But also it is a work of amazing grace, lifting God's beloved child out of the depths of the effects of sin into the heights of the blessings of Christ's redemption.

The resurrection of the body that mainly concerns us, as it mainly concerns holy Scripture, is the resurrection of the elect believers. It is the resurrection that John 5:29 calls "the resurrection of life." There is also a resurrection of the body of the reprobate wicked. This is a resurrection unto eternal death. Daniel 12:2 speaks of the awaking of some "to shame and everlasting contempt." This resurrection is contrasted with the awaking of others "to everlasting life." As the bodies of the godly will be glorious, the bodies of the ungodly will be shameful and ugly. The punishment will correspond to the sin: the ungodly devoted their bodies to the shamefulness of sin. What they sowed in time, they reap in eternity.

The everlasting shamefulness of their bodies exposes the utter folly of unbelieving men and women of devoting endless hours and enormous energy of exercise for a strong or an attractive body. They ought rather to exercise themselves unto godliness. This is the way to an everlastingly strong and beautiful body.

Jesus prophesies that at one and the same hour all who are in the graves "shall hear his voice, and shall come forth; they that have done good, unto the resurrection of life; and they that have done evil, unto the resurrection of damnation" (John 5:28–29). All humans will be raised. The Lord Jesus will raise all at his coming. But there is radical difference between the resurrection of the elect believers and the resurrection of the reprobate unbelievers. Whereas the resurrection of the godly is the work of love—almighty love, but love—the resurrection of the ungodly is an act of sheer power. Whereas the resurrection of the godly brings about the fullness of blessed salvation, the resurrection of the ungodly, with the final judgment that is its goal, realizes fully their awful damnation. Whereas the resurrection of the godly is their ardent and supreme hope, the

---

1 Hoeksema, *Reformed Dogmatics*, 2:582.

resurrection of the ungodly is their ultimate dread. Whereas the resurrection of the godly is the dominating motivation of all their lives, the resurrection of the ungodly is the inescapable truth that spoils all their godless, lawless lives.

There is this difference also, that the resurrection of the godly is based on, and effected by means of, the bodily resurrection of Jesus. This remarkable relation between the resurrection of Christ and the resurrection of the members of his church is expressed in 1 Corinthians 15:16: "For if the dead rise not, then is not Christ raised." The argument of the apostle is striking. He is contending for the resurrection of the believer on account of doubt in the Corinthian church concerning the bodily resurrection of the saints. One would expect the apostle to argue from the resurrection of Christ to the resurrection of the saints: "Since Christ rose, we will rise." Putting the argument negatively, one would expect him to argue that if Christ be not risen, then also we will not rise.

But the apostle's argument runs differently. So close is the relation between Christ's resurrection and our resurrection, so intimately is our resurrection bound up in his, that if we do not rise, neither did Christ rise. To deny the resurrection of the godly is necessarily to deny his resurrection.

This argument settles the matter for the church. It banishes all doubts. It conclusively defeats all the contrary arguments of unbelieving modernism. No Christian will deny the resurrection of Christ. Denial of the resurrection of Christ Jesus is the denial of the gospel and the Christian faith outrightly and in their entirety. The resurrection of Christ is a fundamental truth of the gospel. Therefore, neither can there be any denial of the resurrection of the godly. To deny the resurrection of the godly would be to deny the resurrection of Christ himself.

Other passages of Scripture also emphasize the dependence of the resurrection of the bodies of the godly upon the resurrection of Christ. According to Acts 4:2, the apostles proclaimed "through Jesus the resurrection from the dead." The Greek preposition that the KJV translates as *through* is literally *in*, so that the message was, "*in* Jesus the resurrection from the dead." The gospel message of the apostles was "the resurrection from the dead [of the believers]." And this resurrection is *in Jesus*. Such is the union of faith with Jesus that the believer shares in the resurrection of Jesus. His resurrection is the extension of the resurrection of Jesus himself. The church does not simply proclaim resurrection, it proclaims an *in Jesus* resurrection.

That the resurrection of the godly is their sharing in the resurrection of Jesus is also the message of all the passages of Scripture that teach that in his resurrection Jesus was the "firstborn from the dead" (Col. 1:18), the "first begotten of the dead" (Rev. 1:5), the "firstfruits of them that slept" (1 Cor. 15:20, 23), and the "first that should rise from the dead" (Acts 26:23). In all these passages, *first* does not describe mere temporal precedence. But it announces the resurrection of Jesus as his rising for others in such a way that it made certain their rising as the full reality of his own. *First* does not merely imply a second. But *first* assures, and itself fully consists of, the second that must follow.

The goal of the resurrection of the godly regarding the body itself is its conformity to the body of the risen Christ: "Who [the Savior, the Lord Jesus Christ] shall change our vile body, that it may be fashioned like unto his glorious body, according to the working whereby he is able even to subdue all things unto himself" (Phil. 3:21). The body of the believer is fashioned like the body of Christ as the body not simply of glory, but of *his* glory. That the resurrection body of the believer is like the body of the risen Christ indicates both the astounding glory that awaits the child of God and the difficulty, in reality the impossibility, of comprehending the glorious resurrection body. Still, Scripture enables us to know something of that wonder.

The resurrection of the body will be the salvation of the *very body itself* that the believer has (better, *is*) in his earthly life, in which he dies, and which is lowered into the grave. There is identity of the body that is raised with the body that lived an earthly life and that died. Resurrection is not a new creation. The body that died and decayed in the grave, or in the depth of the sea, is restored to life: "raised out of the earth," according to article 37 of the Belgic Confession.[2] The Heidelberg Catechism declares the identity of the resurrection body with the present earthly body in these words: "This my body, raised by the power of Christ, shall again be united with my soul."[3] The Westminster Confession of Faith emphasizes the identity of the resurrection body with the present, earthly body in these words: "the self-same bodies, and none other," adding that the resurrection body will possess "different qualities."[4]

The resurrection must be the raising of the very body in which the child of God lives and dies, for salvation is the salvation of the child of God in his entirety, body and soul. He is body and soul—*this* individual, unique body and *this* individual, unique soul. If the resurrection is not the raising of the very body in which one lives and dies, *he* is not raised, and the promise of God to raise *him* is proved false.

Although it is hazardous to speculate further about the resurrection body, one may safely deduce several other aspects of the resurrection body of the saved

---

2 Belgic Confession 37, in Schaff, *Creeds of Christendom*, 3:434. The article continues, "their proper bodies in which they formerly lived."
3 Heidelberg Catechism A 57, in Schaff, *Creeds of Christendom*, 3:325–26. The German original is "*diesz mein Fleisch*," literally, "this my flesh." In preaching this phrase, the minister should be pointing at his body.
4 Westminster Confession of Faith 32.2, in Schaff, *Creeds of Christendom*, 3:671.

from what is expressly revealed in Scripture. First, all defects that are due to the effects of sin on the bodies will be removed, for example, blindness, deafness, and all malformations. Second, the body that is raised will be in its adult form, at least the form in which the elect is able to know and praise God. There will be no baby who died at birth, or even before birth, in the form of his or her infancy. Neither will there be an old man or woman in the wrinkled, gnarled form of old age. Third, the saints will be recognizable in their distinctiveness just as is the case in their earthly lives. Their resurrection bodies will distinguish them, just as they do during their earthly lives. Even though too much cannot be made of this in a parable and although the setting of the parable is what is called the intermediate state, prior to the resurrection of the body, it is significant that Abraham and Lazarus retained their identities and were identifiable in Jesus' parable of the rich man and Lazarus (Luke 16:19–31).

Fourth, to the consternation of the contemporary, mad advocates of sexual indifference and unimportance and frenzied opponents of the sexuality that the Creator has established (not that any of them will be where they can notice that God everlastingly maintains this creation order, unless they repent), the sexual difference between male and female will be maintained. This belongs to the resurrection of the very body in which one lives on earth. The male will be raised as a male; the female, as a female. That there will be no marriage in the new world, and therefore no sexual desire or sexual congress, does not imply the obliteration of sexual distinction.[5]

Clearly implied by the resurrection of the body itself is that the body, as a body, will be material, or substantial. It will be a *body*, not a ghostlike, immaterial cloud in the shape of a body. That it will not be flesh and blood as we now know flesh and blood does not imply unsubstantiality. Here the difficulty—and a difficulty it is, exceeding comprehension—is to harmonize 1 Corinthians 15:50 with Luke 24:39. First Corinthians 15:50 declares that "flesh and blood cannot inherit the kingdom," in the context of the promise that we shall "be changed" (v. 51). Luke 24:39 teaches that the risen Jesus, after whose body the resurrection body of the believer will be fashioned, has flesh and bones. Jesus denies that he is a spirit. So much is he flesh and bones that he can and does eat (vv. 41–43). In addition, his hands and feet bear the wounds of his crucifixion, and he can be handled (vv. 39, 40).

---

5 Jesus taught that there is no marriage in the resurrection, and by implication no sexual desire or fulfillment, in Matthew 22:30: "For in the resurrection they neither marry, nor are given in marriage, but are as the angels of God in heaven." This reality as concerns the body of the resurrection is not to be explained in terms of any inherent evil of sex, but in light of marital bliss's being enjoyed and satisfied in the marriage of the entire church to Christ Jesus.

The solution to the difficulty of harmonizing these aspects of the resurrection body of Jesus and therefore also of the resurrection body of the saint—or at least as much of the solution as we are privy to on this side of the experience of the solution—is that the resurrection body will be *heavenly* flesh and bones, not earthly flesh and bones. This is the solution that 1 Corinthians 15 provides. The distinction between the present body and the resurrection body is not between a substantial body and an unsubstantial body, which would be no body at all. But the difference is between an earthly body and a heavenly body. "As is the earthy, such are they also that are earthy: and as is the heavenly, such are they also that are heavenly" (v. 48). Previous to the resurrection, "we have borne the image of the earthy"; in our resurrection body, "we shall also bear the image of the heavenly" (v. 49). In the resurrection, we will be "flesh and bones." But we will be heavenly flesh and bones.

We have some indication of the unique, mysterious nature of this heavenly body in that in the risen Jesus it could pass through the graveclothes without disturbing the wrapping of the cloth, could exit the grave without rolling away the stone that blocked the entrance and exit, and could appear in a room without passing through the locked door.

Fundamentally, the evidence both of the resurrection of the body and that this body is the very same body in which one lived and died is the empty tomb of Jesus on the morning of Resurrection Sunday. "Come, see the place where the Lord lay," the angel said to the women and to the church today (Matt. 28:6).

If the body of the resurrection is not substantial, be it heavenly substance, it is not a genuine body, and therefore the resurrection is not truly the resurrection of the believer (who is *body*). Indeed, it is not resurrection at all, but merely the appearance of resurrection. Thus the resurrection of the body is stripped of its wonder, as well as of its comfort for the child of God.

Insistence on the necessary identity of the resurrection body does not minimize, much less deny, the radical change of the body of the godly in the resurrection. "This my body" will not be the same in its resurrection form as it is in earthly life, with regard to the qualities of the body. According to Philippians 3:21, the change consists of its being made conformable to the risen body of Christ: "Who ['the Saviour, the Lord Jesus Christ,' v. 20] shall change our vile body, that it may be fashioned like unto his glorious body." The preceding context teaches the motivation of the Christian life consisting of the desire to know the power of Christ's resurrection (v. 10) and to "attain unto the resurrection of the dead" (v. 11). The resurrection is the "prize" that the apostle strives for (v. 14). This longing for the resurrection safeguards the apostle, and every Christian, against the sin of minding earthly things (v. 19).

Philippians 3:21 describes this resurrection of the dead. The believer's body is changed. Clearly implied is the identity of the body that is raised with the body that died. The earthly body that died is *changed*; it is not replaced. Resurrection is change; it is not the creation of a new body. But the body of earthly life undergoes change, *radical* change. It is transformation of the body. This is the literal meaning of the word that the KJV translates *change*. One might more accurately translate the Greek verb as *transform*: Who shall *transform* our vile body. To *transform* the body is to change its *form*. The root of the Greek verb that the KJV translates as *change* is *schema*, which means *form* or *fashion*. Resurrection is a change of *form* or *fashion*. That resurrection is the change of form or fashion is emphasized by what follows in the text: "that it [the body of the resurrection] may be *fashioned* like unto his glorious body."

The trans*form*ation of the body is from "our vile body," literally "the body of our humiliation," unto con*form*ity to "the body of his [Christ's] glory" (Phil. 3:21). From a form than which nothing could be lower or more shameful, unto a form than which nothing could be higher or more glorious! From a body that is, as is the translation of the KJV, "vile" (not because the body is inherently base, but because the body suffers the shameful ravages of sin; the Greek original has "body of our humiliation") unto a body that shares in the glory of the risen Christ!

This wonderful resurrection with its marvelous change of the form of the body is the work of the Lord at his coming: "The Lord Jesus Christ…shall change our vile body" (Phil. 3:20–21). The possibility of this impossibility is the ability of the risen Christ: "according to the working whereby he is able" (v. 21). All difficulties, indeed impossibilities, of the resurrection of dead bodies, and they are enormous, fade into nothingness before this ability of the eternal Son of God in the flesh of his exalted, risen human nature. Because of the ability of Jesus Christ, the resurrection of the body of the believer is certain: "Who *shall* change our vile body" (v. 21). Faith lives and dies in this certainty: with regard to this *my* body, he shall change its form, in raising it (me) from the dead.

The resurrection of the dead humans by no means exhausts the ability of Jesus Christ regarding resurrection. Not only is he able to raise dead humans, specifically all the members of his elect church, but also he is able to raise the world of the heavens and the earth. Philippians 3:21 continues: "whereby [that is, by the working of the risen Jesus] he is able even to subdue all things unto himself." As the apostle confesses the truth of resurrection that is promised, and really included, in the resurrection of Jesus, the perspective widens from the members of Christ's body to the universe. "All things" are the world of the heavens and the earth. Subduing the heavens and the earth is the raising of them from their present form, which is the lowliness of their involvement in the fall of their lord Adam into sin, unto a new form in which they share in the glory of the resurrection of their lord Jesus Christ. Christ Jesus will raise not only the human race, but also the world, the cosmos. Of this Romans 8:19–22 speaks more fully. Only let it be noted here that the future of the created world of the heavens and the earth is not destruction in order to be replaced by a newly created world. Like the body of the elect believer, the *form* of the creation will be changed. First Corinthians 7:31 is explicit: "The fashion of this world passeth away."

All of this grand doctrine of resurrection—the Christian's hope—is introduced in Philippians 3 with the practical purpose of exhorting and encouraging believers to live in holiness in the body here and now, in contrast to the sensualists "whose God is their belly, and whose glory is in their shame, who mind earthly things" (v. 19). This present earthly life with its pleasures is not all there is to human existence. There is a future life and glory for those who believe on Jesus Christ, even as there is a future existence of death and shame for the ungodly. The way to the future life and glory of the resurrection body and to bodily life in the renewed creation in the day of Christ is a heavenly way of life, or "conversation," now (v. 20). One might better say that the power of resurrection that one day will raise the body already energizes the believer so that he begins to live the heavenly life, *in the body*, that he will live perfectly in the resurrection body in the day of Christ.

Scripture is not content to hold before the believer the general promise of a change of form of the resurrection body. It specifies the outstanding elements of the change. It does this especially in the main passage on the resurrection of the body as a leading truth of the doctrine of the last things, 1 Corinthians 15, particularly verses 35–58. In these verses the apostle is answering the question, expressing doubt concerning the resurrection, "With what body do they come?" (v. 35). The change is from mortality to immortality, from death to such victory over death as to live a life in the body that is incapable of dying. Already this indicates that the salvation that is Jesus Christ surpasses the creation life of Adam in paradise, for the life of Adam, glorious as it must have been, was mortal, that is, capable of dying. By his death and resurrection, Christ has swallowed up death in his victory over death. He himself lives immortal life in the body. In the resurrection of the body of the believer, God gives the believer the victory over death through the immortal Lord Jesus Christ.

This immortality of the resurrection body of the Christian consists of the following four elements or aspects. First, there is the change from corruption to incorruption, indeed to incorruptibility. Second, there is the change from dishonor to glory. Third, there is the change from weakness to power. Fourth, there is the change from a natural body to a spiritual body.

The first three aspects of the change in the resurrection of the body are clearly deliverances of the body from the ravages of sin upon the body. Sin corrupts the body; sin renders the body inglorious or dishonorable; sin makes the body weak. But the fourth change is quite independent of sin. It is applicable to the change of the body in its unfallen condition in Adam before the fall unto the body of the risen Christ and the resurrection body of the child of God. Adam's body before the fall was natural. The resurrection body of the believer will be spiritual.

It is helpful in explaining this change to know that the Greek word that the KJV translates as *natural* in 1 Corinthians 15:44–46 is literally *soulish*. The distinction in the passage is between a body that is animated merely by the soul and a body that is animated by the spirit. A body that is animated merely by the soul is fitted to live an earthly life. This was Adam in paradise. Had Adam not fallen, this would have been the life of the human race. A body that is spiritual is a body that is fitted to live a higher, better, more glorious life—a heavenly life. This is the higher, better, more glorious life of the body that Jesus acquired for himself by his death and resurrection. His bodily life is spiritual because his body is spiritual in nature. It is still a real, substantial, genuinely human body, but its substance is not "soulish" but spiritual. Sharing in the quality of his body in the resurrection, the elect too will undergo the change from their formerly "soulish" bodies to spiritual bodies. They will be fitted to live the new, different, better, more glorious heavenly lives.

An example of this change might be the change from the life of a man in a prison cell unto a life of a man at liberty. Both states are life—*human* life, indeed the human life of one and the same man—but the quality, or nature, of that life is radically different.

The full understanding of the change from "soulish" to spiritual in the resurrection of the body awaits the experience of this change in that great resurrection morning. This we know: we will not come out of death in the same "soulish" state of the body in which we passed into death. Nor will the quality of life of the resurrection body be the merely earthly life we lived before. After all our struggle, suffering, and dying, we do not merely regain the paradise that was lost. "As we have borne the image of the earthy, we shall also bear the image of the heavenly" (1 Cor. 15:49). Ultimately, this radical change in the quality of our bodily life in the resurrection is due to the fact that, whereas the "first man is of the earth, earthy: the second man is the Lord from heaven" (v. 47).

That the resurrection body is spiritual implies that the agent of the resurrection of the body is the Holy Spirit as the Spirit of the risen Jesus Christ. All that is spiritual is the work of the Spirit. Even as he raised Jesus from the dead with his spiritual body, so also will he raise the members of the body of the spiritual Jesus—the church—unto their spiritual bodies. Romans 8:11 attributes the resurrection to the Spirit, who is the infinite power of God, and connects the resurrection of believers to the resurrection of Christ: "If the Spirit of him that raised up Jesus from the dead dwell in you, he that raised up Christ from the dead shall also quicken your mortal bodies by his Spirit that dwelleth in you."

But the Spirit is always the efficacy of the Son of God, Jesus Christ. And Jesus exerts his efficacious power by his word. Such is true in the raising of the dead: "The hour is coming…when the dead shall hear the voice of the Son of God: and they that hear shall live" (John 5:25). The voice of Jesus will sound like the imperious trumpet: "The trumpet shall sound, and the dead shall be raised incorruptible" (1 Cor. 15:52); "For the Lord himself shall descend from heaven with a shout, with the voice of the archangel, and with the trump of God: and the dead in Christ shall rise first" (1 Thess. 4:16). As befits such a wonderful event, the resurrection of the dead saints will not be a silent, secret, unobtrusive happening as is the teaching of the rapture, but as noisy and public a celebration of the glorious presence and work of Jesus Christ as is imaginable. A shout, a trump, and a voice resounding throughout all the world announce the raising of the dead in Christ and the decisive glorification of God in Jesus Christ.

FEATURES OF THE RESURRECTION

Certain important, particular features of the resurrection of the dead call for attention and defense especially because they are called into question in our day. Already in apostolic times, the truth of the resurrection was controversial. It was denied by some in the Corinthian church: "How say some among you that there is no resurrection of the dead?" (1 Cor. 15:12). Exactly this denial became the occasion for the most splendid proclamation and thorough explanation of the resurrection in all of Scripture. Unbelief concerning the resurrection was not limited to the church at Corinth. Prominent men in the church at Ephesus were teaching that the resurrection "is past already" (2 Tim. 2:17–18).

Already among the people of God of the Old Testament there was a prominent school of teachers that denied the resurrection. These were the Sadducees, "which say that there is no resurrection" (Matt. 22:23).

Today also, the doctrine of the resurrection is questioned in the churches. Ecclesiastical modernism always makes the doctrine of the resurrection the prominent object of its unbelief. But the denial of the resurrection is found also in the Reformed churches. Well known Dutch Reformed theologians have recently denied the resurrection of the body. Every true church of Jesus Christ is called to confess and proclaim the resurrection of the body as a fundamental of the Christian gospel and faith, explain it thoroughly, and defend it vigorously.

Resurrection is not "deification," as was taught by some in the early post-apostolic church according to J. N. D. Kelly.[6] This is the doctrine that in the resurrection the godly share in the being of God. The nature of humans does not become divine in the resurrection. Not even did Jesus become divine in his resurrection. His human nature, body and soul, remained a fully human body and soul.

Another important feature of the resurrection is that there is one, and one only, future resurrection of the body. This occurs at the *parousia*, or coming, of Jesus. This is the clear teaching of John 5:28, 29. There is coming "[one] *hour*" in which "all that are in the graves shall hear his voice, and shall come forth." The doctrine that there will be two or more resurrections is false, and the theology that demands such falsity is exposed as false in its entirety. This is the heresy of premillennial dispensationalism, which has a resurrection at the time of the rapture and another at the close of the millennium, if not a third at the end of the seven years of the persecution of the Jews by the antichrist.

Yet another important feature of the resurrection is that the resurrection of the body is not only a fundamental of the Christian gospel, but also a peculiarly Christian hope. The pagan religions and their philosophers have taught the immortality of the soul, but they know nothing of the resurrection of the body. When Paul proclaimed in Athens, the headquarters of Greek philosophy, that God raised Jesus from the dead, the philosophers mocked: "When they heard of the resurrection of the dead, some mocked" (Acts 17:32).

SAVING IMPLICATIONS OF THE RESURRECTION

Scripture is at pains to bind the implications of the resurrection for the Christian life upon the believing church. First, the truth of the resurrection gives the elect believer hope, that is, the confident expectation of a great good in the future. Apart from the expectation of the resurrection of the body and the everlasting life that resurrection implies, human life is hopeless. After a few, trouble-filled years, life ends in the grave. Implied is that the brief life of humans is vain, empty, without meaning or purpose. Whatever achievements one has accomplished are meaningless and soon forgotten. All the disappointments and

---

6 Kelly, *Early Christian Doctrines*, 469–70. The quotations that Kelly adduces to prove his charge do not, in fact, substantiate the charge. That "the eternal salvation of the righteous… will take the form of that incorruptibility and impassibility which fellowship with God will impart," as Justin taught, is not the teaching of deification, but Christian orthodoxy.

all the suffering only add to the worthlessness of the brief life. In recognition of the vanity of life apart from the resurrection, regardless whether they had resurrection in mind, the unbelieving philosophers gave expression to the hopelessness and vanity of life apart from the resurrection of the body unto eternal life by asserting, in effect, that the best thing is never to have been born and that the next best thing is to die young.

Lack of the hope of resurrection is the explanation of the wasting of the hopeless by drugs and drunkenness; of suicides; of the disturbance and even overthrow of civilizations by senseless revolutions; and of irresponsible addiction to pleasures, legitimate and illicit. Often these expressions of hopelessness are the destructive acts of the young, and then often of the young who have been educated in the public high schools and in the colleges. They have taken to heart the hopelessness of their instruction in atheistic evolutionism. "Without God and immortal life," Dostoyevsky has written, in *The Brothers Karamazov*, "all things are lawful."[7] "All things are lawful," because human life is without hope.

Adding to the misery of the hopeless ungodly is the inescapable testimony of God to their souls that when this brief life is finished, afterward there is the judgment by the holy God. Not only is the unbeliever depressed by the hopelessness of his life, but also he is terrified by the knowledge of impending judgment, and an eternity of suffering to follow. There is no escaping expectation of the future as resurrection. Either one has the expectation of the great good of the resurrection unto life, or one has the dread of the great evil of the resurrection unto death.

Such is the importance of the resurrection for the hope of the Christian that without it even the hope he might have for good in this earthly life is rendered null and void. This is the thought of the apostle in 1 Corinthians 15:19: "If in this life only we have hope in Christ, we are of all men most miserable." Here the apostle is addressing the peculiar denial of the resurrection of the body in the church at Corinth. Believers there denied or questioned the resurrection of the body, while confessing that they had hope in Christ for their present, earthly lives, evidently that he would bless them with the benefits of salvation while they lived. This, the apostle denies. Not only is there no hope pertaining to this present earthly life, apart from hope in the resurrection of the body, but in fact the life of the Christian is the most miserable life of all men apart from the resurrection. For the earthly life of the Christian is a life of struggle with sin and the devil, a life of self-denial, a life of suffering for Christ's sake, a life

---

7 Fyodor Dostoyevsky, *The Brothers Karamazov*, tr. Constance Garnett (New York: New American Library, 1960), 534.

of dying daily. Hopeless as it is, the life of the ungodly is spared all this painful struggle and sorrow.

Becoming personal, the apostle cries out that his own earthly life is a standing in jeopardy every hour (1 Cor. 15:30), a matter of dying daily (v. 31), and the misery of having fought with the beasts at Ephesus (v. 32). What advantage is all this to him, he asks, "if the dead rise not" (v. 32)? With reference not to the ungodly but to Christians who suppose that there will be no resurrection of the body, and that in this life only we have hope in Christ, the apostle shouts the reasonable, and likely inevitable, implication of this denial of the resurrection: "Let us eat and drink; for to morrow we die" (v. 32).

By hope—*this hope* of the resurrection of the body—the child of God is saved: saved in his own experience, saved with regard to the Christian life, and saved in that hope brings him surely to the resurrection unto life everlasting.

A second implication of the resurrection for the Christian life is that the truth of the resurrection requires holiness of the body in this earthly life, particularly regarding sexual chastity on the part both of the married and of the unmarried. To the members of the church at Corinth, in an environment that regarded fornication, including the use of whores by married men, as little more significant than eating, Paul had to give a strong warning against sexual sin. Although he gives other motivations as well, including that the members of the body of the Christian are united to Christ, one motivation for sexual purity is that the body of the believer will be raised. Therefore, the body is not insignificant but is for the Lord, as the Lord is also for the body of his child. "Now the body is not for fornication, but for the Lord; and the Lord for the body. And God hath both raised up the Lord, and will also raise up us by his own power" (1 Cor. 6:13–14).

A body that is destined for the glory of resurrection may not be abased by shameful indulgence in sexual sin. A body that is so for the Lord that he will raise it may not be devoted to fornication, which is obnoxious to the Lord.

The abased culture of North America comes not a whit behind shamefully sex-saturated Corinth. Members of Christian churches need the application of resurrection to sexual purity that the apostle gives in 1 Corinthians 6. It is not enough to warn against such consequences of illicit sex as disease and the harm to marriage and family. The church must admonish in light of the resurrection of the body.

But it is not only that aspect of the Christian life consisting of sexual purity that depends upon the resurrection of the body. Resurrection also guards against the evil of earthly-mindedness. This is no less a danger to the church in the twenty-first century in North America than is sexual sin. Philippians 3:17–21 finds the apostle weeping over an evil that is evidently a threat to members of the church at Philippi. The evil is that they "mind earthly things" (v. 19). One aspect of this evil is that men and women make a god of their belly. Implied is a total devotion of their lives to other members of the body and their earthly pleasures. The antidote to this idolatry is faith's expectation of the risen Christ's fashioning of the bodies of believers unto his glorious body in the resurrection. The hope of the resurrection prohibits and prevents gluttony and dedication to gourmet dining.

And then there is the application of the truth of the resurrection that the apostle makes at the very end of his grand proclamation of the resurrection, in 1 Corinthians 15:58: "Therefore [because death is swallowed up in victory for them, in the resurrection of the body], my beloved brethren, be ye stedfast, unmoveable, always abounding in the work of the Lord, forasmuch as ye know that your labour is not in vain in the Lord." The believer is exhorted to live his entire life in the hope of the resurrection. Doing so, he will abound in the work of the Lord. The "work of the Lord" is not passing out tracts on the street corner. But it is engaging in all the normal elements of human life as work assigned by the Lord Jesus and as work that has its purpose in pleasing and honoring the Lord Jesus. It is the work of being a faithful husband and wife; of raising a family of children according to the will of the Lord, including sending them to the good, Christian school, often with financial struggle; of doing the "menial" labor of a mother in the home and of a father at his metaphorical workbench; of giving a cup of cold water to a thirsty neighbor; and of supporting the ministry of the church.

Often this work is difficult, demanding, and sacrificial. The apostle does not use the normal word for *work*, but the word that translates correctly as *labor*. Often no one notices the labor. There is no reward here. On the contrary, there may simply be loss, even mistreatment. The labor of the wife to be submissive to an ingrate of a husband meets with further cold ingratitude. The zealous, faithful labor of the minister is rewarded by harsh criticism on the part of some in the congregation. The temptation is that the woman or the minister throws up her or his hands, crying out, "What's the use?" Comes back the answer of the apostle in 1 Corinthians 15: by virtue of the promise of the resurrection of the body, "ye know that your labour is not in vain in the Lord."

The resurrection motivates unto steadfastness in the duties of the Christian life, whether resisting temptations to depart from the Christian life altogether or continuing in the positive calling of this life. Indeed, it motivates unto *abounding* in the work of the Christian life. Abounding is doing the work wholeheartedly and doing more of the work than the bare minimum (going the extra mile, as the saying has it, and as one might judge).

The resurrection of the body is the motivation for this abounding labor inasmuch as it itself is the gracious, public recognition and reward by Christ himself before the church and the entire world of the labor of his faithful servants, including the mistreated wife and the unjustly criticized minister. In the resurrection itself, Christ says, "Well done, good and faithful servant." In addition, there are in the resurrection of the bodies of the saints degrees of glory corresponding to the labor that the child of God performed. Abounding work is rewarded with abounding glory.

"Therefore," because of the resurrection, "*therefore*…be ye…always abounding in the work of the Lord."

Resurrection of the body that is coming trans*forms* earthly life and work already now.

10

THE FINAL JUDGMENT

INTRODUCTION

The second of the two great acts of Christ at his coming will be the conducting of the final judgment. Jesus himself prophesies and describes the final judgment in Matthew 25:31–46. The passage forms the conclusion of Jesus' eschatological discourse in answer to the disciples' question about his coming and the end of the world. The Son of man will ascend the throne of his glory. From the throne he will judge all nations. Also Revelation 20:11–15 foretells the final judgment in what is called "the great white throne judgment." All the dead stand before God in the judgment.

Although this study of the last things treats the resurrection of the dead before treating the final judgment, as is logical in that humans must first be raised in order then to be judged, the final judgment is not inferior to the resurrection in importance, nor is it any less the purpose of Christ with his coming. The importance of the judgment is indicated by the Christian and the Reformed creeds when they view the judgment as the purpose of the coming of Christ. The Apostles' Creed confesses that Christ shall come again "to judge the quick and the dead." Interpreting this confession of the creed, the Heidelberg Catechism explains the coming of Jesus Christ as the coming of the "Judge from heaven."[1]

Such is the importance of Jesus' being judge that Jesus himself mandated the apostles to "testify that it is he which was ordained of God to be the Judge of quick and dead" (Acts 10:42). That the apostles fulfilled this mandate and how they worked the truth of the judgment into their evangelistic message is evident in chapter 17:31: "Because he hath appointed a day, in the which he will judge the world in righteousness by that man whom he hath ordained; whereof he

---

1 Heidelberg Catechism A 52, in Schaff, *Creeds of Christendom*, 3:324.

hath given assurance unto all men, in that he hath raised him from the dead." This truth of the judgment was part of the apostle's sermon to the philosophers and other heathen Greeks in Athens on Mars Hill. It served to underscore the seriousness of the apostle's command to all men to repent (v. 30). Such is the relation of resurrection and judgment, according to Acts 17, that the resurrection of Jesus certifies the conducting of the judgment.

The truth of the final judgment must be a vital element of all the preaching by the church, not only in the congregation but also in missions and evangelism. Saints and unbelieving sinners must be confronted by the awesome truth that their lives, especially their response to the call of the gospel to believe on Jesus Christ, will come into judgment, and not only any judgment, but the *final* judgment.

WHAT THIS JUDGMENT IS

The final judgment is that public work of God in Jesus Christ, his servant, of examining the lives of all rational, moral creatures according to the standard of his law, showing them to be either righteous or unrighteous, and of pronouncing upon them the verdict of innocence or guilt in accordance with their works, which verdict determines their eternal state. For the elect, this judgment is another, indeed the final, work of their gracious salvation in that the verdict of innocence is based solely upon the obedience of Jesus Christ in their stead and on their behalf, which work is imputed to them as their own by their faith in him. The final judgment therefore is the last stage of God's gracious salvation of them.

The final judgment is God's work of examining and exposing all angels and humans with regard to their works, in order justly to pass sentence upon them of justification or condemnation, which sentence decides their eternal state, heaven or hell.

Those who are judged are angels and humans. That angels will be judged is the teaching of 1 Corinthians 6:3: "Know ye not that we shall judge angels?" Evidently, the angels who are judged include both those who fell with Satan in the beginning and the multitude that remained faithful. That the wicked angels will appear in the dock of the heavenly courtroom is the teaching of 2 Peter 2:4 and of Jude 6. Peter declares that the angels that sinned are "reserved unto judgment." Jude adds that this judgment of the angels is the "judgment of the great day," indicating something of the importance and awesomeness of the final judgment.

Regarding the judgment of humans, it has been a controversial question in the Reformed tradition whether the elect will be judged, that is, whether their works will be exposed and examined, especially including their sins. Some Reformed theologians have denied this, including men of repute, as though the inclusion of the elect in the final judgment would conflict with the truth of salvation by grace alone. It has been argued that the prospect of the judgment of the elect believers would destroy the hope of the saints for the coming of Christ, shrinking as they naturally do from the exposure of their sins.

In his authoritative work on the Reformed theological tradition, Heinrich Heppe suggests that the denial that the elect will appear in the final judgment has been the Reformed tradition:

> But Christ will deal with the elect godly otherwise than with the ungodly...[in that] there will be no mention of their sins, forgiveness of which has long ago been assured to them. Hence the godly will not really be judged, but Christ will separate them from the others, that they may be witnesses of the righteousness of his real judgments, by which he turns over ungodly angels and men from their own works to their godlessness and worthy condemnation.[2]

Heppe quotes the Reformed theologian Amesius to the effect that "Amesius teaches precisely, that only the ungodly should be described as the object of judgment."[3]

There is good reason to suppose, however, that Reformed theologians only meant to deny that in the judgment of the godly their sins would be exposed. These theologians agreed that the elect would be judged. But their sins, having been blotted out by Jesus, would not be brought up. This was certainly the thought of Francis Turretin:

> If it is asked here whether the sins of the pious equally as well as of the wicked will be revealed, we answer that the negative seems more probable to us. (1) On account of the Judge, who, since he has been most fully satisfied for us and now intercedes for us in heaven, will then come as their Redeemer and Savior, not to reproach them for their sins, but to fulfill his promises in them and to manifest the wonders of his grace...(3) The gratuitous mercy of God does not wish our sins to be remembered anymore, but casts them behind its back. Now what God has once wished to be covered in this life, he will not reveal in the other...
>
> Although all men universally are to be judged, it does not follow that the sins of the pious are to be published.[4]

---

2   Heppe, *Reformed Dogmatics*, 705.
3   Heppe, *Reformed Dogmatics*, 705.
4   Turretin, *Institutes of Elenctic Theology*, 3:602.

The question remains, however, whether a judgment that fails to take into account all the works of the defendant, in any sense whatsoever, is truly a judgment, as the final judgment is and must be.

Those who proclaim that the grace of the final judgment for the elect believer consists of his being exempt from the judgment appeal to John 5:24. In this text Jesus promises that the one who believes on God "shall not come into condemnation." The argument is that the word translated *condemnation* is the Greek word *krisis*, which often means *judgment*. Then Jesus teaches that the believer "shall not come into *judgment*." However, the word can mean, and usually does mean, *condemnation*. This is the meaning in the text, as the KJV rightly translates. In the final judgment, elect believers will not be condemned; they will be judged.

The text itself demands this understanding of the word and this translation. The opposite of *krisis* in the text is "everlasting life": "He...that believeth on him that sent me, hath *everlasting life*" (John 5:24). This is not escape from judgment, but the outcome of the judgment. The one who believes in God is not delivered from the judgment itself, but from the outcome of the judgment that consists of condemnation.

Yet another ground for the denial that the godly are judged in the final judgment is the teaching of 1 Corinthians 6:2–3 that "the saints shall judge the world," including "angels." The argument is that if the saints participate in the activity of judging, they cannot be the object of the judging.

Scripture, however, is clear and conclusive that also the saints appear in the judgment as those who are judged. This is the teaching of Jesus at the conclusion of his great eschatological discourse in Matthew 25:31–46. Before him who is seated on the seat of judgment are all nations. Also the sheep stand before him. They stand safely on his right hand, but they stand before him as their judge. Their works have some place in his judgment of them. These works are their good works, but they are their works. Upon the sheep, he pronounces the saving verdict: "Blessed of my Father, inherit the kingdom." The outcome of the event is their entrance into eternal life—an entrance *by way of judgment*, let it be carefully noted, and an entrance of themselves as shown, *in the final judgment*, to be *righteous*.

Also the great white throne judgment of Revelation 20 has the elect being judged in the final judgment. The outcome of their judgment is determined by their inclusion in the "book of life" (v. 15).

If the testimony of Matthew 25 and Revelation 20 might be contested on the issue, 2 Corinthians 5:10 is incontestable: "For we must all appear before the judgment seat of Christ; that every one may receive the things done in his body, according to that he hath done, whether it be good or bad." This judgment lies in the future. It is the judgment in which the judge is Jesus Christ, the man. The saints appear before Christ to be judged: "*We* must all appear," not "they," the ungodly only. It is a genuine judgment in that the works, and thus the lives, of those who are judged are examined. The verdict is rendered in accordance with the lives of those on trial. The judgment is shown to be just, therefore. And this judgment of the godly as well as of the ungodly is necessary: "We *must* all appear." The Greek original has "it is necessary." To deny the judgment of the saints, or to weaken the nature of the judgment as they do who deny that the works of the saints come up in their judgment, is to oppose a reality that is necessary for the salvation of the saints and for the glory of God. The final judgment of the saints is *necessary*.

The necessity of the final judgment of the saints, first of all, is the *theodicy*. Theodicy is the justification of God, that is, the demonstration that God is righteous in his judging of the human race, specifically righteous in his justifying of the godly and righteous in his damning of the ungodly. God must be, and must be shown to be, just when he judges (Rom. 3:4, 26). In part the theodicy consists of this, that the verdict is in accordance with the nature of the lives of humans. Even as the lives of some were ungodly, so also the verdict upon them is condemnation. Thus, justice is done to the evil of their lives. The evil of unbelief and disobedience is finally exposed for the wickedness that it is. And thus the righteousness of God, which the sinners themselves and the watching world mocked at, is vindicated.

On the other hand, as the lives of some were godly, so also the verdict upon them is justification. Thus, there is the divine testimony to the goodness of their lives. Faith and its obedience are finally manifested as the goodness that they are. And thus the righteousness of God in the lives of God's people, which sinners contemned, is vindicated. This purpose of God with the judging of his people is expressed by the Belgic Confession in article 37: "Their [the elect's] cause, which is now condemned by many judges and magistrates as heretical and impious, will then be known to be the cause of the Son of God."[5]

This judgment of the godly according to their works does not jeopardize the truth of salvation by grace alone. For the works that God recognizes and honors in the final judgment are the product of his own working in his people. God ordained the works (Eph. 2:10). Still more, God himself worked the willing and the doing of these works in his people (Phil. 2:13). In addition, in order to display and approve these works in the judgment, God must cleanse even the good

---

5 Belgic Confession 37, in Schaff, *Creeds of Christendom*, 3:436.

works that his people performed from all the corruption of sin that defiles them and would otherwise render them unfit to qualify as good works at all. Rightly, the Belgic Confession states that the good works performed by the believer are "good and acceptable in the sight of God, forasmuch as they are all sanctified by his grace."[6]

Even though the good works of the elect are the working in them of the grace of God, and even though God must sanctify the works themselves if they are to be approved by him as good, the final judgment would still compromise the gospel of grace if these good works are the *basis* of God's justifying verdict in this judgment. In fact, if the justifying of the believer in the final judgment were *based* on his good works, even in part, as is the teaching of Rome and lately also of those Reformed and Presbyterian theologians who promote the heresy that calls itself the federal vision, the final judgment would nullify justification by faith alone without works in time and history. For the final judgment is, in a way, the decisive judgment.

But the justifying of the believer in the final judgment is not *on the basis of*, or *on account of*, his works. Rather, it is *according to* his works: "according to that he hath done, whether it be good or bad" (2 Cor. 5:10). The verdict of the final judgment is in accord with the nature of one's life, whether good and holy or bad and unholy. There is harmony between one's holy life and the declaration pronouncing one righteous, as also between one's unholy life and the declaration pronouncing one guilty. This is because whom God justifies he also sanctifies. God's verdict of righteousness in the final judgment is in accord with God's salvation of the elect believer in time of sanctifying him.

The good works of the saints *manifest* their justification; they do not *constitute* their righteousness with God. The function of good works in the final judgment is that which James teaches about the role of good works in every phase of justification: "I will shew thee my faith by my works" (James 2:18).

The truth that God justifies elect sinners by faith alone, without works, applies to the judgment in the final assizes as it does to the judgment in time and history. Every saving judgment of God is "by faith without the deeds of the law" (Rom. 3:28). Also in the final judgment, "to him that worketh not, but believeth on him that justifieth the ungodly, his faith is counted for righteousness" (4:5).

Theodicy is not the only reason for the judgment of the saints according to their works. Knowledge of this truth is motivation for the child of God to abound in good works, particularly in confessing the truth of the gospel and in

---

6   Belgic Confession 24, in Schaff, *Creeds of Christendom*, 3:411. For a work of the believer to be good, not only must God sanctify the believer, but also he must sanctify the work itself.

helping the needy neighbor, especially the needy fellow Christian. The latter is the implied exhortation of Christ in Matthew 25:31–46. The setting is the final judgment. The good works that the judge remembers in a public way are those of feeding the hungry, allaying the thirst of the thirsty, housing the homeless, clothing the naked, visiting the sick, and ministering to those in prison. These needy were the brothers and sisters of Jesus. Helping them, therefore, was a helping of Jesus himself.

Merely giving a cup of cold water to one of Jesus' little ones has its reward in the final judgment (Matt. 10:42).

Failing or refusing to help them is, in effect, failing or refusing to show love to Jesus.

Surely, Jesus intended to motivate his church and her members to be active in helping the needy. The importance of the office of the diaconate is emphasized, without any negation of the necessity of personal help as the opportunity arises.

As for the motivation of judgment according to works to abound in the good work of confessing the truth of the gospel, this is the implication of Matthew 10:32: "Whosoever therefore shall confess me before men, him will I confess also before my Father which is in heaven."

This leaves the question whether also the sins of the elect believer will be brought up in the final judgment. It is especially this prospect against which some in the Reformed tradition reacted, as though this would compromise the truth that the sins of the godly have already been forgiven, and forgiven in such a way that God has cast them behind his back and into the depths of the sea (Isa. 38:17; Mic. 7:19). It is inconceivable that having thus disposed of the sins of believers, God would once again raise them in the final judgment. To do so would expose the believers to shame and detract from their comfort regarding the judgment.

Powerful as the argument seems and appealing as the sentiment against any raising of the sins of the saints in the judgment is, the denial that the judgment includes exposure of the sins of the people of God is mistaken. For one thing, it is really the denial that the saints will be judged. That some drew this conclusion from the denial of any appearance of the sins of the godly is understandable, indeed warranted. If one is not judged according to all his works, he is not judged at all. If the evil works of the believer have no place whatever in the final judgment, the believer is exempt from judgment. But Scripture includes the believer in the final judgment, and includes him as one who is judged. Scripture has him being judged "according to that he hath done, whether it be good or bad" (2 Cor. 5:10). Not only according to what he has done that was "good," but also according to what he has done that was "bad"! His judgment is a real judgment. His life—all of it—comes into view in the judgment.

But this is no cause of terror, nor even apprehension of deepest shame. Neither is it contradiction of Isaiah and Micah concerning God's casting the believer's sins behind his back and into the depths of the sea. For God will bring up the sins of believers as obliterated by the blood of Christ; as thoughts, desires, words, and deeds that with regard to guilt and shame have been completely covered by the atonement of the lifelong suffering and shame of Jesus for them; as sins that cannot weigh in the verdict regarding the believer in the final judgment, because they have already been fully weighed in the verdict of the judgment of the cross; as deeds that enter into the final judgment only as fully taken care of, fully dealt with, and fully excluded, therefore, from the outcome of the judgment. The sins of the godly appear in the judgment as that aspect of the life of the believer about which divine justice has been completely satisfied, so that this justice has no objection—none whatsoever!—to the judge's decision of justification. Divine justice has not ignored them, has not overlooked them, has not disregarded them, but has been satisfied concerning them, satisfied by Christ's suffering the punishment due them in the place of those who have done them. The shame of them will not in that day accrue to the believer, for they will appear as foul deeds, thoughts, and desires the shamefulness of which has fully accrued to the humiliated and crucified Christ.

But the sins of the elect do come up in this manner, that is, as obliterated with regard to their guilt and shame. And it is necessary that they do. Simply to ignore them would be to compromise the very nature of the judgment. Some of the evidence pertinent to the judgment would be overlooked or deliberately left out of view. In addition, the justice of God must be honored. No one, including Satan, may be allowed to charge that God is unjust in justifying his people in that he simply ignored their sins and unworthiness to inherit eternal life. God himself cannot be thus unjust.

It is also necessary for the experience of salvation on the part of the children of God that their sins appear in the final judgment. Before they step into the fullness of their salvation, they must know, as they have never so deeply and thoroughly known before, the grace of their salvation in the blotting out of their sins by the blood of God the Son in human flesh. In addition, they must be confident that the verdict that opens up to them the glories of the most intimate fellowship with God, the pleasures of the new world, and the certainty of life everlasting is solidly grounded upon a righteousness that did not ignore, but justly accounted for, their wickedness. To enter into the kingdom with the nagging fear that their sins were overlooked in the judgment would be to deprive the saints of the assurance of salvation.

As for the argument that the saints will participate in Christ's judging the world, particularly the angels (1 Cor. 6:2, 3), this does not at all imply that the saints shall not themselves be judged. Having judged the saints, Christ will honor them by having them join himself in judging others. Such is the union of Christ and the church and such is his goodness in allowing his people to share in his own glory that he will permit them to share even in this, the manifestation of his greatest glory at the end. In the language of Matthew 25:31–40, after he has judged the sheep on his right hand, *according to their works*, Christ will call to the sheep, "Come up, ye unimaginably greatly blessed of my Father, and share with me the glory of my throne by joining me in my judging of the world and of the angels." But the basis of this glory is the saints' own justification in the judgment.

That the comfort of the saints regarding the final judgment is the graciousness of the judgment, rather than their escaping the judgment altogether, is the doctrine of the Heidelberg Catechism. In answer to the question concerning their comfort regarding the final judgment, the catechism responds: "I look for the self-same One who has before offered himself for me to the judgment of God, and removed from me all curse, to come again as Judge from heaven."[7] Comfort regarding the final judgment is not that the believer will not be judged, but that the Judge is Jesus, who removed the curse, and thus all guilt and shame, from the believer.

In this question and answer about the final judgment, the catechism leans heavily on John Calvin:

> Hence arises a wonderful consolation: that we perceive judgment to be in the hands of him who has already destined us to share with him the honor of judging [cf. Matt. 19:28]! Far indeed is he from mounting his judgment seat to condemn us!…How could our Advocate condemn his clients?…No mean assurance, this—that we shall be brought before no other judgment seat than that of our Redeemer, to whom we must look for our salvation! Moreover, he who now promises eternal blessedness through the gospel will then fulfill his promise in judgment.[8]

Calvin's consolation regarding the final judgment is not at all that the elect will escape the judgment, not even that their sins do not at all come

---

7 Heidelberg Catechism Q&A 52, in Schaff, *Creeds of Christendom*, 3:323–24.
8 John Calvin, *Institutes of the Christian Religion*, ed. John T. McNeill, trans. Ford Lewis Battles, 2 vols., Library of Christian Classics 20–21 (Philadelphia: Westminster Press, 1960), 2.16.18, 1:526.

up, but that the judge will be Christ, who has redeemed them, thus satisfying divine judgment regarding the guilt of their sins, which *do* come up as blotted out.

THE JUDGE

The judge in the judgment is Jesus Christ, as the servant and representative of God. Although Jesus is qualified for this demanding task by his deity, he judges as the exalted man: "[God] will judge the world in righteousness by that man whom he hath ordained; whereof he hath given assurance unto all men, in that he hath raised him from the dead" (Acts 17:31). Jesus himself claims this work for himself, as the Father's honoring of him: "For the Father judgeth no man, but hath committed all judgment unto the Son: that all men should honour the Son" (John 5:22–23).

That Jesus is the judge is fitting since he is the one man who sought God's glory. He conducts the judgment with the whole-souled purpose that God be vindicated in all his works and ways.

At the same time, being judge is glory for Jesus, the culmination of the exaltation that began with the resurrection. Jesus himself calls his seat of judgment "the throne of his glory" (Matt. 25:31). Then is realized that every knee shall bow at the name of Jesus and every tongue shall confess "that Jesus Christ is Lord, to the glory of God the Father" (Phil. 2:10–11).

As even a merely earthly courtroom has its awe, all the more will the court of the final judgment be awesome. An especially dramatic moment in the proceedings will be the appearing before Judge Jesus of those who cooperated in the shaming, condemnation, and crucifixion of him: the members of the Jewish council, Ananias, Caiaphas, Pilate, Herod, the Roman soldiers who nailed him to the cross, and all those who mocked him, without repenting: "and they also which pierced him" (Rev. 1:7). The impenitent malefactor will remember his unbelieving challenge to Jesus (Luke 23:39). The spittle of those who spat upon him in the time of his humiliation will dry up in their mouths (Mark 14:65).

But Jesus is judge as the representative of God, so that, very really, in him God is judge. Thus with the judgeship of Jesus is to be harmonized the truth that God is judge at the final judgment: "And I saw the dead…stand before God" (Rev. 20:12). It has pleased God to perform all his works, from creation to re-creation, including the final judgment, by Jesus Christ. So must the church honor Jesus, and thus also must the church end all its praise of Jesus in praising the triune God and his glory.

STANDARD, BASIS, AND SOURCE

As has already been demonstrated, the final judgment is a real judgment—a judgment of every human and every angel as to his or her works according to the standard of the law of God. The judgment examines men's works, including the motives of the heart. The standard is the law of God, as the spiritual law of love for God and for the neighbor. For those who had the revelation of the will of God in the ten commandments, the standard is that law as made known in the Bible. For the heathen, who did not have the written or spoken law of the ten commandments but only the law made known in creation itself, including their conscience, the standard is the "work of the law written in their hearts" (Rom. 2:15). No human, whether the pagan whom the gospel never reached or the most avowed atheist, escapes the knowledge that God—the *true* God—is and that he must be served and obeyed. Therefore, all can and will be judged by the standard of the law of God.

If the standard of the judgment for the believer is the law, the basis of his judgment is the obedience of Christ, which obedience counts for the believer's own in the judgment. The verdict from the bench sounds in the ears and heart of the believer like this: "Because of my suffering the punishment of your sins in your stead and because of my obedience to the law of God on your behalf, which suffering and obedience are yours by means of your faith in me, I declare you righteous with regard to all the demand of the law of God upon you, and worthy of eternal life. Your holy life and good works demonstrate the reality of this your righteousness by faith in me."

There is also a source of the justification of the believer in the final judgment, which source is prominent in Scripture's teaching about the final judgment. This is often overlooked in discussion and debate concerning the final judgment, just as this is often overlooked in the debate over justification in time and history. What, ultimately, is the *source* of justification? What, ultimately, is the source of the happy outcome of the judgment for some? The source is eternal, gracious, unconditional election. Ultimately, the explanation of the salvation of the child of God in the final judgment is God's free choice of him unto salvation. Christ proclaimed this source in his great treatment of the final judgment in Matthew 25. The verdict of the judge is not simply "inherit the kingdom," but "inherit the kingdom *prepared for you from the foundation of the world*" (v. 34). This is Christ's declaration that the source and explanation of the favorable outcome of the judgment, including the justification of the sheep in that judgment, is God's election of the sheep in eternity.

The account of the final judgment in Revelation 20 emphatically teaches the same. In the judgment, "the books were opened: and another book was opened, which is the book of life: and the dead were judged out of those things which were written in the books, according to their works…And whosoever was not found written in the book of life was cast into the lake of fire" (Rev. 20:12, 15). The book of life is God's eternal decree of election, in which he graciously chooses some humans unto eternal life. This book determines who are justified in the final judgment. Even though those who are written in the book of life are still judged according to their works (v. 12), it is not the judgment according to their works, that is, justification by faith alone demonstrated by their works, that determines their salvation in the final judgment, but that their names are written in the book of life. For election is the source of their faith and of their justification by faith. What governs the final judgment, specifically the verdict of innocence and the outcome of everlasting salvation, is not good works but the book of life.

The great question for every human as he faces the final judgment (and every human faces the judgment) is: "Is my name written in the book of life?" And the assurance that one's name is written in the book of life is faith in Jesus Christ. Although a life of impenitent performance of evil works (for a time) is destructive of any assurance of standing in the final judgment, even as this is destructive of assurance of justification in this life, assurance of justification in the final judgment does not depend on one's good works but is the confidence that is faith—faith *alone*, without works.

Such is the importance of predestination regarding the outcome of the final judgment for humans—and angels—that Revelation 20:15 teaches that the condemnation of the ungodly in the judgment is in accord with God's eternal decree of reprobation: "And whosoever was not found written in the book of life was cast into the lake of fire." The ultimate explanation of the casting of some into the lake of fire, as the execution of the verdict of their guilt in the judgment, is that their names are not found written in the book of life. The judicial ground of their condemnation and damnation is their evil works as recorded in the book of their earthly conduct. This does not fall outside the will of God's eternal decree of predestination—his predestination of some to eternal damnation—or in the language of the text, his not writing their names in the book of life.

The Reformed creeds faithfully reflect the teaching of Scripture that the source and ultimate explanation of the justification of the godly in the final judgment is God's election. In explanation of Christ's coming again to judge the quick and the dead, the Heidelberg Catechism deliberately describes those who are justified in the judgment as "all his chosen ones": "shall take me, with all his *chosen ones*, to himself, into heavenly joy and glory."[9]

While at the same time doing full justice to the truth that the judgment will be according to works, the Belgic Confession affirms that gracious election is the ultimate explanation of the justification of some in the final judgment: "The consideration of this judgment is…most desirable and comfortable to the righteous and the *elect*…The faithful and *elect* shall be crowned with glory and honor."[10]

FURTHER FEATURES OF THE JUDGMENT

One feature of the place of good works in the final judgment of believers is the testing of preachers' exercise of their office. The result of this examination of the work of ministers of the gospel will be that the ministerial works of some will be burned, although they themselves will be saved. This is the sobering aspect of the judgment Paul warns of in 1 Corinthians 3:12–15. The final judgment will be a fiery testing of the work of ministers. There will be a reward of sound, zealous ministers for their good work in their office, which consisted of sound building upon the foundation, Jesus Christ. But the trying, or testing, of the work of ministers will also reveal that the work of others was "stubble." The fiery judgment will burn this work up as worthless. Thus, these ministers, who to a certain extent are unsound or careless, even lazy, will "suffer loss," but they themselves shall be saved, "yet so as by fire." This warning is an incentive to ministers to be faithful and zealous in the work of their office. Even though one is saved in the end, no one wants to have his life's work in his office "burned."

What is specified in Scripture concerning the sins of ministers, who nevertheless are saved in the judgment, holds also concerning the sins of others who may be considered children of God. The final judgment is more than only pronouncing the final verdict upon elect and reprobate. It also exposes and condemns actions of believers that were approved by the church and society as good and right, or at least were never condemned, and at the same time vindicates behavior of believers that even churches condemned in time and history. For example, there are the orthodox ministers whom their envious colleagues successfully blackened with false charges, even expelling them from the fellowship of the denomination. If somehow or other we may regard the sinful, envious,

---

9   Heidelberg Catechism A 52, in Schaff, *Creeds of Christendom*, 3:324; emphasis added. The importance for the Reformed faith of election for the final judgment may be inferred from the fact that this is one of the very few times that the catechism expressly mentions election.
10 Belgic Confession 37, in Schaff, *Creeds of Christendom*, 3:435–36; emphasis added.

treacherous officebearers as yet elect children of God, their sin will be exposed before the world, especially the church world, and the faithful, orthodox minister will be publicly vindicated before all. Or the lie of the church member to discredit a brother or sister, which was "successful" in history, will be undone in the final judgment, and the brother or sister who had been defamed in the church will be delivered finally of the defamation.

The final judgment will be thorough. All injustice will be set right. All falsehood will be corrected. All clandestine plots will be exposed to the brightest light. Truth will prevail, fully and finally. Justice alone will hold victorious sway in the entire field of human life and history. Coming is *judgment*, *God's* judgment, God's *thorough* judgment, God's *just* judgment, God's *final* judgment. Every unjust judgment, whether of the Supreme Court of the United States or of Reformed synods, will be reviewed, exposed, and condemned, with consequences for the impenitently unjust judges. Since all of this is the public defense of the righteousness of God, all is theodicy.

"Every valley shall be exalted, and every mountain and hill shall be made low: and the crooked shall be made straight, and the rough places plain" (Isa. 40:4). The prophet adds, "And the glory of the Lord shall be revealed" (v. 5). This is the glory of theodicy. And the child of God, especially the child of God who is abused and persecuted in this life, earnestly responds, "Come, Lord Jesus, come as judge!"

Awareness of this judgment of his work by the Lord is the reason why the apostle could say to the Corinthian church that "it is a very small thing that I should be judged of you, or of man's judgment" (1 Cor. 6:3). Indeed, this is why his own judgment of his ministry was not the important verdict upon his office for the apostle: "Yea, I judge not mine own self" (v. 3). The judgment of his work that mattered to him and that motivated him in his labor was the Lord's judgment at the end: "He that judgeth me is the Lord" (v. 4). Often the faithful minister is encouraged to persist in his official labors by this confidence, that the Lord Jesus will judge his work to have been sound and right, work that built on the foundation, work that was "gold, silver, precious stones" (3:12), despite the criticism of an unthankful congregation and even the rejection of his work on the part of a large and influential segment of the wider Christian church, or even, for that matter, on the part of unjustly critical colleagues.

Not to be overlooked in the carrying out of the judgment is the Holy Spirit. It is he who brings the totality of one's life and work to the immediate consciousness of everyone who is judged, as well as the true nature of that life and work, and then impresses upon the soul of every man the justice of the verdict. God must be just in his judging in the conscience of every human, whether justified or condemned.

The judgment at the *parousia*—the presence of Christ—will be final. The finality is not only that it is the last in a series of judgments, including the judgment at the cross; the judgment in time by faith; and the judgment at death. But it is final also because it determines the everlasting destiny of every human and angel *decisively*. There will be no subsequent and different judgment. There is no appeal to a higher court.

Jesus' coming has as its purpose the final judgment of all humans, a judgment of two distinct kinds of humans, sheep and goats, and a judgment with two different outcomes for these two kinds of humans—justification and condemnation and then eternal life and eternal death. The coming does not promise what is known as *apokatastasis*. This Greek word means *restoration* or *restitution*. It occurs once in the Bible, at Acts 3:21, where it is translated by the KJV as *restitution*: "the times of *restitution* of all things," with reference to the work of Christ at his coming of restoring both the human race, in the elect among all nations, and the world of the heaven and the earth.

This word has come to refer to the heretical doctrine that at his coming Christ will restore the human race by saving every human without exception, as also all demons, including Satan himself. Among its other errors, this doctrine denies that Christ comes for judgment. There will be no judgment according to works with a twofold outcome, as is the teaching of Christ in Matthew 25:31–46. There will rather be a universal salvation that dispenses with judgment.

The well-known Old Testament Bible commentator C. F. Keil proposed a variation of this *apokatastasis* or universal salvation. He himself described his theory of the accomplishment of the salvation of humans by Jesus at his coming as *apokatastasis*. But Keil's version was not necessarily the salvation of all humans. Rather, Christ's coming will be a proclamation of the gospel once again to all humans, specifically including the Sodom of the Old Testament. All those humans who have died in unbelief and impenitent disobedience will have the "prospect" of yet being saved. The "possibility of eventual pardon [will be] open still." Those who remain unbelieving, if such there will yet be, will be damned. Christ does not come for judgment, but to offer all humans a last chance for salvation.[11]

Also this watered-down form of an *apokatastasis* contradicts the biblical and creedal doctrine of the coming of Christ, to say nothing of its attack on the truth of predestination and on the significance of the preaching of the gospel with its working of faith in time and history. "It is appointed unto men once to die,

---

11 C. F. Keil, *Biblical Commentary on the Prophecies of Ezekiel*, vol. 1, tr. James Martin (Grand Rapids, MI: Eerdmans, n.d.), 234–36.

but after this the judgment" (Heb. 9:27)—not "after this another day of grace for the salvation of sinners," but "after this the judgment." The Christian creed confesses that "Christ shall come again to judge" all humans according to what they have done in their life, prior to their death.

THE PURPOSE OF THE JUDGMENT

The purpose of the final judgment is not to discover the destiny of individual humans, much less the destiny of angels. Satan and his crew, "reserved" as they are "in everlasting chains under darkness unto the judgment of the great day" (Jude 6), certainly do not need a final judgment to determine their destiny. God does not need a final judgment to discover the destinies of humans. He has determined the destiny of all in the decree of predestination. Neither do humans themselves need a final judgment to discover their eternal destiny. Every believer knows and is assured of his justification in the final judgment by his faith in Jesus Christ. The final judgment only confirms the verdict of God to the believer by his faith in time and history. But also the unbeliever knows the outcome of the final judgment for himself. He lived his entire life in the consciousness of his guilt before God and of the wrath of the just God upon him: "knowing the judgment of God, that they which commit such things are worthy of death" (Rom. 1:32).

In addition, prior to the conducting of the judgment, every human will have been raised in his new body, whether gloriously fitted for eternal life or shamefully fitted for everlasting death. Before the Son of man begins conducting the final judgment, he sets the sheep on his right hand and the goats on his left. The outcome of the judgment is not in question for the sheep or for the goats, and certainly not for the judge.

But the purpose of the judgment is the theodicy, that is, the justification of God, not only in his public, final verdict of salvation or damnation upon all humans and angels, but also in all his dealings with the children of men. He will not defend himself before the judgment of humans, for he is God, but he will display his perfect righteousness in all his works. Finally, he will show to Job his justice in his affliction of that man, a justice that consisted of glorifying himself in that man's confession of God's goodness despite his sufferings. Finally, he will fully convince David of the justice (as well as mercy) of his chastisements of that man in view of David's gross sins against God's law and goodness. Finally, he will display to the world his righteousness in the punishments in World Wars I and II of a world that had grievously departed from him and blasphemed him, as well as his righteousness in the punishment in the twenty-first century of a world that changed the truth of God into a lie, worshiping and serving the creature rather than the Creator, in giving it over to sodomy and lesbianism, with all the miseries attendant upon this wickedness.

Romans 3:4 is clear and conclusive in its assertion that God's purpose in all his judging, including the final judgment, is that he may be "justified in thy sayings, and mightest overcome when thou art judged." Although he makes no reference to the final judgment, Calvin captures the thought of the text when he explains, "God in all His judgments is worthy of praise, however much the ungodly may clamour and with hatred endeavor to efface His glory by their complaints."[12] God will have his day in (his own) court. Not that he must answer for his doings to anyone. As God, he himself is the standard of righteousness. But since the purpose of creation and providence in the end is his own glory, he will demonstrate before all that his government of the history of the world and his dealings with every human were right and good.

This theodicy will center on Jesus Christ. The reality of all things and of their history will be demonstrated to have been right and good in that they all had Jesus Christ as their reason for existence and in that they all served Jesus Christ. "[He is] the firstborn of every creature…All things were created by him, and for him: and he is before all things, and by him all things consist…For it pleased the Father that in him should all fulness dwell" (Col. 1:15–17, 19). The theodicy is Jesus Christ. Such is the meaning of Romans 3:4 in the context of chapters 3–5 and, indeed, in the context of the entire gospel of the book of Romans.

Romans 3:4 is explicit concerning theodicy. But Geerhardus Vos is mistaken when, in opposition to theodicy, he declares that this verse is the only text that conceivably teaches theodicy: "The only passage which in Paul actually contains the thought of a forensic vindication of God occurs in Romans 3:4."[13] Verse 26 explicitly declares that the purpose of God in justifying sinners by faith in the crucified Jesus Christ is "to declare…his righteousness: that he [God] might be just." Although the reference is to the judgment by faith under the gospel, the implication is that demonstrating God's righteousness is the ultimate purpose of all his judging, including his judging at the final judgment. Implied too is that his judging of the condemnation of unbelievers also has as its ultimate purpose the declaration of God's justice. In all his judging of humans, God declares "his righteousness."

Every statement in Scripture that the final judgment is according to the works of the one judged is, and intends to be, the justification of God in his

---

12 John Calvin, *The Epistles of Paul the Apostle to the Romans and to the Thessalonians*, tr. Ross Mackenzie (Grand Rapids, MI: Eerdmans, 1961), 61.
13 Vos, *The Pauline Eschatology*, 279.

judging. Second Corinthians 5:10 is one instance among many in the writings of Paul, as also of the other apostles. In the final judgment, "every one… receive[s] the things done in his body, according to that he hath done, whether it be good or bad." This is justice. This is the justice of God. And this demonstration of the justice of God is a purpose of the final judgment. This is theodicy.

The thought of 2 Thessalonians 1:6–10 is the second coming of Christ and the final judgment that Christ will conduct regarding all humans at that coming. The outcome of this judgment will be that those who "trouble" the church are "punished with everlasting destruction from the presence of the Lord, and from the glory of his power" (v. 9). This punishment is just with regard to the enemies of God and his church. It is also, as the apostle is at pains to declare, "a *righteous* thing with God to recompense tribulation to them that trouble you" (v. 6). In the judgment of the wicked, God displays his righteousness. The final judgment will be the justification of God, the theodicy.

THE PURPOSE OF PROCLAIMING THE FINAL JUDGMENT

God has a purpose with the church's proclamation of the final judgment for the unbelievers in the audience. The truth of the final judgment lends urgency to the call to repent and believe. This purpose the apostle expresses, in a lively fashion, in his own preaching in Acts 17:30–31: "God…now commandeth all men every where to repent: because he hath appointed a day, in the which he will judge the world in righteousness by that man whom he hath ordained; whereof he hath given assurance unto all men, in that he hath raised him from the dead." In that some believed this message, we may conclude that God made this urgent message of the coming judgment effective in them, to realize his purpose of election.

Even when the message of the final judgment does not save those to whom the message is addressed, it accomplishes the purpose of God to render reprobate unbelievers accountable for their unbelief and to add to their condemnation. This evidently was the case with the Roman official Felix, according to Acts 24:25. Paul witnessed to him of "judgment to come" (which again indicates the prominent place of the truth of the judgment in the apostolic preaching). The effect of this message was not that Felix believed and was saved. But there was an effect: "Felix trembled." The truth of the coming judgment is an awesome reality. Even the thoroughly worldly politician trembles at the thought of it, under the conviction that it is coming, and coming for him. Unjust himself (this official of the Roman government knew Paul was innocent, but kept him imprisoned and desired a bribe), Felix cannot escape the conviction that the God who is, and who is just, will judge the world, including Felix, in righteousness. The Holy

Spirit binds the truth of the coming judgment upon the soul of the unbeliever to his greater condemnation when he does not believe.

The main purpose of God with the preaching and teaching of the final judgment is the salvation of the elect. First, it is an incentive to the believer to persevere in righteous behavior, doing battle with the temptation to live unjustly. This is especially the function of the truth of the judgment when righteous behavior finds no reward in this life, but even meets with persecution and opposition. It belongs to the incentive of the expectation of the final judgment that the believer desires that God shall be publicly vindicated in the believer's life on that occasion. God's cause shall be vindicated in the righteous life of the believer.

Another aspect of the incentive provided by the final judgment is that the believer desires and expects to receive the reward of his righteous life on that occasion. That righteous conduct in this life will be rewarded in the final judgment and that this should be an incentive to this righteous conduct are the message of the parable of the talents in Matthew 25:14–30.

Second, the truth of the final judgment is the comfort of the saints regarding present persecutions and regarding the discrediting of their cause in the world. The Westminster Confession of Faith captures this saving function of the truth of the final judgment in the lives of God's people in these words: "for the greater consolation of the godly in their adversity."[14]

Third, the final judgment is the saving hope of the believer, both inasmuch as that event will be the final, decisive, public justification of the believer by which he will be saved and inasmuch as by means of this judgment he shall be redeemed, that is, enter into the complete and perfect enjoyment of redemption in the new world: "Therefore we expect that great day with a most ardent desire, to the end that we may fully enjoy the promises of God in Christ Jesus our Lord. Amen. Even so, come, Lord Jesus."[15]

In light of the description of the Christian's attitude regarding the judgment as "knowing…the terror of the Lord" in 2 Corinthians 5:11, the question ought to be raised whether the Christian is at all afraid of the final judgment. *Terror* in the text is a poor, indeed misleading, translation of the word that means *fear*. And fear ought to be understood as *reverence*, as is often the case with the word in the New Testament. The Christian reverences the Lord Jesus. He reverences him particularly as the one who will conduct the final judgment. In this reverence, the believer now labors so that he may be "accepted of him" (v. 9).

---

14 Westminster Confession of Faith 33.3, in Schaff, *Creeds of Christendom*, 3:672–73.
15 Belgic Confession 37, in Schaff, *Creeds of Christendom*, 3:436.

But no Christian who is living in faith in Jesus Christ is terrified at the thought of Jesus Christ as his judge in the final judgment. Nor does the final judgment terrorize him. Jesus the judge is the one who has removed all curse from the believer. The believer is now justified by faith alone in this Jesus; the verdict in the final judgment will be, and by the righteousness of God *must* be, the same as his verdict now: justification. Rather than being terrified at the prospect of the judgment, the believer ardently desires the judgment.

Terror at the thought of the final judgment on the part of a believer is a spiritual disease, from which he must be healed by the medicine of the gospel of grace. Those who instill terror into a believer over the judgment, whether at his death or on the world's last day, as some ministers do, are bad physicians of souls.

Another question concerning the judgment about which there is confusion and error has to do with the function of the gospel in the judgment. The error is to posit the gospel rather than the law as the standard of the judgment. Humans, it is said, will be judged by the standard of the gospel, rather than by the standard of the law. This is the error of those who really deny that the believers will be judged according to their works. As has already been demonstrated, to deny judgment according to works, and thus according to the law, is to deny the reality of the final judgment for believers. It is to exempt believers from the final judgment, contrary to the clear and repeated testimony of Scripture that also the believers will stand in the final judgment.

The great compiler of the Reformed tradition Heinrich Heppe is guilty of the error of denying that the standard of the judgment is the law and of proposing that the standard is the gospel: "The norm according to which Christ will pronounce judgment upon individuals is the gospel revealed by him, whereby Christ will consider man's works as the fruits and proofs of his faith or unbelief in himself."[16]

Heppe then quotes approvingly another Reformed theologian: "The voice, not so much of the law as of the gospel, which the apostles preached, will be the norm (of the last judgment)."[17] Taking note, rightly, of the implication of this denial of a judgment according to the law, Heppe frankly denies that the godly will be judged in the final judgment: "Hence the godly will not really be judged."[18]

---

16 Heppe, *Reformed Dogmatics*, 704.
17 Heppe, *Reformed Dogmatics*, 704. The Reformed theologian whom Heppe quotes is Bucan.
18 Heppe, *Reformed Dogmatics*, 705.

The standard of the judgment will be the law, not the gospel. This is the plain teaching of the outstanding passage on the judgment, 2 Corinthians 5:10: "According to [in other words, by the standard of] that he hath done, whether it be good or bad." The standard is not "that he hath believed or not believed," but "that he hath *done*, whether it be good or bad." The deeds of his life, whether good or bad, as determined by the law, are the standard of judgment. This is necessarily the standard inasmuch as the judging God must maintain the demands of his righteous law. God cannot dispense with his own law in judging. And the believer meets the standard not in himself, but in Jesus Christ who obeyed the law perfectly and in the judgment reckons his obedience to the law to the believer.

In addition, to the standard of judgment (not the *basis*, let it be repeated) belongs the beginning of obedience to the law by the believer, all his disobedience being forgiven by the sacrifice of Christ on his behalf and his good works being cleansed from the defilement of sin.

Regardless of the good intentions of Heppe and others, the gospel is not the standard, or norm, of the judgment of the believer in the final judgment, but the law is. The gospel is the judgment itself, or the word and content of the judgment. The verdict of the final judgment upon God's elect is the pronouncement of the gospel, the good news of gracious justification, based upon the work of Jesus Christ.

CONTEMPORARY CONTROVERSY OVER THE FINAL JUDGMENT

Any consideration in the twenty-first century of the doctrine of the final judgment that ignores the heresies of the federal vision and of the new perspective on Paul thereby makes itself guilty of conniving at these false doctrines. As the name itself expresses, the federal vision is a doctrine of the covenant. By its own confession, this doctrine is essentially a doctrine of the covenant. The doctrine is that the covenant of God in Jesus Christ is conditional. The conditions are one's act of faith and the good works that faith ought to perform. Upon the sinner's act of believing and good works depend God's covenant with the sinner and the salvation that this covenant conditionally promises.

How this concerns the final judgment is that in the final judgment the verdict of justification depends upon the sinner's having maintained his activity of faith to the very end and upon his performance of good works throughout all his life. According to this heresy, faith is merely another work of the sinner, along with the other good works that the sinner is required to perform. God's justifying judgment in the final judgment depends upon one's faith and good works. The decisive justification of the sinner is *on account of* faith and the good works of faith. It is characteristic of the federal vision, as of the new perspective on Paul with which the federal vision is one doctrinally, to appeal to Romans 2:13 as teaching what is actually the case in the final judgment: "For not the hearers of the law are just before God, but the doers of the law shall be justified."

The implications of this heresy, which the men of the federal vision are themselves happy to draw, are God-dishonoring and destructive of the comfort of the believer, especially with regard to his facing the final judgment. One can originally have been saved, in the sense of being justified, but lose this salvation, coming under the eternal condemnation of God. Like the Arminian heresy, of which it is a form, the federal vision teaches that salvation, in the end, is the achievement of the sinner himself. With Rome, the federal vision teaches justification by works, the works being the activity of faith and the good works that faith produces. It is terrifying in that it sends the sinner into the awesome courtroom of the final judgment depending upon his own works and worth for his righteousness with God. The ultimate wickedness of the theology of the federal vision is that of Pelagianism, Roman Catholicism, and Arminianism: it robs God of the glory of the salvation of sinners and, in the words and sense of Galatians 5:4, makes Christ "of no effect."

This heresy, which in a special way is false doctrine of the final judgment, has appeared in most of the reputedly conservative Reformed and Presbyterian churches in North America; has been either exonerated or approved by most of them; and is entrenched in some of them. Its appeal to the Reformed and Presbyterian churches and theologians is its doctrine of a conditional covenant.

The advocates of the federal vision in North America lean heavily on the movement that calls itself the new perspective on Paul. Even more plainly than the federal vision, the new perspective links its heretical doctrine of the final judgment, as a judgment based on the sinner's works, to its doctrine of justification (in time) on the basis of the sinner's own works. For the new perspective contends that the Reformation of the sixteenth century, and all the Reformation creeds, radically misunderstood the doctrine of justification by faith without works in Romans and Galatians. In fact, according to the new perspective, Romans and Galatians teach only that one becomes a member of the church by faith. They are not teaching about righteousness with God. They are not soteriological, but ecclesiastical. Regarding salvation, so teaches the new perspective, one is saved on the basis of faith as a work and on the basis of the good works of faith. This holds true also for the salvation of the final judgment. Prominent theologians, influential with evangelicals in North America, and indeed everywhere, embrace and promote the new perspective.[19]

THE OUTCOME OF THE FINAL JUDGMENT

The outcome of the final judgment for angels and humans is twofold: everlasting life and glory for those whom God justifies in the judgment, and everlasting death and shame for those who are condemned in the judgment. According to Jesus, at the conclusion of his thorough treatment of the last things in Matthew 24–25, "These shall go away into everlasting punishment: but the righteous into life eternal" (25:46).

Hell as a place of unending suffering of the reprobate, unbelieving wicked is an awful reality. No one taught the reality and awfulness of hell more often and more emphatically than Jesus. Hell is not the invention of Paul, or of grim, unfeeling Calvinists. It was Jesus who warned against behavior that would be punished with going "into hell, into the fire that never shall be quenched: where their worm dieth not, and the fire is not quenched" (Mark 9:43–48).

The explanation of hell is the awesome holiness of God and the unutterable evil of sin as offense against this holiness. The readiness of the modern church to deny hell is not its profound sympathy or its vehement love, but its complete lack of knowledge of the holiness of God and of the wickedness of sin. The true God is the one who inflicted the full torment of hell upon the Son of his love: "He descended into hell." The denial of hell is the effective denial of the cross of Jesus Christ and thus of salvation.

The human who knows God as holy and himself as sinner is tempted to stumble not at the reality of hell but at the existence of heaven, at least for himself. The heaven that is the gracious reward of those judged righteous in the final judgment is the place of bliss and glory that defy imagination. "Eye hath not seen, nor ear heard, neither have entered into the heart of man, the things which God hath prepared for them that love him" (1 Cor. 2:9). Such is

---

19 For a thorough examination of the theology of the federal vision and of the new perspective on Paul, including the identification of churches and theologians that defend and promote the heresy, cf. David J. Engelsma, *Federal Vision: Heresy at the Root* (Jenison, MI: Reformed Free Publishing Association, 2012) and *Gospel Truth of Justification* (Jenison, MI: Reformed Free Publishing Association, 2017). It ought to be noted here that Romans 2:13, upon which the federal vision and the new perspective hang their Pelagian hats, does not teach that in fact those who have done the law will be justified in the final judgment. Rather, the text teaches that one who looks to the law for justification and salvation must then do the law, that is, do it perfectly, without any lapse or failure. It is not enough to hear the law; one must do it. This is an utter impossibility for any and every human. Romans 2:13 is a basic premise in the apostle's argument that justification can only be by faith in Jesus.

the exalted state of heaven and its life and glory that Scripture makes little or no attempt to describe it.

The last two chapters of Revelation stretch the sanctified imagination with a figurative description of heaven and its life and glory. The passage promises a new heaven and a new earth, as the everlasting abode of those whose names are found written in the book of life. The blissful life of the elect is communion with God in the person of the incarnate Son of God, Jesus, the Lamb who was slain. Their bliss and honor are that they are the bride of the Lamb. The life of heaven for them is the intimate union and communion with God in Jesus Christ—the real marriage. This is the reality of the covenant. One last time in Scripture, salvation is promised as fellowship with God, this time in its perfection: "I will be his God, and he shall be my son" (21:7).

Excluded from the new world are all reprobate ungodly sinners and all sin. Impenitent sinners will have been banished to the "lake which burneth with fire and brimstone" (21:8). Even in the description of heaven and eternal life, Scripture is antithetical. There is a heaven, the life and glory—and *grace*!—of which is accentuated by the death and shame—and rigorous *justice*!—of hell.

Forever outside the new world also are all the effects and consequences of sin, that is, tears, death, sorrow, crying, and pain. Death with all its effects is the wages of sin. These wages have been fully paid for the inhabitants of the new world by Jesus Christ. Death is the infliction of the curse of God, and in the new world "there shall be no more curse" (22:3).

The outcome of the final judgment for those written in the book of life has been that "death and hell were cast into the lake of fire" (20:14). They have no place, or possibility of place, in the new world. Hell with its prisoners is "outside," even as the valley of Hinnom in the Old Testament was "outside" the city of God.

Adding to the grandeur and to the promise of life in the new world as fellowship with God and with each other is the representation of it as a great and grand city. The city is massive and magnificent. It is as large as the new world itself, for it is the new world in the form of the city. Its magnificence is pictured by the garnishing of the foundation of the city walls with all manner of precious stones. Again the emphasis is on the life of the new creation as fellowship, for the very idea of a city is that of the citizens of the city living together in unity. But fundamental to the life of this city is that in it God and Christ dwell with the people, for they are the temple of it.

That the new heaven and new earth take on the form of a city—the holy Jerusalem—and not of a garden, a paradise restored, emphasizes that the redeeming work of Jesus Christ is a development of the life of the church and of the creation itself beyond the garden of Eden and the life of the human race in Adam the first. The life of the city is civilization, whereas the life of a garden is rudimentary. God's goal with humanity was never that it continue cultivating plants in a garden, regardless how lovely the garden was and forever might have continued to be, had Adam not fallen. Exactly what forms this civilized life in the city might take, it is presumptuous to speculate.

Whatever forms the life in the city may take, all the citizens "shall reign for ever and ever" (Rev. 22:5). In their reigning, the citizens "shall serve [the Lamb]" (v. 3).

In this new creation, the bliss and glory of the elect, and God's being all in all in Jesus Christ, God realizes his *telos*—the end, or goal, of all things. This is the goal of God in his eternal council regarding all things and regarding all of history. In the hope of this glorious end, believers are patient in their present afflictions, grievous though they may be, reckoning that "the sufferings of this present time are not worthy to be compared with the glory which shall be revealed in us" (Rom. 8:18).

On the other hand, comfortable as his earthly circumstances may presently be, the believer yet longs for an infinitely greater good and prays earnestly, "Come, Lord Jesus"—come for *judgment*.

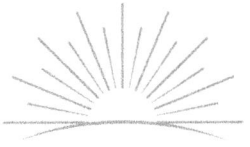

11

THE FINAL STATE

INTRODUCTION

Two important truths of eschatology make up the final state. The first is the eternal destinies of those who have been judged in the final judgment: heaven and hell. The second is the future of the creation, that is, the universe, or to use the biblical, Greek term for the heavens and the earth, the cosmos.

These two truths are related to the twofold achievement of the *parousia*, the coming or presence of Christ. The outcome of the final judgment is the verdict that sentences some humans to damnation and opens the way for others to blessedness. Also, the resurrection is the coming forth from the grave of some to eternal life. Others are raised unto damnation.

Regarding the future of the heavens and the earth, or the cosmos, the present form of it cannot continue, since the goal of earthly history has been reached and also since the present form of the cosmos is corrupted by sin and death. Besides, the creation must be made suitable to be the dwelling place of the glorified saints with their exalted head, the glorious Jesus Christ.

Although the Reformed creeds say little about this aspect of the last things, concentrating as they do upon the resurrection of the dead and upon the final judgment, as indeed is true also of Scripture, article 37 of the Belgic Confession has Jesus Christ "burn[ing] this old world with fire and flame to cleanse it."[1] A renewed creation, as well as the eternal state of humans, therefore, is creedal for the Reformed church and the Reformed believer.

To this final state of humans and of the creation, we turn now in our study of the last things, keeping in mind that the little that Scripture reveals on these subjects is not intended to satisfy our curiosity but to confirm and direct our hope.

---

1 Belgic Confession 37, in Schaff, *Creeds of Christendom*, 3:434.

THE ETERNAL DESTINIES OF HUMANS

Wherever they may be, heaven and hell are places. Heaven is the dwelling of God. To it, the risen Jesus ascended in the body. There, presently he sits in his glorified body at God's right hand. From this place, he will come again to the earth on the world's last day. In this place are the hosts of angels. The soul of the believer is taken up to this place at the instant of his death. Into this place, as their everlasting home, the saints will be taken in the body upon the resurrection of the dead. Out of this place, according to Revelation 12, Satan was evicted at the ascension of Christ.

The heaven that is the home of the resurrected saints at the presence (*parousia*) of Christ is not, of course, the blue, star-studded sky. The firmament of Genesis 1 belongs to the earthly creation. The dwelling in which God reveals himself in his majesty, at the right hand of whom Christ is enthroned, and which is the home of the departed saints is rather the "third heaven," into which Paul was caught up, whether in the body or out of the body, and where he heard "unspeakable words." This heaven is the reality of "paradise" (2 Cor. 12:2–4). Into it, the spirit of Jesus went, as did the spirit of the penitent malefactor, at the moment of their deaths (Luke 23:43).

Concerning the location of this heaven, as well as many details about it, we do well to heed the warning of John Calvin concerning these details of the third heaven. Scripture sets "bounds to knowledge." It does not satisfy our "curiosity." It does not answer our "frivolous questions." Believers are to be content with "what the Lord has seen it good to reveal to his Church."[2] It is sufficient that the believer think of this heaven as "up": Paul was "caught *up* to the third heaven." Regarding this heaven's being the "third," Calvin explains that "the number *three* is made use of…*by way of eminence*, to denote what is highest and most complete."[3]

Also hell is a place. It is the proper abode of Satan and his demons, although at present they are permitted to make their forays upon the church in the world (Jude 6). To this infernal place, the reprobate wicked are sent at the moment of their death. Upon his death, the rich man of the parable of the rich man and Lazarus "in hell…lift up his eyes, being in torments" (Luke 16:22–23). It will be the place of the everlasting punishment of the ungodly upon their final judgment. To this place, Christ, upon his resurrection, went by his Spirit to preach to the spirits in that prison (1 Pet. 3:18–20).

---

2 John Calvin, *Commentary on the Epistles of Paul the Apostle to the Corinthians*, vol. 2, tr. John Pringle (Grand Rapids, MI: Eerdmans, 1948), 370–71.
3 Calvin, *Commentary on the Epistle to [2nd] Corinthians*, 368.

Heaven and hell are not merely states of being. They are places of the existing of created beings. Created beings require places in which to live (in the case of the saints) or in which to suffer (in the case of the wicked). It is inevitable that with the questioning of the local nature of heaven and hell is increasingly denied the resurrection of the dead. Denial of the resurrection of the dead saints, as the implication of the denial of the locality of heaven, must end in the denial of the resurrection of Jesus, and not only because of the inseparable relation of the resurrection of the believers and the resurrection of Jesus. If heaven is not a place, where then is the risen Jesus, in his (human) body?

The heaven of the new world will be the place in which the justified, risen elect enjoy the perfection of eternal life and glory in body and soul. The essence of heaven's life and glory will be the sight of God in the face of Jesus Christ, God in human flesh, what the ancients referred to as the *visio Dei*, the vision of God. There will be the fullest knowledge of God that is possible for humans. Because God is infinite, and because the life of heaven is not static, the life of heaven will be the steadily increasing knowledge of God. Everlastingly, the glorified saint will know God more and more, as it were continually exploring the depths of the riches of the truth of God in Jesus Christ.

This knowledge of God will not be academic and scientific, any more than this is the knowledge of God by the believer today. It will be the knowledge of fellowship, the knowledge of God's everlastingly drawing closer to the believer and of the believer's becoming more intimate with God. It will be the knowledge of love, symbolized by the husband's knowledge of his wife and the wife's of her husband. With the passing of every year, he knows her more intimately, as she also knows him more fully and deeply, with the knowledge of love.

The Bible and sound Reformed theology know this life of heaven as the perfection of the covenant. As a place, heaven is the locale of the covenant. The life of heaven will be the consummation of the covenant of grace. Revelation 19 describes heaven as the celebration of the marriage of the Lamb and his bride, the church (v. 7). This is the fellowship of the covenant. Revelation 21 depicts heaven as the realization of the tabernacle of God with men (v. 3). This is God's communion with his people in the covenant. Both Revelation 19 and Revelation 21 present the end (Greek: *telos,* "end" as goal or divine purpose) of all things as the perfection of the covenant of God with his people in Jesus Christ.

It is striking that, in contrast with the representation of the covenant as a mere, cold contract by much of contemporary Reformed theology, the conception of the covenant as communion with God, and therefore the conception of heaven as the perfection of the covenant, have deep roots in the Christian tradition. Ambrose viewed heaven in its perfected bliss as "the blessed fellowship which the saints have with one another and with God, and of the mutually sympathetic charity which binds them together."[4]

Summarizing the Reformed tradition, Heppe writes that the return of Christ will be the consummation of the "covenant of grace," and that the "bliss of the righteous" in this consummation of the covenant will be "their communion with God," just as "the non-blessedness of the damned, eternal death, rests upon separation from God."[5]

With insight that many conservative Reformed theologians lack, contemporary Reformed theologian Hendrikus Berkhof has written, "To sense the full implication of that [eternal life], we have to go back to the often-used term 'covenant.' It expresses the union of God and man."[6]

As for the quality and nature of the life of heaven, there will be no sorrow, suffering, and tears, for "death is swallowed up in victory" (1 Cor. 15:54). The life of the inhabitants will be life in the highest and most blessed degree, far above, and better even than, the life of Adam in the first paradise. It will be the life of the risen Jesus Christ, which the risen saints now share in beginning. That life will be the most delightful joy, the most tranquil peace, and the most blessed bliss.

The life of heaven will also be the most satisfying work. With regard to peace, every man "shall sit under his vine and under his fig tree; and none shall make them afraid" (Mic. 4:4). But this description of the life of the child of God in the new world does not do justice to the activity of this life. If sitting under a vine and fig tree were all there were to life in the new world, that life would be unutterably boring. There will be more to it, much more. As Adam worked in the old paradise, prior to the fall, dressing and keeping it (Gen. 2:15), so the saints will work in the new paradise. As they had been faithful to their callings in earthly life, they will have responsibility in the new world, as is the teaching of the parable of the pounds in Luke 19:11–27: "have thou authority over… cities" (vv. 17, 19). This authority will be exercised in the activity of reigning over the new creation with the Lord Jesus (Rom. 5:17; 2 Tim. 2:12; Rev. 3:21; 5:10). Revelation 3:21 has the saints sitting with Christ on his throne. This is not only glory; it is also work.

According to Revelation 5:10, the work of the glorified saints will be priestly, as well as royal: "And hast made us unto our God kings and priests: and

---

4 Ambrose, quoted in Kelly, *Early Christian Doctrines*, 488.
5 Heppe, *Reformed Dogmatics*, 697, 710.
6 Hendrikus Berkhof, *Christian Faith*, tr. Sierd Woudstra, rev. ed. (Grand Rapids, MI: Eerdmans, 1986), 540.

we shall reign on the earth." Also the priestly work will be satisfying, rewarding, valuable, honorable, demanding work. The saints will be busy consecrating the new creation and all creatures to God.

About heaven, Irenaeus wrote: "We should hope to receive and learn more and more from God, because He is good, and possesses boundless riches, a kingdom without end, and knowledge beyond measure."[7]

Heaven's duration for everyone who enters into it upon the verdict of innocence in the final judgment is that it is everlasting. Of the sheep on the judge's right hand, who have been publicly justified, Scripture states that they go away "into life eternal" (Matt. 25:46). Life eternal is not only the highest quality of life; it is also life that does not and cannot end, exactly because of its quality as the immortal life of Jesus. First Thessalonians 4:17 assures the believers that upon the coming of Christ they shall be caught up into the air "to meet the Lord," and "so shall we ever be with the Lord." *Ever* being with the Lord is life *everlasting*. The explanation of the everlasting life of the elect child of God in heaven is that his life is a participation in the immortal life of the risen Jesus Christ. If the resurrected child of God can die, the risen Jesus can die also. But "Christ being raised from the dead dieth no more; death hath no more dominion over him" (Rom. 6:9).

With Scripture, the Reformed faith believes and teaches hell as the place in which the resurrected reprobate ungodly suffer the fullness of eternal death and shame in body and soul as punishment for their unbelief and other sins. The essence of this torment is the death and shame of separation from God, what Heppe calls "the unbliss of abandonment by God,"[8] although this separation from God carries with it also the active infliction of the fire of God's wrath: "Whosoever was not found written in the book of life was cast into the lake of fire" (Rev. 20:15). No one, not even the damned in hell, can escape God. If he is not present in his blessing, he is absent with the presence of his curse. In the New Testament, especially prominently in the teaching of Jesus, the admittedly awful reality of hell is taught by the Greek word *gehenna*. This is the Greek word translated *hell* in Mark 9:43, where Jesus warns that it is better to go into life maimed, than having two hands "to go into hell" (Greek: *geennan*).

This word for hell derives from a site on the outskirts of Jerusalem that was altogether dreadful and shameful. It was a valley on the southeast side of the city known as the "valley of the children of Hinnom" (2 Kings 23:10; Hebrew: *gee…*

---

7   Irenaeus, *Against Heresies*, II, 28, 3, in *The Scandal of the Incarnation: Irenaeus Against the Heresies*, tr. John Saward (San Francisco: Ignatius Press, 1990), 110.
8   Heppe, *Reformed Dogmatics*, 710.

Hinnom, hence *Gehenna*). In this valley, idolatrous Israelites burned their little children on the fiery arms of the idol Molech as sacrifices to the cruel god (2 Kings 23:10; 2 Chron. 33:6; Jer. 7:31–32). The valley served as the dump of the city. There the flames of fire continually flickered, burning not only the garbage of the city, but also the carcasses of dead animals and unburied criminals. The valley of Hinnom was outside the holy city! *Outside*!

Gehenna in biblical times was the place of dreadful sin and disgusting shame. Thus, it came to represent the place of the suffering of the terrible punishment of sin as a fire that is never extinguished and the place of indescribable shame.

The reality of hell is awesome. Even though the common use of it by the world in everyday discourse trivializes hell, the ungodly exert utmost effort not to think on the reality. Even the child of God finds it almost unbearable to think seriously for more than a few minutes on the reality of hell and the endless, awful suffering of hell by humans. The denial of hell by nominal Christians as well as by the unbelieving world is understandable—inexcusable in light both of the testimony of Scripture and of the glimmerings of natural light, but understandable. Hell in all its awful reality is due, first, to the dreadfulness of sin and, second, to the infinite righteousness and holiness of God against whom sin is committed. In explanation of God's punishment of sin in time and in eternity, the Heidelberg Catechism states that "God is…just; wherefore his justice requires that sin, which is committed against the most high majesty of God, be also punished with extreme, that is, with everlasting punishment both of body and soul."[9]

The duration of hell is that it is everlasting—without end. The explanation is that hell is punishment of sin, not a purifying of the sinner with a view to eventual deliverance from the suffering. In the words of Christ Jesus, he will send those whom he condemns in the judgment "into everlasting fire" (Matt. 25:41), "into everlasting punishment" (v. 46).

As there will be degrees of bliss in heaven, so also there will be degrees of suffering in hell. The punishments will be commensurate with the offenses. Those with a fuller knowledge of God's will "shall be beaten with many stripes," whereas "he that knew not, and did commit things worthy of stripes, shall be beaten with few stripes. For unto whomsoever much is given, of him shall be much required" (Luke 12:47–48). It will be more tolerable in the day of judgment for heathen Tyre and Sidon than for Chorazin and Bethsaida, in which cities Christ performed his mighty works and taught the gospel. The fire of hell will be less hot for vile Sodom than for religious but unbelieving Capernaum

---

9 Heidelberg Catechism A 11, in Schaff, *Creeds of Christendom*, 3:311.

(Matt. 11:20–24). The punishment of the apostate, disobedient, nominally Reformed man will be more severe than that of the pagan who never heard the gospel.

Hell does not represent the defeat of the God of grace in Jesus Christ, as is charged against the doctrine of hell by contemporary theologians, unless God desires and wills the salvation of all humans without exception. If God in grace desires the salvation of all humans, hell is indeed God's defeat—his everlasting defeat. But God has not purposed the salvation of all humans. The biblical doctrine of predestination teaches that God has elected some only and reprobated others. The damnation of the lost is fully and truly their own responsibility; it is the punishment they deserve. But this damnation is in accordance with God's eternal decree appointing them to this punishment (Rom. 9). Hell spells no defeat of God also in that God is glorified by "the terrible vengeance which God shall execute on the wicked."[10] God's glorification of himself in the damnation of the unbelieving and disobedient is especially the illustration and recommendation of his grace in the salvation of the elect, who are equally deserving of the punishment of hell with those who perish.[11]

In spite of the revelation of Scripture, the denial of hell abounds among professing Christian theologians, as well as the cults. The denial takes many forms. There is outright universalism, that is, the doctrine that eventually, perhaps by way of purification for a time in the fires of hell, all will be saved. This was the teaching of the early theologian Origen. His theology of the eternal destiny of all rational, moral creatures demanded that even Satan be saved in the end.[12]

In our day, the theory of universalism becomes popular and respectable through the doctrine of the enormously influential Karl Barth. Barth's espousal of universalism is evident, although he proposes it cautiously. The doctrine has his heart, although his theological head, unable to ignore the clear and conclusive testimony of Scripture to the contrary, cannot be certain.

> In grateful recognition of the grace of the divine freedom we cannot venture the opposite statement that there cannot and will not be this final opening up and enlargement of the circle of election and calling [that is, that all humans in the end will be saved]…No one outside or alongside Him [Jesus Christ] is rejected…There is, therefore, no place outside or alongside Him for…Esau.[13]

---

10 Belgic Confession 37, in Schaff, *Creeds of Christendom*, 3:435.
11 See the Canons of Dordt 1.15, in Schaff, *Creeds of Christendom*, 3:584.
12 See Kelly, *Early Christian Doctrines*, 469–74.
13 Karl Barth, *Church Dogmatics*, II/2 (Edinburgh: T. & T. Clark, 1967), 419–23.

Even more revealing is what Barth says about the likelihood of the final salvation of all humans at the very end of his treatment of "The Holy Spirit and Christian Hope." Here, Barth is bold to describe his doctrine as "*apokatastasis* or universal reconciliation."

> There is no good reason why we should forbid ourselves...openness to the possibility that in the reality of God and man in Jesus Christ...there might be contained the super-abundant promise of the final deliverance of all men...[that is] of an *apokatastasis* or universal reconciliation.[14]

Since Barth's universalism is based on his conviction that the saving lovingkindness of God and the atoning death of Christ have all humans as their objects and beneficiaries, his conclusion of universalism is sound—on Barth's thinking. The saving love of God and the atoning death of Christ assure the salvation of all their objects. They cannot fail. If they fail, God fails. A love of God and a cross of Christ for all humans rule out eternal punishment. Indeed, they rule out punishment entirely.

The Dutch Reformed theologian Hendrikus Berkhof gives credence to and advances the false doctrine of universalism: "The darkness of rejection and God-forsakenness cannot and may not be argued away, but no more can and may it be eternalized. For God's sake we hope that hell will be a form of purification."[15] Not to be overlooked in Berkhof is that he suggests that an eternal hell reflects badly on God: "For God's sake..." The implied charge is that God would not be good, were he to punish sinners in hell. This is, in fact, a denial of the grace of salvation. Salvation is no longer gracious but necessary. According to Berkhof, it is necessary that God save sinners. Thus is evident what the Canons of Dordt confesses, namely, that the truth of reprobation with its end in the punishment of hell illustrates the grace of salvation, so that the denial of hell carries with it the denial of the grace of salvation. Denial of eternal punishment is a form of the denial of the grace of salvation.

Historically, annihilationism, that is, the doctrine that those who are not saved pass out of existence, has been the heresy of the cults, for example, the Jehovah's (false) Witnesses. Of late, the detestation of the reality of hell moves nominal evangelicals to deny eternal punishment. A number of reputedly evangelical theologians advance what is called "conditional immortality." This is the teaching that immortality, which for them is everlasting existence, is conditioned

---

14 Barth, *Church Dogmatics*, IV, 3, 1, tr. G. W. Bromiley (Edinburgh: T. & T. Clark, 1961), 477–78.
15 Berkhof, *Christian Faith*, 536.

upon faith in Jesus Christ. Only believers exist forever. Those without faith perish in the sense of passing out of existence. These theologians include John R. Stott; Greg Boyd; Philip E. Hughes; Michael Green; Clark Pinnock; Edward Fudge; and F. F. Bruce.[16]

In addition to these explicit denials of hell, much of evangelical Christianity is silent about hell in its preaching and teaching. It is as if there is no hell, or if there is a hell, as though hell has no place in the preaching of the gospel. The same becomes increasingly true of orthodox Reformed preaching. Hell is denied by silencing the teaching of it. There is today a sore, and likely cowardly, lack of the preaching of hell.

The preaching of hell makes known the holiness, righteousness, and majesty of God—of the God who *is*. The preaching of hell impresses upon the believing congregation the enormity of the suffering of Jesus in our stead and on our behalf, who, according to the church's creed, descended into hell. It brings home to the believing soul the greatness of the love of God, who gave his Son into this misery on behalf of the people whom he elected. The preaching of hell is a warning to the unbeliever: the end of his way of unbelief and disobedience is hell. He must be left without excuse. And not only a warning to the unbeliever! God uses the preaching of hell to warn his impenitent children that the wages of the sins they are presently living in is the death of hell. Such warning, in the context of the fullness of the gospel, is blessed by God to bring the sinning child to repentance. In an article confessing the truth of the perseverance of the saints, the Canons of Dordt admonishes that God preserves his saints by the "threatenings" of his word.[17] These threatenings include the warning of eternal punishment in hell.

No one is scared into salvation. But many are admonished into salvation, when the admonition is an aspect of the call of the gospel.

Hell must have much more of a place in the preaching of Reformed churches than it presently has, at the beginning of the twenty-first century. It is biblical truth. It was prominent in the teaching of Jesus. In its own antithetical way, it is part and parcel of the gospel of grace.

The human who knows God as holy and himself as sinner is not tempted to stumble at the reality of hell but, on the contrary, at the existence of heaven, at least for himself. The heaven that is the gracious reward of the righteous is the place of blessing and glory that defy imagination, and for the most part the ability even of the word of God to describe it to us earthly mortals. The apostle

---

16 See https://www.jewishnotgreek.com.
17 Canons of Dordt 5.14, in Schaff, *Creeds of Christendom*, 3:595.

made no attempt to describe the things that he saw and heard when he was caught up to "the third heaven" (2 Cor. 12:2–5).

The most that Scripture does say about heaven is its figurative description of the new creation, heaven and earth, in the last two chapters of the Bible, Revelation 21 and 22. This brings up the second grand work of Christ upon the completion of the final judgment: the glorious future of the cosmos (or universe of the heaven and the earth).

THE FUTURE OF THE COSMOS

The *parousia*, or coming, or presence, of Christ as judge of all will bring about the destruction of the universe, the cosmos of the heaven and the earth created by God in the beginning. This destruction of the world is fitting because it has been corrupted by the sin of Satan and the angels that rebelled with him and by the sin of Adam and the human race. But Christ will destroy the world in such a way that the destruction will serve the purpose (or goal) of his renewal of the universe as the new heaven and the new earth. The *parousia* and judgment will be the end of the old, earthly history; of the old, earthly time and space; and of the entire old creation.

Christ will shake the old creation away by a massive earthquake: "Yet once more I shake not the earth only, but also heaven" (Heb. 12:26). The destroying earthquake will be accompanied by an intense fire that will dissolve the very elements of the creation: "the day of God, wherein the heavens being on fire shall be dissolved, and the elements shall melt with fervent heat" (2 Pet. 3:12). Out of the fire, Peter adds at once, will emerge "new heavens and a new earth, wherein dwelleth righteousness" (v. 13). Speaking more precisely of the purpose and effect of the destroying earthquake and fire, 1 Corinthians 7:31 declares that "the *fashion* of this world passeth away." Not the world absolutely, not the very essence of the world, but the *fashion*, or *form*, of the present world is destroyed and passes away. The transliteration of the Greek word translated *fashion* is *scheme*: the scheme of this world passes away in the earthquake and fire.

With the passing away of the world passes away also all the cultural works of humans: paintings; music; statuary; books; philosophy; technology; and all else invented, constructed, and produced in any way by man. Barth's supposition that he would listen to the music of Mozart, for all its appreciation of good, earthly music, is mistaken. In comparison with the melody of the music of the angelic host and of the songs of the redeemed, the music of Mozart would sound raucous noise. Besides, the music of Mozart is corrupted by the sinfulness of that ungodly composer. Even Handel's *Messiah* will have been burned and destroyed. For all its beauty, and even quotation of holy Scripture, the oratorio is part of the sin-cursed world. Hendrikus Berkhof is in error in understanding Revelation 21:24, 26 as teaching that "the cultural treasures of the nations are brought into it [the new world]."[18] The "glory and honour of the nations" are the spiritual riches worked into them in the salvation of them by the Spirit of Christ. These are not cultural but spiritual.

Revelation 20:11 makes the destruction of the present creation with all its cultural artifacts, whether Beethoven's 9th Symphony or Van Ruisdael's *The Storm,* part of the final judgment and explains the destruction: "from whose face [the face of God in Jesus Christ as the judge, sitting on the great white throne of judgment] the earth and the heaven fled away; and there was found no place for them." The heaven and the earth are tainted, and in the case of the earth thoroughly corrupted, by sin. It is as if the creation knows its corruption and guilt and therefore willingly and hurriedly passes away in abject acknowledgment of its unworthiness in its judgment. Mozart's music does not plead its cultural goodness but acknowledges its spiritual corruption and, in its corruption, willingly submits to the judgment of Christ that destroys it. Implied by the guilty flight of the earth and all its contents from the face of Christ is that the source of all earthly culture was not a (common) grace of God, but only the sinful mind and will of depraved mankind. A grace of God, even if common, would stand its ground in the judgment, not flee away.

If it is understandable that the earth and all its culture must be destroyed because of its guilt and corruption in the rebellion of Adam, its head, why must the heaven also be destroyed? The answer is that it too was defiled by sin. In fact, sin originated in heaven with the revolt of Lucifer/Satan and the angels who followed him. That rebellion stained the precincts of heaven. Neither may heaven endure in its present condition. Heaven too, in its present form, must be destroyed, so that it may be renewed by Jesus Christ. Heaven also flees from the awesome face of Jesus Christ on his throne of judgment (Rev. 20:11).

Yet the destruction of the present world (biblically: *kosmos*) of the earth and the heaven will not be annihilation. The shaking away of the old world by the

---

18 Berkhof, *Christian Faith,* 543. Also Richard J. Mouw is mistaken in supposing that the cultural products of the human race will find a place in the new world. As Calvin explains in his commentary on the passage, Isaiah 60, upon which Mouw largely bases his eschatology, is a prophecy of the adding to the church of the elect among the Gentiles, which elect converts include "princes and nobles." As for the riches and various "cultural products" that accompany the kings, Calvin remarks: "That benefit which Isaiah puts into the possession of the Church is spiritual, and the brightness which he promises is spiritual; and consequently, these things relate to the spiritual kingdom of Christ" (*Commentary on Isaiah,* vol. 4 [Grand Rapids, MI: Eerdmans, 1956], 276). See Richard J. Mouw, *When the Kings Come Marching In,* rev. ed. (Grand Rapids, MI: Eerdmans, 2002).

massive earthquake is the destruction of its present form. The earthquake shakes the world into existence in its new, re-formed form. The coming fire melts down the old world to its basic elements, its atoms, as it were. These basic elements of the creation Christ then cleanses and refashions as the new world. There will be the same radical change but fundamental identity with regard to the creation as will be true of the resurrected bodies of the saints.

In salvation, God does not annihilate his works, in order to start over with new and different works. But the salvation of the creation of the heaven and the earth will be a "regeneration" of the creation (Matt. 19:28). It will be a "restitution [or restoration] of all things" (Acts 3:21). It will be the deliverance of the creation "from the bondage of corruption into the glorious liberty of the children of God" (Rom. 8:21). The new world will not be completely other than the old world; it will be the very same world completely renewed.

By way of the judgment of earthquake and fire, the Spirit of the exalted Jesus Christ renews the original creation with the life of Christ, so that the creation itself in its own creaturely manner shares in and manifests the glory of Christ. Only thus can it be the dwelling place of Christ and his church.

Beyond all doubt and contradiction, the new world does not come by natural, evolutionary development, but by wonder and catastrophe—by earthquake and fire. "In the end a catastrophe, a divine act of intervention, terminates the rule of Satan here on earth and brings about the completion of the unshakable kingdom of heaven…The crisis, or judgment…that he [Christ] precipitated by his first coming he consummates at his second coming."[19]

In this new creation, as the home of the elect church in her bliss and glory and as the world in which God shall be all in all, God will have realized his goal, his end, his purpose with all things. This goal is to "gather together in one all things in Christ, both which are in heaven, and which are on earth; even in him" (Eph. 1:10).

In order that the creation of the heaven and the earth might be worthy of this honor, Jesus redeemed it, along with those who will live in it, by his death. By the blood of the cross of Christ, God reconciled "all things unto himself; by him, whether the things on the earth, or the things in the heavens" (Col. 1:20; literal translation of the Greek original).

Sharing thus in the saving, eternal purpose of God and in the redemption of the cross of Christ, the world of the heaven and the earth will be delivered from its present bondage of corruption in order to share in the liberty of the glory of the children of God (Rom. 8:21).

---

19 Bavinck, *Reformed Dogmatics*, vol. 4: *Holy Spirit, Church, and New Creation*, 684–85.

For this grand salvation of itself in the day of Christ, the non-human creation of the heaven and the earth now groans in its present misery and eager expectation of its deliverance in the day of Christ (Rom. 8:22). Occasionally the listening believer hears the groaning, as, for example, in the rumbling of the earthquake and in the roaring of the storm. As creation is vast, so its groaning is loud.[20]

This groaning of the creation is not merely the expression of its misery, under the curse of God on account of man's sin. Rather, it is the groaning of intense hope. It is the groaning of travail: the present creation is in labor, to bring forth the new creation. As the mother groans, in the pain of giving birth to be sure, but also, and especially, in the eager anticipation of her offspring, so is the travail of the creation. In its own non-conscious, providentially increated way, creation hopes for the day of Christ.

Romans 8:19 uses another figure to express the hope of the inanimate creation for the presence (parousia) of Christ and the "manifestation of the sons of God." Creation has an "earnest expectation" of the coming of Christ, where *earnest expectation* is the translation of a Greek word that literally describes one's stretching his neck to the utmost limits in order to see what is desired in the distance. It is as though creation extends its neck in hope of catching the first glimpse of the presence of Christ at the end, inasmuch as Christ will deliver it from its present bondage of corruption.

All of this striking testimony to the hope of the inanimate creation, astounding as it is, serves the purpose of confirming, or, if the hope has waned, restoring, the hope of the children of God for the presence of Christ at his coming again. "And not only they, but ourselves also, which have the firstfruits of the Spirit, even we ourselves groan within ourselves, waiting for the adoption, to wit, the redemption of our body. For we are saved by hope" (Rom. 8:23–24).

With creation, we groan.

"Come, Lord Jesus."

---

20 I write this as a powerful hurricane strikes the southern coast of the United States. Advanced science, which for all its knowledge cannot penetrate to the fundamental truth of earthly realities, analyzes the storm only in terms of atmospheric pressures, ocean temperatures, and the like. The truth of such earthly realities having been revealed to him by holy Scripture, the believer hears creation groaning, loudly (with a voice that even the atheist hears, although in his spiritual deafness he does not perceive), for its deliverance from the bondage of corruption into the liberty of the glory of the children of God. The noise and turbulence of the hurricane are creation's travail in bringing forth the new world.

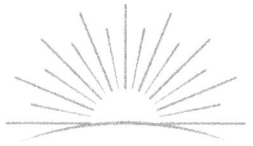

EPILOGUE

In its confession of the gospel truth of eschatology—the doctrine of the last things—the Reformed, Christian faith stands alone.

The belief of the heathen is that history is an endless cycle and that the heavens and the earth, having come into existence accidentally, will likewise perish, in one way or another, accidentally. As for the individual human, at death either he is translated into a hall of pleasure (but only in the soul) in which he can discuss philosophy with Socrates forever (a prospect of dubious eternal pleasure for most), or he passes out of existence entirely.

Speak to a heathen, whether of the first or of the twenty-first century, of the resurrection of a dead body, of a judgment to come, and of an everlasting death or life in body and soul, and the reaction is that of the Athenians of old: they mock (Acts 17:32).

Evolution, which forms the thinking concerning eschatology of multitudes of moderns, consigns every human to a brief, meaningless life ending in the decay of the grave. For some, the hopeless "science" of evolution results in the despairing behavior of "eat, drink, and be merry, for tomorrow we die." For others, it results in the sudden suicide of shooting oneself or the drawn-out suicide of drunkenness and drugs. Still others put on a show of bravado, putting the thought of death and the final judgment out of mind, as best they can. "As best they can," because God's witness to himself and testimony of the coming judgment are inescapable. He impresses this witness and testimony upon the souls of all. When Paul "reasoned of…judgment to come, [the pagan] Felix trembled" (Acts 24:25).

The original source of the saying is uncertain, but the sense of it is unmistakable: "Life is one d---thing after another, and death is the thing after that." The saying gives expression to the unbeliever's awareness of death as a prominent, unavoidable, decisive element of the reality of eschatology for himself and all humans who die outside of Christ. Not only did this anguished outcry give expression to the unbeliever's despair in the face of death, but also it rightly recognized that a hopeless death renders all of life meaningless as well, accomplished as that life may seem. Ending in a death without hope, all of life is merely "one d--- thing after another."

Similar was the declaration of the hopelessness of human life by the German atheist philosopher Friedrich Nietzsche, expressed in his translation of an ancient Greek text: "The best of all things is not to be born, not to be, to be nothing. But the second best thing for you is to die soon."[1] This statement too is the analysis of life apart from the eschatology of the Christian gospel.

Also much of evangelicalism is riddled with unsound theories of the last things. Therefore, the hope it offers is vain. Hordes expect a future millennium of an earthly victory of the kingdom of Christ within history, prior to the very end, whether of a postmillennial or of a premillennial stripe. Volume 1 of this set of works on eschatology exposes this vain hope.

Prominent evangelical theologians now promote a groundless universalism, or a conditional immortality. According to the latter, there will be no hell, at least, no everlasting hell. The "gospel hope" of many, then, is simply that they pass out of existence. Some hope!

Within Presbyterian circles today, influential theologians terrify all who pay heed to them with the doctrine that there comes a final judgment that will be conditioned upon their works (the federal vision). No one who believes this false gospel can die in peace. Like the theology of the Roman Catholic Church, both with its teaching of purgatory for nearly all and with its doctrine of salvation by works, the theology of the federal vision is an eschatology of hopelessness.

Only the creedal Reformed Christian faith proclaims the biblical, hopeful gospel of the end. This gospel is good news, as a fundamental aspect of the gospel of grace. It is good news in itself, and as such. But it is not good news for all humans. There will be a final judgment of all humans, and the judgment will be according to the works of those who are judged. This judgment will have a happy outcome for those Christians whose faithful confession of Christ made them burning torches in the garden of Caesar Nero. In this hope, they sang the psalms as they died. For Nero, the outcome will be the righteous punishment of everlasting suffering in the fires of hell.

The good news of the biblical doctrine of the last things, like the good news of the gospel in its entirety, is particular. It is good news for the elect alone, who believe in Jesus and, by this faith, walk in obedience to the law of God, even though not perfectly.

---

1 Friedrich Nietzche, *The Birth of Tragedy and Other Writings*, ed. Raymond Geuss and Ronald Speirs, trans. Ronald Speirs (Cambridge: Cambridge University Press, 1999), 23.

For them, eschatology is a message of hope—hope for themselves in the resurrection of the body, sharing in the immortality of the risen Christ Jesus; hope for a favorable verdict in the final judgment; hope for everlasting life and glory with Jesus and all the saints in the new world.

The content of this book on the last things is fundamentally the hope of the believer: the risen and glorified Jesus Christ is coming, coming for him or her.

This is the future!

INDEX

A
Abel, 1:252
abomination of desolation, 2:94–2:97
abortion, 2:15–2:16
Abraham, 1:312, 1:314, 1:315–1:316, 1:318–1:319, 1:320, 1:330
AD 70, 2:22, 2:24, 2:28, 2:96, 2:115
Adam, 1:252
Alexander, Charles D., 1:276
Alexander, Joseph Addison, 1:63
Amesius, 2:139
amillennialism
    great tribulation viewpoint within, 2:99
    introduction to, 1:165
    messianic kingdom victory and, 1:166–1:167, 1:174
    overview of, 1:87–1:88
    postmillennialism *versus,* 1:129–1:130, 1:142–1:143, 1:211, 2:23n2:6
    precursory signs and, 1:84
    premillennialism *versus,* 1:331–1:332
    Reformed, 1:88–1:96
    Revelation understanding within, 2:27
    spiritual victory and, 1:167–1:169
    teachings of, 1:232
    untimely victory and, 1:169–1:170
    warning within, 1:258–1:259
Amos, 1:187, 1:262
Anabaptist movement, 1:7–1:8
An Eschatology of Victory (Kik), 1:211
angels, 2:107, 2:138, 2:140, 2:145, 2:159
animal sacrifice, 1:264–1:266, 1:328n1:23
annihilationism, 2:170–2:171
antichrist
    as ape of Christ, 2:86

apostasy and, 2:35, 2:54–2:57
appearance of, 2:15
battle of Armageddon and, 2:100–2:102
as beast, 2:78
church *versus,* 1:139, 2:67–2:68, 2:98–2:99
coming of, 1:20
within Daniel 9, 1:288
defeat of, 1:132–1:133, 1:136, 1:213, 1:259, 2:88–2:91
empowerment of, 2:86–2:87
faith and, 2:90–2:91
false church and, 2:77–2:85
futurity of, 2:66–2:68
God and, 2:88
gospel of, 2:78
identity overview of, 2:71–2:72
Jesus' control over, 2:43, 2:88–2:89
against the Jews, 1:257–1:258
kingdom of, 2:72–2:77
man of, 2:85–2:88
within the millennium, 1:103
miracles of, 2:87
nature of, 2:64–2:66
overview of, 2:63–2:64, 2:93
persecution from, 1:136, 2:31, 2:75
personal, 2:56
as political, 2:83, 2:84
preaching of the gospel and, 2:41–2:44
as precursory sign, 2:5, 2:11, 2:13, 2:18, 2:68–2:69
preterism viewpoint regarding, 1:151
providence of God and, 2:58
realization of, 2:14
restraint of, 2:43–2:44

rise of, 2:42–2:43
Roman Catholic Church and, 1:155, 1:159, 2:82–2:83
Satan and, 2:65–2:66, 2:75
similarity to Christ of, 2:86
spiritual nature of, 2:75
spiritual warfare against, 2:27
unpreparedness for, 1:231–1:233
Westminster Confession of Faith writings regarding, 1:30
wickedness of, 2:87–2:88
work of, 1:132
worship of, 2:54–2:55, 2:76
anti-Judaism, 1:300–1:302
antinomianism, 1:336–1:346, 2:48–2:49
Antiochus Epiphanes, 2:75, 2:94–2:95
anti-semitism, 1:320–1:321
apostasy
    antichrist and, 2:35, 2:54–2:57
    as beast, 2:78
    of the church, 1:121, 1:124–1:125, 1:150, 2:17, 2:47, 2:51, 2:52, 2:59
    defined, 2:16
    as ecclesiastical, 2:48
    examples of, 2:17, 2:60
    faith and, 2:58–2:61
    generational aspects of, 2:47–2:48
    as God's punishment, 2:57
    gradual development of, 2:17
    as "in here," 2:51
    iniquity and, 2:16
    within Jeremiah's day, 2:17
    nature of, 2:46–2:54
    overview of, 2:45–2:46
    as precursory sign, 1:119, 2:4, 2:46, 2:51
    of present day, 2:59–2:60
    providence of God and, 2:57–2:58
    white horse and, 2:40–2:41
apostles, 1:20, 2:137
Apostles' Creed, 1:4, 1:43, 1:223, 2:110, 2:137
appearing (epiphaneia), 2:108–2:109
Aristotle, 1:75
Arius, 1:14
Armageddon, battle of, 1:132–1:133, 1:134, 1:140, 1:211, 2:74, 2:100–2:102

Arminianism, 2:52, 2:56, 2:158
Arminius, James, 2:52
Artaxerxes, King, 1:283
ascension of Jesus Christ, 1:21–1:22
Athanasian Creed, 2:50, 2:110
Athanasius, 1:56–1:57
Augsburg Confession, 1:24
Augustine, 1:4, 1:8

B

Bahnsen, Greg, 1:13, 1:105, 2:23
Banner of Truth, 1:13
Barak, 2:101
Barker, Kenneth L., 1:299, 1:332
Barth, Karl, 1:10–1:11, 1:27, 2:169, 2:170
Bavinck, Herman, 1:91, 1:186, 1:247–1:248, 1:286–1:287, 2:12
beasts, four, significance of, 2:72–2:73
Before Jerusalem Fell (Gentry), 2:22–2:23
beheaded souls, 1:90, 1:91, 1:94, 1:116–1:117, 1:209
Behold, He Cometh! (Hoeksema), 1:15, 1:140
Belgic Confession
    overview of, 1:24–1:25
    quote within, 1:6, 1:50–1:51, 1:72–1:73, 1:78, 1:214–1:215, 1:224, 1:249, 1:250–1:251, 1:315, 1:317, 1:330, 2:100, 2:111–2:112, 2:124, 2:142, 2:149, 2:163
believers
    coming of Jesus Christ (parousia) and, 2:111–2:112
    daily life of, 2:19–2:20
    death of, 2:8
    eternal destinies of, 2:164–2:172
    falling away of, 2:5
    final judgment and, 1:24, 2:155
    grief of, 1:224
    immortality of, 1:79–1:80
    intermediate state of, 1:26, 1:61–1:62, 1:64–1:65
    judgment of, 2:142–2:144
    justification for, 2:147
    resurrection of, 1:24, 1:60
    virtues of, 2:19
    work of the Lord by, 2:134
    See also saints

Benedict XVI (Pope), 1:103n1:8
Berkhof, Hendrikus, 2:166, 2:170, 2:173
Berkhof, Louis, 1:83
Berkouwer, G. C., 2:55
biblical realism, 1:195–1:196
birth pangs, 2:11, 2:18
black horse, significance of, 1:168
Blaising, Craig A., 1:324, 1:328
blessed hope, 1:86, 1:100, 1:214, 1:223, 1:226, 1:238, 1:243. *See also hope*
Bock, Darrell L., 1:268, 1:328
body, resurrection, 2:126–2:127, 2:128–2:130, 2:166–2:167
body sleep, 1:49–1:51
Boer, Harry R., 1:11
Boettner, Loraine, 1:86–1:87, 1:112, 1:123–1:124, 1:142
Bonda, Jan, 1:11
book of life, 2:68, 2:90, 2:148, 2:160, 2:167
Boyd, Greg, 2:171
Brakel, Wilhelmus à, 1:109, 1:159, 1:159–1:160, 1:177, 1:199–1:201
Brown, David, 1:109–1:110
Bruce, F. F., 2:171
Bullinger, Heinrich, 1:21
Bultema, Harry, 1:336, 1:342–1:345, 1:346, 1:348
Burns, J. Lanier, 1:298–1:299, 1:304

C

Caesar Nero, 1:151–1:152
Calvin, John, 1:9, 1:58, 1:66, 1:67, 1:185–1:186, 1:268–1:269, 1:276, 1:319–1:320, 2:39, 2:106n2:2, 2:109, 2:145, 2:153, 2:164
Calvinism, 2:26
Canons of Dordt, 1:14, 1:27–1:29, 1:230, 1:317, 2:52, 2:171
catastrophes, as precursor sign, 2:11, 2:15
Chafer, Lewis Sperry, 1:38, 1:324, 1:337, 1:339
Chardin, Pierre Teilhard de, 1:102–1:103
Charity in Truth (Chardin), 1:102–1:103
Charles I, 1:218
chiliasm, 1:241, 1:286–1:287

Chilton, David, 1:86, 1:101, 1:105, 1:115, 1:141–1:142, 1:150, 1:192, 1:199, 1:206, 1:227n1:21, 2:30, 2:116
Christian hope, 1:220–1:221, 1:349. *See also hope*
Christianizing, defined, 1:166
"Christian nations," hardening of, 2:32
Christian reconstructionists, 1:105–1:107, 1:143–1:144, 1:199, 1:221
church
    amillennialism viewpoint regarding, 2:24–2:25
    antichrist *versus,* 1:139, 2:67–2:68, 2:98–2:99
    apostasy within, 1:121, 1:124–1:125, 1:150, 2:17, 2:47, 2:51, 2:52, 2:59
    Belgic Confession viewpoint regarding, 1:215
    as bride of Christ, 1:322, 2:10
    carnal victory of, 2:26
    coming of Jesus Christ dread of, 1:6
    confessional, Reformed doctrine regarding, 1:248–1:249
    deliverance of, 1:130, 1:134
    dominion of, 1:117, 2:26
    earthly future of, 2:23
    earthly victory of, 1:141–1:144
    eschatology doctrine within, 1:3–1:4
    expectancy of, 2:20
    failure of, 1:163–1:164
    final judgment proclamation by, 2:154–2:157
    as fulfillment, 1:332–1:333
    golden age for, 2:23n2:6, 2:24
    great tribulation of, 2:14
    history of, 2:32
    hope of, 1:131, 1:223
    Jesus as head of, 1:249, 1:315
    as kingdom of God/Christ, 1:183, 1:330, 1:331
    last battle of, 1:231–1:233
    lawlessness and, 2:16
    marriage to Jesus Christ by, 2:112–2:113
    as martyr, 1:276

millennium preparation of, 1:95
New Testament, 1:333
organizational form of, 1:329
origin of, 1:251–1:252
as people of God, 1:250–1:251
persecution of, 1:136, 1:151–1:152, 2:14
within postmillennialism, 1:113, 1:114, 1:117, 1:128–1:129, 1:130–1:131, 1:147, 2:23–2:24
prayer of, 2:20
preaching of the gospel by, 2:41
within premillennialism, 1:38, 1:246, 1:251, 1:310
removal of, before the end, 1:133–1:136
rule of, 1:215
salvation of, 1:278, 1:323–1:324, 1:327
Satan *versus*, 1:125, 1:163–1:164
signs of the coming of Jesus Christ for, 1:225–1:226
spiritual warfare of, 2:27
tribulation of, 2:9
as true witness, 1:134, 1:139
unpreparedness of, 1:229–1:230
victory of, 2:32
visible, 1:217
churches, seven, within Revelation, 2:9
clouds, significance of, 2:106, 2:107–2:108
Clouse, Robert G., 1:87
coming of Jesus Christ (parousia)
biblical terminology regarding, 2:108–2:110
as bodily, 2:105
cloud within, 2:106, 2:107–2:108
confessional statements regarding, 2:110–2:112
denial of, 1:158–1:159
description of, 2:14, 2:104–2:108
dread regarding, 1:6
as the end, 1:36
exaltation within, 2:107
expectancy of, 2:20
fanfare within, 2:13–2:14
as goal, 2:1–2:2
hope of, 1:222, 1:223, 2:19
judgment and, 2:112

as marriage ceremony, 2:112–2:114
nearness of, 2:114–2:119
overview of, 2:103–2:104
as personal, 2:106
phases of, 2:7
preterism denial of, 2:28–2:30
purpose and nature of, 2:112–2:114
resurrection of the dead and, 2:131
saints within, 1:138
Second Helvetic Confession writings regarding, 1:21–1:22
signs of, 1:225–1:229
as sudden, 2:105–2:106
theologian viewpoints regarding, 1:4
as unexpected, 2:105
unprepared for, 1:229–1:230
See also end of all things; rapture
common grace, 1:40–1:42, 1:120n1:8
communion, with Jesus Christ, 1:55, 1:64
condemnation, judgment *versus*, 2:140
cosmic eschatology, 1:83. *See also millennium*
cosmos, future of, 2:172–2:175
Council of Trent, 1:69–1:70
covenant, 1:36, 1:57, 1:203–1:204, 1:292, 1:293, 1:303, 2:165–2:166
creation, 2:11, 2:18, 2:175
cremation, 1:51
cultural works of humans, passing away of, 2:172–2:173
culture, common grace viewpoint regarding, 1:40–1:41
Cyrus, King, 1:283, 1:289, 1:294

D

Dabney, Robert L., 1:110–1:111
Daniel, 1:19, 1:23
Daniel 9, 1:281–1:289, 1:290–1:294
Daniel Apocalypse, 2:55
Dante, 1:6, 1:73–1:74
Darby, John Nelson, 1:12
death
  believer's existence following, 1:24
  effects of, 1:69
  fearlessness regarding, 1:56–1:58
  gain through, 1:61

intermediate state and, 1:47–1:48
of Jesus, 1:62
resurrection from, 1:50
salvation following, 1:53
Socrates' viewpoint regarding, 1:75–1:76, 1:77
solemn burial following, 1:51–1:52
soul following, 1:224
soul sleep *versus*, 1:48
tearing apart within, 1:52–1:53, 1:62
unbelievers and, 1:24, 2:177–2:178
as wages of sin, 2:160
Deborah, 2:101
defeatism, 2:26
deification, 2:131
De Jong, James A., 1:104
"delay of the parousia" theory, 2:6–2:7
deliverance, through Jesus Christ, 1:179–1:180
DeMar, Gary, 1:13, 1:105, 1:227, 2:5, 2:116–2:117
desolation, abomination of, 2:94–2:97
despair, 1:32–1:34
Dies Irae (day of wrath), 1:6
disciples, fearlessness of, 1:56–1:57
dispensation, defined, 1:245–1:246
dispensationalism, 1:38–1:39, 1:113–1:114, 1:136, 1:200, 1:245–1:246, 1:256–1:257, 1:312, 1:323–1:327
Dispensationalism, Israel and the Church, 1:248, 1:265–1:266
Divine Comedy (Dante), 1:6
dominion, significance of, 1:106
Dominion & Common Grace (North), 1:120n1:8
Domitian, 2:21, 2:31
Dooyeweerd, Herman, 1:67
Dostoyevsky, Fyodor, 1:180, 2:132
Dutch Reformed, 1:109

E

earthquake, 2:172, 2:174
Edwards, Jonathan, 1:104, 1:107–1:109, 1:119, 1:145, 1:155, 1:156n1:5, 1:161–1:162, 1:170–1:171
election, 1:29, 1:203–1:204, 1:317–1:321

Elijah, 1:203
Eliot, T. S., 1:33
encouragement, great tribulation and, 2:99
end, defined, 2:1
end of all things
  beginning of, 1:42–1:44
  common grace viewpoint regarding, 1:40–1:42
  covenant within, 1:36
  despair within, 1:32–1:34
  evolution viewpoint regarding, 1:37, 1:42
  glory of God within, 1:37
  goal of, 1:31–1:32
  God's appointment within, 1:34–1:35
  Jesus Christ within, 1:35–1:36
  kingdom within, 1:36
  overview of, 1:31–1:32
  promise fulfillment within, 1:42
Engelsma, David J., 1:172
Erigena, John Scotus, 1:6
eschatological universalism, 1:121, 1:122–1:123, 1:126, 1:208
eschatology, 1:3, 1:3–1:4, 1:22, 1:47–1:48, 1:154
eternal destinies, 2:164–2:172
eternal life, 2:167
Euphrates River, 2:102
Evangelicals and Catholics Together (ECT), 2:79
Eve, 1:252
evolution, 1:31, 1:37, 1:42, 2:177
Ezekiel, 1:19, 1:130, 1:186–1:187, 1:263–1:266
Ezra, 1:289

F

faith, 2:58–2:61, 2:90–2:91
falling away, as precursor sign, 2:5. *See also* apostasy
false Christs, 2:13
false church, 2:77–2:85
false prophet, 2:49
fear, 2:155
federal [covenant] vision, 2:53, 2:158
Felix, 2:154–2:155

final judgment, 1:24–1:25, 1:271, 1:279, 2:137–2:146, 2:147–2:161, 2:178
final state, 2:163
1 Peter 2:9, 1:322–1:334
first coming of Jesus Christ, 2:103–2:104
first resurrection, 1:276–1:278
free-will theology, 1:317
"from now on," 2:8
Fudge, Edward, 2:171
Fuller, Daniel, 1:328
further reformation (nadere reformatie), 1:159

G

Gabriel, 1:281, 1:288, 1:294
Galatian churches, 2:48
Gehenna (Hinnom), 2:167–2:168
Geneva Bible, 1:201
Gentiles
    falling away of, 1:198
    as Israel of God, 1:331
    Jewish oneness with, 1:330–1:331
    within New Testament church, 1:248–1:249, 1:286
    premillennialism viewpoint regarding, 1:310
    salvation of, 1:39, 1:104, 1:122, 1:144–1:145, 1:187, 1:198, 1:199, 1:204–1:205, 1:295–1:296, 1:298–1:299, 1:301, 1:304–1:306, 1:307
Gentry, Kenneth L., Jr., 1:13, 1:105, 1:151–1:152, 1:158, 2:22–2:24, 2:25, 2:26, 2:27–2:28, 2:29, 2:30–2:31, 2:116
George, Timothy, 1:7–1:8
Glenny, W. Edward, 1:332
globalization, 2:77
God
    abandonment of (hell), 2:167
    antichrist and, 2:88
    appointment by, 1:34–1:35
    denial of, 2:16
    within dispensationalism, 1:38–1:39
    election of, 1:317–1:321
    forms of, 1:338
    glory/glorification of, 1:37, 2:169
    as immanent deity, 1:102
    justice of, 1:56
    justification of, 2:141, 2:153–2:154
    as longsuffering, 2:6, 2:37
    rage against, 1:231–1:232
    reckoning of, 2:6
    sovereignty of, 1:34
Gog, 1:126, 1:128, 1:130, 1:133, 1:135–1:136, 1:139–1:140, 1:232, 2:64, 2:102
golden age, 1:260
Goodwin, Thomas, 1:207
good works, judgment of, 2:141–2:143
gospel, 1:16, 2:156
grace, 1:40–1:42, 1:120n1:8, 1:337, 2:37
great tribulation
    amillennialism viewpoint regarding, 2:99
    church and, 1:23, 1:100, 1:108, 1:130, 1:136, 1:160, 1:191, 1:192–1:194, 1:279–1:280, 1:307, 2:14
    as completion of suffering, 2:100
    escape from, 1:192–1:194
    Hoeksema's viewpoint regarding, 1:140
    Ironside's viewpoint regarding, 1:243
    Jews and, 1:148, 1:228
    Murray's viewpoint regarding, 1:157, 1:198
    overview of, 2:97–2:100
    postmillennialist viewpoint regarding, 1:84, 1:100, 1:108, 1:130, 1:136, 1:192–1:194, 1:195–1:196
    premillennialist viewpoint regarding, 1:244, 1:257–1:258, 2:99
    preterism viewpoint regarding, 1:151, 1:154
    prophecies regarding, 1:19
    signs of, 1:258–1:259
    viewpoints regarding, 1:148
Greek Orthodox Church, 1:71
Green, Michael, 2:171
Gregory the Great, 1:6, 1:71
grief, of the Christian, 1:224
Gruber, Dan, 1:305

H

harbingers, precursory signs as, 2:7
heathen religions, 1:33
heaven, 2:159–2:160, 2:164–2:172

the heavens, 2:18, 2:172–2:175
Heidelberg Catechism
    church discussion within, 1:250–1:251
    criticism regarding, 1:67
    intermediate state theme within, 1:26, 1:54–1:55
    overview of, 1:25–1:26
    persecution theme within, 1:26
    quote within, 1:6, 1:43, 1:48, 1:178, 1:182–1:183, 1:214, 1:215, 1:216, 1:223–1:224, 1:249–1:250, 1:277, 1:313, 1:330, 1:338, 2:111, 2:145, 2:148–2:149
    resurrection of the body theme within, 1:26
    on second petition, 1:249–1:250
hell, 1:6, 1:11–1:12, 1:62, 2:159, 2:160, 2:164, 2:167–2:172
Henry VIII, 1:208
Heppe, Heinrich, 2:139, 2:156
heresy, premillennialism as, 1:307–1:308
heretics/heresies, 2:49, 2:50, 2:51, 2:53–2:54
Hinnom (Gehenna), 2:167–2:168
History of Redemption (Edwards), 1:107
Hitchens, Peter, 1:231–1:232
Hitler, Adolf, 1:103, 1:320
Hoch, Carl B., Jr., 1:341
Hodges, Zane, 1:338
Hoekema, A. A., 2:10
Hoeksema, Herman
    Behold, He Cometh!, 1:15, 1:140
    Daniel 9 interpretation by, 1:293–1:294
    influence of, 1:198, 1:343
    as martyr, 1:276
    quote of, 1:77–1:78, 1:134–1:135, 1:204–1:205, 1:228, 1:295, 1:321, 1:347, 2:104, 2:122
    support regarding, 1:120n1:8
    viewpoint of, 1:83, 1:132–1:140, 1:346–1:348
Hofmann, Melchior, 1:7, 1:8
Holy Spirit, 1:54, 1:74, 1:88, 1:104, 1:154, 1:166, 1:167, 1:197, 1:202, 1:275, 1:289, 2:7, 2:26, 2:44, 2:150
homosexuality, 2:15

hope
    blessed, 1:86, 1:100, 1:214, 1:223, 1:226, 1:238, 1:243
    Christian, 1:220–1:221, 1:349
    of Christian reconstructionists, 1:221
    of the church, 1:131, 1:223
    of the coming of Jesus Christ, 1:222, 1:223, 2:19
    of the creeds, 1:223–1:225
    diversion of, 1:220–1:222
    within millennium, 1:102, 1:207
    misdirection of, 1:222
    overview of, 1:349–1:350
    of Paul, 1:61
    of premillennialism, 1:243
    of the Puritans, 1:221
    Reformed, 1:224–1:225
    of Scripture, 1:223
hopelessness, 2:131–2:132
Horner, Barry E., 1:298, 1:300–1:302, 1:305, 1:320, 1:323, 1:332
horns, four, significance of, 2:73
horns, ten, significance of, 2:88
Hughes, Philip Edgcumbe, 2:42, 2:171
Hut, Hans, 1:7

I

idols, worship of, 2:94, 2:97
immediate state, 1:23–1:24
immortality, 1:79–1:80
incarnation, 2:7
individual eschatology, 1:47–1:48
iniquity, apostasy and, 2:16
intercalation, 1:38
intermediate state
    of believers, 1:26, 1:61–1:62, 1:64–1:65
    body sleep and, 1:49–1:51
    creedal statements regarding, 1:48–1:49
    defined, 1:47
    exceptions to, 1:58
    glorification within, 1:55
    as Heidelberg Catechism theme, 1:26
    immortal Christian and, 1:79–1:80
    immortality of the soul and, 1:74–1:76
    indestructibility of the soul and, 1:78–1:79

individual eschatology and, 1:47–1:48
king of terrors and, 1:56–1:58
last enemy and, 1:52–1:53
martyrs within, 1:90
modernism and, 1:65–1:66
morality of the soul and, 1:77–1:78
naturalism and, 1:65–1:66
New Testament witness to, 1:60–1:62
Old Testament witness to, 1:58–1:60
overview of, 1:58, 1:64–1:65
popular errors regarding, 1:48
within postmillennialism, 1:116–1:117
preliminary judgment within, 1:55–1:56
purgatory and, 1:69–1:74
resurrection of the soul within, 1:53–1:55
sanctification within, 1:55
solemn burial and, 1:51–1:52
soul sleep and, 1:66–1:69
souls within, 1:91–1:92
truth of, 1:95
of unbelievers, 1:62–1:63
Irenaeus, 2:21–2:22, 2:167
Ironside, H. A., 1:243
Irving, Edward, 1:12
Isaiah, 1:16–1:17, 1:184–1:186, 1:187–1:189, 1:262
Islam, 2:80
Israel
    blinding of, 1:304–1:305, 1:306
    Cyrus' decree to, 1:283, 1:289
    Daniel 9 prophecy and, 1:281–1:282
    election determination regarding, 1:202–1:204
    identity of, 1:318
    premillennialism viewpoint regarding, 1:267–1:269
    restoration discussion regarding, 1:202, 1:259
    salvation of, 1:296–1:297, 1:298, 1:303–1:304, 1:319–1:320
    See also Jews

J

Jenkins, Jerry B., 1:12
Jerusalem
    destruction of, 1:23, 1:147–1:150, 1:152, 1:153–1:154, 1:156–1:157, 1:191, 1:192–1:193, 1:194–1:195, 1:227, 1:290, 1:291–1:292, 2:12–2:13, 2:24, 2:28, 2:96
    new, 1:223, 1:237, 1:239–1:240, 1:241, 1:250, 1:256, 2:160–2:161
    prophecies regarding, 1:19, 1:23
    rebuilding of, 1:109, 1:199, 1:201, 1:283, 1:288–1:289, 1:294
    temple within, 1:265–1:266, 2:95
Jesus Christ
    antichrist control by, 2:43, 2:88–2:89
    ascension of, 1:21–1:22
    as the beginning and the end, 1:35–1:36
    charges against, 1:181–1:182
    communion with, 1:55, 1:64
    control of, 2:8
    death of, 1:62
    dominion of, 1:117–1:118, 1:179–1:180
    as end of the law, 1:341–1:342
    enemies of, 1:211–1:212
    as eternal King, 1:175–1:177, 1:208, 1:315, 1:330
    as everlasting king, 2:111
    exaltation of, 2:107
    as fulfillment, 1:16
    as head of the church, 1:249
    within heaven, 2:164
    as history-bender, 2:10–2:11
    hope through, 1:349–1:350
    humanity raising by, 1:41–1:42
    immortality of, 1:79
    instructions of, 1:19
    as judge, 2:146, 2:156
    as king, 1:313–1:315
    as the lamb, 2:78
    last days purpose of, 1:24–1:25
    as Lion of the tribe of Judah, 1:176
    marriage of the church to, 2:112–2:113
    as mediator, 1:313
    within postmillennialism, 1:117–1:118
    power of, 2:127–2:128
    promises regarding, 1:17
    prophecies regarding, 1:58–1:59, 1:312
    reconciliation through, 1:17–1:18

redemption through, 1:17–1:18
rejection of, 2:52
resurrection of, 1:50–1:51
reverence of, 2:155
sacrifice of, 1:264–1:265
salvation work by, 1:53
as seed of Abraham, 1:315–1:316
suffering of, 2:100
supremacy of, 1:93
teachings of, 1:60, 1:62–1:63, 1:191, 2:11–2:15

Jews
antichrist against, 1:257–1:258
anti-semitism and, 1:320–1:321
blindness of, 1:307
conversion of, 1:144–1:146, 1:197–1:202, 1:205, 1:259, 1:329
Cyrus' decree to, 1:283, 1:289
Gentile oneness with, 1:330–1:331
God's casting away of, 1:202–1:203
identity of, 1:318
messianic kingdom dreams of, 1:179–1:180
millennial kingdom for, 1:241
oppression of, 2:25
as people of God, 1:322–1:323
persecution of, 1:257–1:258, 1:284
premillennialism viewpoint regarding, 1:100, 1:267–1:269
rejection by, 1:251, 1:300–1:302
salvation of, 1:296–1:297, 1:302–1:303, 1:323–1:324
See also Israel

Jezreel, 2:101
Joachim of Fiore, 1:5
John, 1:88, 1:115–1:116, 2:21, 2:25
Judas, 1:63
judgment, 1:24–1:25, 1:55–1:56, 1:271, 1:279, 2:112. *See also* final judgment
justification, 2:53–2:54, 2:141, 2:142, 2:147, 2:153–2:154, 2:158

K

Keil, C. F., 2:151
Kelly, J. N. D., 2:131
Kik, J. Marcellus

Puritans and, 1:155–1:156
quote of, 1:113, 1:114, 1:119, 1:124–1:125, 1:142, 1:162, 1:163–1:164
viewpoint of, 1:104, 1:106, 1:112, 1:124–1:125, 1:147–1:148
writings of, 1:211
king, significance of, 1:314
kingdom of God, 1:36, 1:103, 1:131, 1:183, 1:215–1:216, 1:250, 1:314, 1:330, 1:331, 2:38
king of terrors, 1:56–1:58
Kung, Hans, 2:81–2:82
Kuyper, Abraham, 1:40, 1:239, 2:85

L

LaHaye, Tim, 1:12
lake of fire, 2:148
The Late Great Planet Earth (Lindsey), 1:245
law, 1:105, 1:336, 1:341–1:342, 1:344, 1:345, 1:346–1:348, 2:157
The Lawful Use of the Law (Bultema), 1:348
lawlessness, 2:4, 2:15–2:16, 2:51, 2:75
Lazarus, 1:60, 1:62–1:63
Left Behind book series, 1:239
Lenin, Vladimir, 1:103
Leonard, J. E., 1:149, 2:115–2:116
Leonard, R. C., 1:149, 2:115–2:116
lesbianism, 1:231, 2:53
liberalism, 1:10, 1:76
licentiousness, 2:53
life eternal, 2:167. *See also* millennium
Lindsey, Hal, 1:245–1:246
longsuffering, God as, 2:6, 2:37
lordship controversy, 1:338
Lord's prayer, 1:250
Louis XIV, 2:85
Lowery, David K., 1:341
Luther, Martin, 1:70, 1:74, 1:276, 2:40, 2:52, 2:71, 2:71n2:1, 2:72n2:3

M

MacArthur, John, 1:338–1:340
Machen, J. Gresham, 1:247
Magog, 1:126, 1:128, 1:130, 1:133, 1:135–1:136, 1:139–1:140, 1:232, 2:64, 2:102
man, deification of, 2:74
manifestation (epiphaneia), 2:108–2:109

marriage, 2:112–2:113, 2:125, 2:125n2:5
Marsden, George, 1:107–1:108
martyrs/martyrdom, 1:90, 1:91, 1:209, 1:213, 1:276
McClain, Alva J., 1:240, 1:250, 1:260, 1:268, 1:273–1:274, 1:300, 1:317
The Meaning of the Millennium: Four Views (Clouse), 1:87
Messiah the Prince, 1:283, 1:290, 1:292, 1:294
messianic kingdom
    earthly conception of, 1:178–1:179, 1:207, 1:212
    earthly fulfillment of, 1:185
    Edwards' viewpoint regarding, 1:170–1:171
    goal of history and, 1:173–1:175
    as heavenly, 1:181–1:182
    as holy nation, 1:182–1:184
    Jesus forever within, 1:175–1:177
    Jewish dreams regarding, 1:179–1:180
    perfection of, 1:197
    premillennialist viewpoint regarding, 1:269–1:271, 1:309–1:310
    reconstructionist viewpoint regarding, 1:171–1:173
    righteousness within, 1:174
    spiritual fulfillment of, 1:185–1:187
    spiritual victory and, 1:167–1:169
    temporary, 1:160–1:163
    victory of, 1:166–1:167, 1:213
Miceli, Vincent P., 2:71n2:1
Middle Ages, 1:5, 1:6
millennialism, 1:4–1:5, 1:8, 1:23, 1:86, 1:87, 1:100, 2:4
millennium
    antichrist within, 1:103
    beheaded souls within, 1:90, 1:91, 1:94
    church blame within, 1:163–1:164
    church preparation regarding, 1:95
    conclusion events of, 1:92
    controversy regarding, 1:85–1:86
    ending of, 1:95
    fullness of, 1:89
    hope within, 1:102, 1:207
    introduction of, 1:83–1:84
    Jonathan Edwards' viewpoint regarding, 1:156n1:5
    martyrs within, 1:90
    preliminaries to, 1:256–1:257
    within premillennialism, 1:241–1:242, 1:259–1:261, 1:278–1:279
    Reformation viewpoint of, 1:8–1:9
    reign of Christ within, 1:260
    revival prior to, 1:108
    Satan within, 1:85, 1:89–1:90, 1:95, 1:279
    in Scripture, 1:84–1:85
    Second Helvetic Confession and, 1:22–1:23
    temporary messianic kingdom during, 1:160–1:163
    viewpoints regarding, 1:86–1:88
    See also amillennialism; postmillennialism; premillennialism
The Millennium (Boettner), 1:123–1:124
Milton, John, 2:75–2:76
ministers, 2:57, 2:60–2:61, 2:149–2:150
Miskotte, K. H., 1:142
moderate dispensational premillennialism, 1:325, 1:327–1:328
modernism, 1:65–1:66, 1:101–1:102
Moltmann, Jurgen, 1:11, 1:27–1:28
Montanism, 1:4
Morecraft, Joe, III, 1:145
Muntzer, Thomas, 1:7
Murray, Iain H., 1:13, 1:104, 1:143–1:144, 1:156–1:157, 1:197–1:199, 1:207, 1:221, 1:228

N

nadere reformatie (further reformation), 1:159
National Covenant, 1:222
naturalism, 1:32–1:33, 1:65–1:66
nature, 2:18, 2:172–2:175
Nebuchadnezzar, 2:76–2:77
Nehemiah, 1:289
Nero, 1:151–1:152, 2:25, 2:31
the Netherlands, apostasy within, 2:59
new dispensation, 2:8
new heaven and new earth, 2:160–2:161, 2:172

new Jerusalem, 1:223, 1:237, 1:239, 1:239–1:240, 1:241, 1:250, 1:256, 2:160–2:161
Nicene Creed, 1:14, 1:223, 2:110–2:111
Nietzsche, Friedrich, 2:178
Noah, 1:252, 2:105
North, Gary, 1:13, 1:105, 1:120, 1:120n1:8, 1:124, 1:141, 1:164, 1:192–1:193, 2:23, 2:116
Nott, Eliphalet, 1:206

O

obedience to God, disregard of, 2:53
occupy, defined, 2:19
Olivet Discourse, 1:158
one-world government, 2:73
Origen, 1:4, 1:11, 2:169

P

paganism, 1:33–1:34
pale horse, significance of, 1:168
Palestine, 2:101
parable, rich man and Lazarus, 1:62–1:63
parable of the pounds, 2:6
Paradise Lost (Milton), 2:75–2:76
parenthesis, 1:285, 1:285–1:287
The Parousia (Russell), 1:158
Paul, 1:18, 1:52, 1:61, 1:76, 1:89, 1:203, 2:150, 2:154–2:155, 2:158
peace, 1:167, 1:183
Pelagianism, federal vision of, 2:158
Pentecost, 1:43
people of God, division of, 1:322–1:329. *See also church*
persecution, 1:26, 1:136, 1:151–1:152, 1:257–1:258, 1:284, 2:14, 2:21, 2:25, 2:31, 2:75, 2:95, 2:97, 2:98
Peter, 1:63, 1:89, 1:154
Phaedo (Plato), 1:75
philosophy, despair of, 1:33–1:34
Pinnock, Clark, 2:171
Plato, 1:75, 1:77
polemics, preaching of the gospel and, 2:39
postmillennialism
    amillennialism *versus,* 1:129–1:130, 1:142–1:143, 1:211, 2:23n6
    antichrist viewpoint within, 2:64, 2:67n2:1, 2:71
    apostasy and, 1:150
    biblical realism and, 1:195–1:196
    binding of Satan viewpoint within, 1:112–1:114
    Christian reconstruction, 1:105–1:107
    church role within, 1:113, 1:128–1:129, 1:130–1:131, 1:147, 1:163–1:164, 1:215
    coming of Jesus Christ viewpoint within, 1:84, 1:87
    conversion of the Jews within, 1:144–1:146
    denial within, 1:230
    description and distinctions of, 1:100–1:103
    diversion of our hope within, 1:220–1:222
    Dutch Reformed, 1:109
    earthly conception of kingdom within, 1:178–1:179
    earthly victory of Christ within, 1:117–1:118, 1:141–1:144
    error of, 1:93, 1:127–1:129
    golden age of, 1:126–1:127, 2:23n2:6, 2:24
    heaven on earth and, 1:123–1:125
    intermediate state within, 1:116–1:117
    introduction to, 1:99
    kingdom glory viewpoint within, 1:177–1:178
    latter day glory within, 1:198
    loosing of Satan within, 1:118
    Matthew 24 interpretation within, 1:193–1:196
    messianic kingdom victory and, 1:166–1:167
    millennial viewpoint within, 1:86
    mortal blow to, 1:129–1:131
    Old Testament prophecy interpretation within, 1:184–1:187
    optimism of, 1:120–1:121, 1:125–1:127, 2:23n2:6
    overview of, 1:12–1:14, 1:112
    pessimism of, 1:119–1:120, 2:23, 2:24
    precursor signs and, 1:84, 2:4–2:5
    premillennialism shared view with, 1:99–1:100

Presbyterian (United States),
1:110–1:111
preterism, 1:146–1:154
Puritan, 1:104–1:105, 1:107–1:109, 1:143
redating Revelation within, 1:192
within the Reformed tradition,
1:103–1:104
reign of souls within, 1:114–1:116
resurrection events within, 1:210
Revelation 20 interpretation within,
1:112–1:118, 1:205–1:212
Revelation date viewpoint within, 2:22
Romans 11:25-26 interpretation
within, 1:196–1:197, 1:201–1:202,
1:203–1:205
Scottish Presbyterian, 1:109–1:110
signs against, 1:226–1:228
temporary messianic kingdom and,
1:160–1:163
typical fulfillment within, 1:194–1:195
unpreparedness within, 1:229–1:233
untimely victory and, 1:169–1:170
power, of messianic kingdom, 1:167
prayers of the church, 2:20
preaching of the gospel, 2:11, 2:14–2:15,
2:35–2:44
precursory signs
of the coming of Jesus Christ, 1:225–
1:229, 1:258–1:259
as harbingers, 2:7
identity of, 2:11–2:18
interdependence within, 2:4
order of, 2:14, 2:14–2:15
overview of, 1:84, 2:3–2:8
practical purpose of, 2:18–2:20
reality of, 2:3–2:4, 2:5
structure of Revelation and, 2:8–2:11
time passage within, 2:6
See also specific signs
predestination, 1:27, 1:28, 1:317, 2:148,
2:169
premillennialism
amillennialism *versus*, 1:331–1:332
antichrist within, 1:257–1:258, 2:64
antinomianism of, 1:335, 1:336–1:337

binding of Satan within, 1:273–1:275
blindness regarding Christ within,
1:333–1:334
church within, 1:246, 1:251
coming of Jesus Christ viewpoint
within, 1:84, 1:87
covenant theology within, 1:248
Daniel 9 and, 1:281–1:294
defined, 1:99
denial of Jesus within, 1:264,
1:310–1:316
doctrine of, 1:255–1:256
election denial within, 1:317–1:321
end of all things and, 1:37–1:39, 1:42
false doctrine of, 1:307–1:308, 1:309
Final Judgment within, 1:271, 1:279
1 Peter 2:9 interpretation within,
1:322–1:334
first resurrection within, 1:276–1:278
fundamental Reformed critique of,
1:309–1:316
golden age within, 1:260
great tribulation within, 1:244, 1:257–
1:258, 2:99
hope within, 1:243
introduction to, 1:237–1:238
Israel/Jews discussion within, 1:259,
1:267–1:269
kingdom within, 1:249–1:250, 1:314
law dishonoring within, 1:342
literal interpretation of prophecy within,
1:262–1:266
lordship controversy within, 1:338
messianic kingdom within, 1:269–1:271
millennium within, 1:259–1:261,
1:278–1:279
necessity of critiquing, 1:238–1:240
overview of, 1:12, 1:113–1:114, 1:240–
1:242, 1:246–1:248
postmillennialism shared view with,
1:99–1:100
precursory signs and, 1:84, 2:4
rapture within, 1:237, 1:238,
1:242–1:244
Reformed confessions against,
1:329–1:330

restoration viewpoint of, 1:304
resurrection of the soul within, 1:275–1:276, 1:277
resurrection viewpoint of, 1:137
Revelation 20 interpretation within, 1:254–1:271, 1:272–1:280
Romans 11 interpretation within, 1:295–1:308
as schismatic, 1:322
Scripture against, 1:330–1:331
temple despising within, 1:266–1:267
timeline of, 1:244–1:245
See also dispensationalism
Presbyterian Church, 1:104, 1:110–1:111, 2:59, 2:178
preterism, 1:146–1:154, 1:155–1:163, 1:190–1:192, 1:193, 1:198, 2:28, 2:29, 2:30, 2:115, 2:116–2:118
progressive parallelism, 2:10
prophecy, literal interpretation of, 1:262
prosperity, 1:167–1:168, 1:183
Protestantism, 2:52, 2:56
Protestant liberalism, 2:56
Protestant Reformation, 1:108
providence of God, 2:57–2:58
Psychopannychia (Calvin), 1:58, 1:67
The Purgatorio (Dante), 1:73–1:74
purgatory, 1:5–1:6, 1:7, 1:24, 1:48, 1:69–1:74
The Puritan Hope (Murray), 1:143–1:144
Puritans, 1:13, 1:104–1:105, 1:106, 1:107–1:109, 1:143, 1:155–1:156, 1:197–1:199, 1:221, 1:222

Q

question and answer 80, 2:79–2:80, 2:80n2:8, 2:82

R

rapture
as blessed hope, 1:100, 1:238
overview of, 1:12, 1:242–1:244, 1:256
premillennialist viewpoint regarding, 1:12, 1:42, 1:84, 1:100, 1:237, 1:238, 1:259, 1:296–1:297, 1:320, 1:323, 1:329, 1:330
theories regarding, 1:136
See also coming of Jesus Christ (parousia)

Rauschenbusch, Walter, 1:10, 1:102
reckoning of the Lord, 2:6
reconciliation, 1:17–1:18
Reconstructionists, 2:24
redemption, 1:17–1:18
red horse, significance of, 1:168
Reformation, 1:6–1:9, 1:155–1:156
Reformed Church Order of Dordt, 2:60–2:61
Reformed confessions, 1:214–1:217
Reformed Ecumenical Synod of 1963, 1:217
Reformed hope, 1:224–1:225
reincarnation, 1:76
restoration, 1:106, 2:151
resurrection, 2:122
resurrection, first, 1:276–1:278
resurrection body, 2:126–2:127, 2:128–2:130, 2:166–2:167
resurrection of Jesus Christ, 1:50–1:51, 1:58–1:59, 1:60, 2:123–2:124
resurrection of the dead/resurrection of the body, 1:50, 1:58, 1:137, 1:209, 1:213, 2:121–2:135
resurrection of the soul, 1:53–1:55, 1:275–1:276, 1:277
Revelation
dating of, 2:21–2:33
as history, 2:28
postmillennialism viewpoint regarding, 1:192
presentation of history within, 2:9–2:10
progressive parallelism within, 2:10
as prophecy, 2:28, 2:31
structure of, 2:8–2:11
revelation (apokalupsis), defined, 2:109–2:110
Revelation 20
amillennialism warning regarding, 1:258–1:259
antichrist against the Jews within, 1:257–1:258
binding of Satan within, 1:273–1:275
gospel within, 1:275
introduction to, 1:254–1:255
Israel/Jews discussion within, 1:259, 1:267–1:269
messianic kingdom within, 1:269–1:271

millennium within, 1:256–1:257, 1:259–1:261
postmillennialism interpretation of, 1:112–1:118, 1:205–1:212
premillennialism interpretation of, 1:254–1:271, 1:272–1:280
reverence, 2:155
revivals, 1:104, 1:108
righteousness, 1:174, 1:341
Roman Catholic Church
antichrist and, 1:155, 1:159, 2:72n2:3
as false church, 2:82–2:83
federal vision of, 2:158
Galileo and, 1:326n1:11
influence of, 2:79
Mass viewpoint of, 2:80n2:8
natural perfecting of man viewpoint of, 1:10
origin of, 2:51–2:52
purgatory viewpoint of, 1:24, 1:48, 1:69–1:74
theology of, 2:56
Roman Empire, 2:21, 2:25, 2:31, 2:73, 2:96
Romans 11
Barker's explanation of, 1:299
Burns' explanation of, 1:298–1:299, 1:304
Horner's explanation of, 1:298, 1:300–1:302, 1:305
McClain's explanation of, 1:300
postmillennialism interpretation of, 1:196–1:197, 1:201–1:202, 1:203–1:205
premillennialism interpretation of, 1:295–1:308
Reformed interpretation of, 1:307
Saucy's explanation of, 1:299
Scofield's explanation of, 1:297–1:298
"so" error within, 1:306–1:307
"until" error within, 1:305–1:306
Walvoord's explanation of, 1:298
Ware's explanation of, 1:299
Rome, defeat of, 1:155–1:156
Rushdoony, Rousas J., 1:13, 1:105, 1:106, 1:113, 1:121, 1:125, 1:142–1:143, 1:147–1:148, 1:211
Russell, Bertrand, 1:33–1:34
Russell, James Stuart, 1:149, 1:158, 2:29, 2:116, 2:116–2:117
Ryrie, Charles C., 1:240, 1:246, 1:248, 1:251, 1:270n1:27, 1:311, 1:324–1:325, 1:326–1:327, 1:328

S

sacrifices, 1:264–1:266, 1:328n1:23
saints
within the coming of Jesus Christ, 1:138, 2:107
good works of, 2:142–2:144
as judges, 2:140, 2:145
millennial reign of, 1:90–1:91
postmillennialism viewpoint regarding, 1:177–1:178
preservation of, 1:140
reign of, 1:115–1:116, 1:205
resurrection of, 1:50, 1:58, 1:137, 1:209, 1:210, 1:213
salvation
admonishment to, 2:171
of the church, 1:278, 1:323–1:324, 1:327
compromising of, 2:59–2:60
covenant of, 1:57, 1:303
creation and, 2:174
denial within, 1:230
dispensationalism teachings regarding, 1:312
extension of, 1:307
final judgment proclamation and, 2:155
of the Gentiles, 1:295–1:296
of Israel/Jews, 1:296–1:297, 1:298, 1:303–1:304, 1:319–1:320
of the Israel/Jews, 1:296–1:297, 1:302–1:303, 1:323–1:324
Moltmann's viewpoint regarding, 1:27–1:28
within the Old Testament, 1:311
through preaching of the gospel, 2:37
universal, 2:151–2:152
within universalism, 1:11
upon death, 1:53
sanctification, 1:55
Sandlin, Andrew, 2:116

Satan
    as adversary, 2:77
    as angel of light, 2:51
    antichrist and, 2:65–2:66, 2:75
    attack by, 2:9
    battle of Armageddon and, 2:102
    beastly kingdom of, 2:31
    binding of, 1:93, 1:112–1:114, 1:124–1:126, 1:205, 1:213, 1:273–1:275
    Christian life struggle against, 1:91
    church *versus*, 1:125, 1:163–1:164
    crushing of, 1:16
    deception of, 1:140
    defeat of, 1:92–1:93
    Edwards' viewpoint regarding, 1:156n1:5
    final rebellion of, 1:120
    heresy and, 2:54
    kingdom of, 1:211–1:212
    loosing of, 1:92, 1:101, 1:118, 1:125–1:126, 1:127–1:129, 1:130, 1:132–1:140, 1:206, 1:213, 2:33
    within the millennium, 1:85, 1:89–1:90, 1:95, 1:279
    preaching of the gospel *versus*, 2:38–2:39
    within premillennialism, 1:242
    unpreparedness for, 1:231–1:233
Saucy, Robert L., 1:299, 1:326, 1:327
Sauer, Erich, 1:255–1:256, 1:263
Savoy Declaration, 1:13, 1:105, 1:218–1:219
Schaff, Philip, 1:21, 1:216
Schwarz, Hans, 1:18, 1:68–1:69, 1:78
Scofield, C. I., 1:245–1:246, 1:251, 1:256, 1:268, 1:297–1:298, 1:323–1:324, 1:337
Scottish Presbyterians, 1:109–1:110
seals, seven, 2:9
second coming. *See* coming of Jesus Christ (parousia)
second death, 1:277
Second Helvetic [Swiss] Confession, 1:8, 1:21–1:24, 1:51, 1:216
Selbrede, Martin G., 1:113, 1:120–1:121, 1:125, 1:129, 1:131, 1:148, 1:153, 1:154, 1:171–1:173, 1:208, 1:212, 1:270n1:28, 2:23, 2:24
servant, defined, 2:19

seven (number), significance of, 1:288
seventy weeks of Daniel 9, 1:281–1:294
seven vials, 1:134, 2:10, 2:101
sexuality, 2:133–2:134
sheep and goats, imagery of, 2:14, 2:140, 2:145, 2:147, 2:152, 2:167
Shekinah-cloud, 2:106, 2:107–2:108
shepherd, characteristics of, 1:59
Shepherd, Norman, 1:124, 1:124n1:24
signs, of the coming of Jesus Christ, 1:225–1:229, 1:258–1:259
signs of the end/signs of the times. *See* precursory signs
666, significance of, 2:74
sixth vial, 1:132–1:133, 1:134
Smalcald Articles, 1:7
Social Gospel movement, 1:101
social turmoil, as precursory sign, 2:15
Socrates, 1:75–1:76, 1:77
sodomy, 1:231, 2:53
Soloviev, Vladimir Sergaevitch, 2:86
sorrows, as precursory sign, 2:11, 2:15, 2:18
soul(s)
    beheaded, 1:90, 1:91, 1:94, 1:116–1:117, 1:209
    following death, 1:224
    hell within, 1:62
    immortality of, 1:74–1:76
    indestructibility of, 1:78–1:79
    within the intermediate state, 1:91–1:92
    judgment of, 1:56
    mortality of, 1:77–1:78
    within postmillennialism, 1:114–1:116
    reincarnation of, 1:76
    relation to God within, 1:53
    resurrection of, 1:53–1:55, 1:275–1:276, 1:277
    second resurrection of, 1:92
    as substance, 1:66
soul sleep, 1:48, 1:66–1:69
special grace, 1:40
spiritual victory, 1:167–1:169
Sproul, R. C., 1:157–1:159, 2:117
Spykman, Gordon, 1:67, 1:68
Stalin, Joseph, 1:103

Staten Vertaling, 1:201, 1:204
Stephen, death of, 1:62
stone, kingdom as, 2:38
Stott, John R., 2:171
submission to God, 1:183
suffering, 1:280, 2:100
Supreme Court, 2:15
syncretism, 2:52, 2:80–2:81

T

Telder, B., 1:67
teleology, 1:31–1:32
temple, 1:263, 1:266–1:267, 2:12, 2:95
temporal succession, 1:273
ten (number), significance of, 1:88–1:89
Ten Commandments, 1:335, 1:339–1:340, 1:344–1:345, 1:346
ten horns, significance of, 2:88
Tertullian, 1:4
Tetzel, 1:70
theodicy, 2:141, 2:152–2:153
theonomy, 1:114
thief, coming as, 2:5–2:6, 2:105
thief on the cross, 1:61
Tillich, Paul, 1:103
time, as progressive realization, 2:11
Toon, Peter, 1:218
transformation of the body, 2:127. *See also* resurrection body
tribulation. *See* great tribulation
tribulation of the church, 2:9, 2:11
trumpet, heralding of, 2:13
trumpets, seven, 2:9–2:10
truth, development of, 1:14–1:15
Turretin, Francis, 1:91, 2:117–2:118, 2:139
Twisse, William, 1:218

U

unbelievers, 1:24, 1:62–1:63, 2:123, 2:131–2:132, 2:164–2:172, 2:177–2:178
universalism, 1:6, 1:10–1:11, 1:27–1:28, 2:52, 2:170
universal salvation (apokatastasis), 2:151–2:152
untimely victory, 1:169–1:170

V

Vatican II, 1:70–1:71
vaticinium ex eventu, 2:13n2:7
Venema, Cornelis P., 1:83
vials, seven, 2:10, 2:101
victory, 1:167–1:170
visible Church, 1:217. *See also* church
Vollenhoven, D. H. T., 1:67–1:68
Vos, Geerhardus, 2:55, 2:153

W

Walvoord, John F., 1:38, 1:241, 1:251, 1:263–1:264, 1:298, 1:325, 2:4
Ware, Bruce A., 1:268, 1:299, 1:326, 1:327–1:328
Warfield, Benjamin B., 1:91, 1:110, 1:116–1:117, 1:122–1:123, 1:125, 1:126–1:127, 1:128, 1:162, 1:172, 1:208, 1:212
wars, as precursory sign, 2:15
Westminster Confession of Faith, 1:13, 1:29–1:30, 1:48–1:49, 1:217–1:219, 2:82, 2:84–2:85, 2:124, 2:155
Westminster Shorter Catechism, 1:217
white horse, 1:168, 1:278, 2:36, 2:39, 2:40–2:41
whore, significance of, 2:84
Why Christian Anti-Judaism Must be Challenged (Horner), 1:300–1:302
wickedness, development of, 1:231
will of man, within antichrist kingdom, 2:75
Wilson, Douglas, 1:105, 1:206, 1:227n1:21
witnesses, two, 1:134, 1:138–1:139, 2:42, 2:98
work of the Lord, significance of, 2:134
World Council of Churches, 2:79
World War I, 1:102
worship, 2:54–2:55, 2:76, 2:94–2:95, 2:97
Wright, N. T., 2:79

Z

Zechariah, 1:262
Zerubbabel, 1:289
Zeus, 2:95

Also by David J. Engelsma

The Christian's hope is the visible, bodily, glorious return of the Lord Jesus Christ on the clouds of heaven with the resurrection of the Christian's body, the public vindication of the Christian at the last judgment, and the enjoyment of the glories of the new creation.

The last things—centrally the coming of Christ—are the purpose and goal of all the revelation of God in Scripture, from beginning to end. This book will encourage the Christian as he heeds Christ's instruction regarding that coming: "Gird up the loins of your mind, be sober, and hope to the end for the grace that is to be brought unto you at the revelation of Jesus Christ" (1 Peter 1:13).

Available in paperback and ebook format at **rfpa.org**,
or by calling the Reformed Free Publishing Association
at **616-457-5970** or emailing **mail@rfpa.org**.

You may also like

These fifty-three expository sermons comprehensively explain the book of Revelation, providing the believing reader with doctrinal clarity and practical comfort.

> "The church organically in principle always longs for the coming of the Bridegroom even though she may not always be equally conscious of this longing for the coming of the Lord. But also individual believers do not always partake in this sigh of longing. But the church responds to this promise of the coming of the Lord not only directly and in earnest prayer, but also in the preaching. Hence, through that preaching of the bride comes the admonition, or exhortation, 'And let him that heareth say, Come.' And again: 'And let him that is athirst come.' And once more: 'And whosoever will (that is: whosoever longs for righteousness and life, and who therefore will), let him take of the water of life freely.'
> — Herman Hoeksema, *Behold, He Cometh!*

Available in paperback and ebook format at **rfpa.org**,
or by calling the Reformed Free Publishing Association
at **616-457-5970** or emailing **mail@rfpa.org**.

"Let us then sit at the feet of the Master, as he instructs us about those things that must come to pass. Let us not fear, for these things concern our salvation."
—Martyn McGeown, *Called to Watch for Christ's Return*

From a review by Rev. Jerome Julien, retired pastor:

"Rev. McGeown has produced an excellent and very readable volume on Matthew 24 and 25, often called 'The Little Apocalypse' ... This book is a gem. It is filled with sound teaching, and at the same time it is filled with comfort and blessing for God's people. For those who want to know more about what the Bible teaches on the important area of biblical truth, these chapters on the Little Apocalypse will be of great spiritual value." — Rev. Jerome Julien

---

Available in paperback and ebook format at **rfpa.org**,
or by calling the Reformed Free Publishing Association
at **616-457-5970** or emailing **mail@rfpa.org**.

www.ingramcontent.com/pod-product-compliance
Lightning Source LLC
Chambersburg PA
CBHW070612170426
43200CB00012B/2665